SMOKE FROM THEIR FIRES

Charley at Seventy

SMOKE FROM THEIR FIRES

THE LIFE OF A
KWAKIUTL CHIEF

BY

CLELLAN S. FORD

Charles J. Nowell

ARCHON BOOKS

© 1941 by Yale University Press, Inc.

Reprinted 1968, 1971 with permission
in an unaltered and unabridged edition and
published as an Archon Book by
The Shoe String Press, Inc.
Hamden, Connecticut

ISBN 0-208-00336-3
Library of Congress catalog card number 68-15344
Printed in the United States of America

To

CHARLES JAMES NOWELL

CONTENTS

ILLUSTRATIONS

ACKNOWLEDGMENTS

THIS volume results from a field study made during the summer of 1940, sponsored jointly by the Department of Anthropology and the Institute of Human Relations, Yale University. The people studied, the Kwakiutl of Vancouver Island, are well known to anthropologists through the valuable and extensive works of Dr. Franz Boas. I should like to acknowledge here my indebtedness to Dr. Boas, without whose pioneering efforts this study probably would not have been made. I should like also to thank him for his advice preliminary to my going into the field and for his courtesy in reading the manuscript. I am especially grateful to my colleagues in the Department of Anthropology and the Institute of Human Relations at Yale. In particular, I wish to thank Professor George Peter Murdock and his wife, Carmen Rothwell, for their helpful criticism and assistance. I am indebted to Professor Ralph Henry Gabriel for his kindness in reading the manuscript. To Lois Jordan I wish to acknowledge my gratitude for valuable aid in assembling this material and in preparing the work for publication. To my wife, Edna Yates, I want to express deep appreciation for her assistance during the field study and while working on the material, as well as for preparing the map of Vancouver Island.

I should also like to thank my many Indian friends who so generously spent their time giving me valuable information. To Alfred Shaughnessy I am grateful for the free-hand drawings in color which illustrate this book. I owe most, of course, to Charles James Nowell whose life story is presented here. His patience in teaching me the complexities of his native culture won my deepest gratitude. Throughout my work with him he displayed an interest, honesty, and faithfulness which left nothing to be desired. At best, this volume could express but a fraction of my indebtedness to him.

Much of my information corresponds to material already published. The occasional discrepancies between the information secured by Dr. Boas and by myself will be readily discovered by those familiar with the literature on the Kwakiutl. The emphasis in this volume is placed on behavior, rather than on formal patterns; the attempt will be made to bring Kwakiutl society to life for the reader by presenting the life story of a Kwakiutl chief.

CLELLAN S. FORD

Yale University,
September, 1941.

CHRONOLOGICAL SUMMARY OF
CHARLEY'S LIFE

1870–1879
1870 Charley is born
1874 His mother dies
1876 He goes to school at Alert Bay

1880–1889
1884 Charley's father dies
1887 Charley goes north to school
1888 He goes to Japan

1890–1899
1895 Charley marries
1897 His first child is born and dies
1899 His *"grandfather"* dies

1900–1909
1901 Charley receives a copper from his father-in-law
1903 His brother builds a community house
1904 Charley goes to St. Louis

1910–1919
1915 His father-in-law dies
1916 His son marries

1920–1929
1920 His son dies
1921 His brother dies

1930–1939
1931 His wife dies
1935 He marries again
1939 He goes to Bella Bella

1940–
1940 Charley tells the story of his life

PRINCIPAL PERSONS IN CHARLEY'S STORY

CHARLEY	Charles James Nowell
MALITSAS	Charley's father
OWADI	Charley's brother
TLAKODLAS	Charley's grandfather (his mother's father's brother)
MR. HALL	The missionary
LAGIUS	Charley's father-in-law
LAGIUS' DAUGHTER	Charley's wife
ALFRED	Charley's second child
JANE	His fifth child
BEATRICE	Sixth child
AGNES	Seventh child
VIOLET	Eighth child

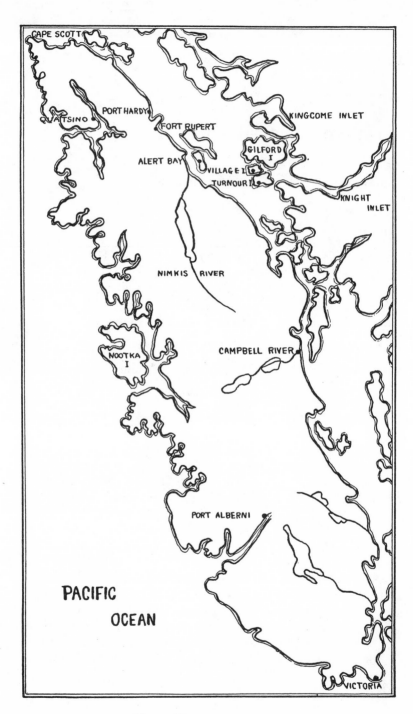

CAPE SCOTT

QUATSINO

PORT HARDY

FORT RUPERT

KINGCOME INLET

ALERT BAY

GILFORD
I

VILLAGE I.

TURNOUR I.

KNIGHT
INLET

NIMKIS RIVER

CAMPBELL RIVER

NOOTKA
I

PORT ALBERNI

PACIFIC

OCEAN

VICTORIA

Map of Vancouver Island

SMOKE FROM THEIR FIRES

CHAPTER I

AN INTRODUCTION TO KWAKIUTL SOCIETY

ON the northeast coast of Vancouver Island live the remnants of a once powerful nation—the Kwakiutl. Bound together by a common language, intermarriage, and a complex system of economic exchange, these people prospered and flourished until the coming of the whites. Since then—about the middle of the nineteenth century—their numbers have decreased, their prosperity has diminished, and their culture has undergone rapid change.

Kwakiutl culture, like that of any society, developed through centuries of experience. It represents all that the ancestors of the present generation learned about the art of living together. This heritage from the past may be compared to an unwritten book of culture. The very first ancestors of the Kwakiutl composed its first edition thousands of years ago. Through trial and error, success and failure, pleasure and pain, those men and women learned something about life. A part of this knowledge became the book of culture which they transmitted to their children. The new generation lived and learned a little more, added a new paragraph or two, blotted out a few sentences here and there, and then passed it on again. In this fashion each generation received its book of culture from the preceding one, revised it, and willed the new edition to its successors. The culture which thus evolved consists of solutions to the problems of life. Techniques for dealing with all phases of existence are contained within it.

In studying the culture of a people it is easy to lose sight of its problem-solving function and to regard it as a mere collection of foreign customs. When studying a primitive society, such as the Kwakiutl, the temptation to regard their culture as exotic is exceptionally great. The ways in which these "ignorant and superstitious people" behave seem, at first, outlandish and senseless, but if one overcomes this temptation and attempts to discover the problems to which their culture represents adjustment, the result is rewarding. An alternative system of techniques for living is revealed. Customs which seemed at first sight outlandish and senseless are found to be common and sensible.

What, then, are these problems which the Kwakiutl learned to solve? In brief, they are the ones involved in the struggle of a group of people to live: wresting from their environment food, clothing, and shelter; harnessing incentives to provide the energy for constructive activity; maintaining peace among their fellows by eliminating situations which provoke envious hatred and by sternly controlling such aggressive acts as theft and murder; perpetuating group membership by providing for the welfare of their children and by forcing them to learn the ways in which, as adult members of their society, they must act. To problems like these, Kwakiutl culture represents adjustment; far from being a meaningless jumble of disjointed curiosities, the ways of thinking and acting which compose it are a meaningful complex of integrated techniques by means of which the problems of group living are solved.

But the task of picturing, in clear-cut outlines, just how Kwakiutl culture functions presents certain difficulties. It is dangerous, for example, to discriminate between the various aspects of their culture, selecting some and discarding others; significant details may be overlooked and others, less significant, may be given an exaggerated importance. At the same time, this is a risk that must be taken. If the culture were presented in its entirety, a mass of intricate detail would clutter the picture and obscure points of vital interest. But even a clear-cut description which pictures accurately the functioning of their culture would, nevertheless, lack living reality. The reality of their culture can only be experienced by living in their society—an experience denied to white people. This difficulty, however, might be overcome, at least in part, by reporting the life story of a Kwakiutl Indian.

To plunge the reader directly into that story would be somewhat like abandoning an Indian who had never been outside of his society in the middle of the Grand Central Station in New York City and telling him to fend for himself. The reader must first have a guide to Kwakiutl society and culture; he must become acquainted with the techniques used by these Indians to exploit their environment and to carry on their social intercourse. He must be able to visualize the material apparatus among which they live: he must know, for example, the kinds of houses in which they live, the types of tools and utensils which they use, and the kinds of boats in which they travel. He must know their social structure: their hierarchies of rank and prestige, their stratification by sex and age, and their social groupings. He must know the life cycle of the individual in this society and the rules and regulations defining expected behavior in such life crises as birth, puberty, and death. If the reader has this knowledge before him as a guide, he will be better equipped to understand the life story which follows and to gain from it an insight into the functioning of Kwakiutl society.

As a prelude to describing Kwakiutl culture, something must be said about the environment in which these people live. The northeastern coast of Vancouver Island is cut into numerous bays and inlets. Directly inland, fir-clad mountains, many of them snow-capped in both summer and winter, tower above their valleys. Rivers flow through these valleys to the sea. At the mouths of these rivers gravel beaches line the shore; elsewhere the coast is forbidding with jagged rocks. Deep waters separate Vancouver Island from the western coast of Canada. Here the tides run swift and the currents are treacherous. Sheltered from the broad sweep of the Pacific, these straits are nevertheless difficult to navigate, especially in the winter when heavy winds and high seas whip through them. Small islands are found here and there in the straits; some of them are inhabited, others are not.

From October to March there is almost continuous rain or snow and the temperature on the coast hovers about the freezing point. During the summer months there is somewhat less precipitation and the temperature averages a little over seventy degrees; on rare occasions during July and August it may go as much as twenty degrees higher. The prevailing coastal winds vary from southeast to southwest. The total amount of precipitation during the year is great, though it changes considerably from one district to another.

Vegetation on the island is prolific. Trees of many kinds grow to great height and reach diameters of five feet and more. Among these are to be found red and yellow cedar, yew, fir, oak, maple, and many others. Forested areas are interspersed with tangled undergrowths of a great variety of bushes, many of them bearing edible berries. The animal life is also prolific; it includes black and brown bear, elk, white-tailed and black-tailed deer, wolves, squirrel, mink, and otter. There are several kinds of birds: grouse, drum partridge, Mexican woodpecker, bullfinch, raven, crow, and eagle. It is the sea, however, which has served the natives best; from it they take seal, sea lions, sea otters, whale, salmon, halibut, olachen or candlefish, cod, and many sorts of shellfish.

It is not known how long the Kwakiutl have lived in this environment. The natives themselves believe that they have always lived where they are today. Their physical type fails to shed much light on this problem. In physique they resemble closely the other Indians of this general region; their faces are typically long, thin, and distinguished by a high and narrow nose which is sometimes markedly hooked. Their skin is a light brown which could easily pass for a coat of sun tan. Their culture gives few clues to their history. There is some evidence that the folktales of the Kwakiutl originated, in part, much farther north, but this tells us nothing about the actual migrations of these people. On the other hand, their culture is so well adjusted to their present environment that they must have lived on the northwest coast of North America for many generations.

The techniques by which they manipulated the raw materials of their environment were fundamental to the native life of the Kwakiutl—the way they prepared their food, manufactured their tools, weapons, and utensils, constructed their houses and canoes, fashioned their clothing and ornaments—in short, transformed their environment into useful possessions and wealth. The objects thus produced were rarely ends in themselves; they were rather means to the solution of other and, from the standpoint of human motives, more basic problems. This, perhaps, is the reason why the technology of these people has changed so rapidly since their contact with white civilization. The Kwakiutl did not make boxes for the sake of making boxes, but to provide themselves with containers. As soon as they discovered that the metal containers of the whites served the same purpose and were, at the same time, easier to get than the boxes were to make, they abandoned the art of manufacturing wooden boxes. The same thing happened with many other items of their material culture, and the majority of the native technical processes fell into disuse and disappeared.

Formerly, the manufacture of wooden objects dominated Kwakiutl technology. Work in stone, shell, bone, and horn merely supplemented this basic craft. They made their weapons and tools of stone or bone and wood. Many of their utensils, their ceremonial masks, their houses and canoes, their cradles and coffins were made of wood—generally cedar or yew. All the wood working was done by the men. Wood carvers of special ability and training made it their sole occupation. They were expert craftsmen and their products were marvels of ingenuity and design. These wood carvers, hired by others who desired their services, were well-to-do and respected members of Kwakiutl society.

Some wood carvers specialized in canoe building. The canoe was made from a single cedar tree which the builder hollowed out and shaped with a stone adz and chisel. After the hull was the required thickness, it remained to make the boat wide enough to be seaworthy. This problem was solved by bending the sides outward until they assumed the desired shape. To make the sides soft enough to bend, the builder filled the dugout with water which he heated with red-hot stones so as to soak the wood thoroughly with boiling water and steam. Knotholes and other imperfections in the wood were caulked by wedging shredded cedar bark into the hole as tightly as possible with wooden pegs and then covering the plug with pitch or gum. The canoes were of various sizes: there were small ones for fishing and large ones, capable of carrying thirty or forty persons, for traveling and transportation. They were propelled by both paddles and sails. In former times the sails consisted of thin cedar planks sewn together. Today gasoline-driven boats have almost completely supplanted the native canoe.

Housebuilding required considerable effort and was generally a cooperative enterprise. With stone adzes the men hewed the posts and beams for the framework from fallen cedar logs. With wooden wedges and stone mauls they split the planks for the walls and roof from standing cedar trees. If the planks were crooked, they were straightened by placing them in a pile on level ground and weighting them down with stones, or by placing each end of a plank between a pair of stakes slanting in opposite directions to give the plank a reverse twist. Formerly, nails were unknown and the various parts of the house were fastened together with cedar withes and spruce roots. The length of time which the construction consumed and the labor which it involved were major factors in influencing the Kwakiutl to adopt the white man's methods of housebuilding which, by contrast, required far less time and effort. Today the native type of dwelling has all but disappeared; the Indians live in modern houses made of boards from the sawmill and put together with hammer and nails.

Whereas wood carving was a specialty of the men, the production of textiles was that of the women. They wove blankets: some of mountain-goat wool with, perhaps, an admixture of dog's hair or feathers, others of soft cedar bark trimmed with fur. They also made blankets of skin. Cordage was an important article of manufacture: thin fishlines were twisted and braided of human hair; thread for sewing was made of animal sinew; heavier ropes were made of cedar bark or strips of skin. They also made fine baskets of various shapes and sizes; these were among the most important articles of daily use. Nowadays it is rare for a woman to make blankets, cordage, or baskets. Some of the women, however, are employed by the canning companies to make gill and seine nets and at this they are very adroit. Moreover, some of the Indian women today knit sweaters and socks. They also sew little dresses for their daughters and occasionally make over their husbands' pants for their little boys.

Fishing was carried on by the men. It was by far the most important exploitative activity of the Kwakiutl. In days before white contact, it was the primary source of food; today it is the chief source of money. Native methods of securing fish included trapping, netting, spearing, and fishing by hook and line. Sea lions, seals, and porpoises were harpooned. Codfish and halibut were caught with hooks attached to fishlines made of kelp, using bait of cuttlefish. Salmon were harpooned and caught in weirs, fish traps, or nets dragged between two canoes. A long rake was used to secure smaller fish such as the herring and olachen. Somewhat less important than fishing was hunting—another male activity. The men caught most of their game in traps and deadfalls. They also hunted with the bow and arrow. This weapon has now been completely replaced by the white man's gun, but some of the native traps are still in use. Fowling was of some importance; they caught the birds in snares and nets or hunted them with the bow and arrow.

While the men fished and hunted the women collected shellfish and seaweed, picked berries, and dug roots. At low tide they combed the shore for crabs, mussels, abalone, sea grass, and kelp, and dug for clams. In the berry season the women set forth early in the morning for the berry patch. Each one took with her a belt to which she fastened a small basket (nowadays a pail) into which she picked. When the basket was filled she emptied it into a larger one on the ground. Roots were dug with digging sticks. The patches where the roots grew were well known and utilized from year to year, but they were never planted. Since inedible plants invariably mingled with the edible ones, training and a keen eye were required to select those with the desired roots. Girls were taught to dig roots by their mothers and, as some of the women say, it was often difficult for them to learn.

The seasonal nature of the food supply dictated the cycle of their activities. In the early summer while the men fished the women collected roots and berries. Some of these foods were eaten; others were dried for winter use. At some time during the summer they would move to where the clams were plentiful so the women could gather and dry them, while the men continued to fish. In the late summer when the salmon sought fresh water to spawn the Indians followed them, moving up deep into an inlet. The fish caught here were smoked and dried for the winter. Thus the spring, summer, and fall provided the Kwakiutl with an excess of food which could be drawn upon during the winter months. The leisure which this procedure afforded was of great importance to their social life. In the winter all the people congregated in their villages to feast, to dance, and to hold their gift-giving ceremonials—the potlatches.

Native methods of preserving food were simple but effective. Roots, berries, and fish were dried over the fire or in the sun, put in baskets or boxes, and then stored in the house near the fire where they would keep dry. The more bulky roots were placed in a pit in the earth near the fire and covered over with boards. Seaweed was put on the beach, covered with a mat for four days and dried in the sun. It was then dampened, pressed into bricks, and dried. Olachen oil was kept in long bottle-like containers made of kelp and these, in turn, were stored in large boxes. Today they dry a few berries and some seaweed. Most of the natives use modern methods, however, to preserve their fish. Using a hand-canning machine, the women can their own salmon—often as many as five hundred pints in one summer.

The Kwakiutl used several methods for preparing their food. They cooked roots and some other foods in an earth oven. Lacking pottery or metal utensils, they boiled or steamed food in open boxes, heating the water with red-hot stones which were dropped into the box. Sometimes meat or fish was

broiled in tongs before the open fire. The Kwakiutl generally
ate three meals a day. Breakfast usually consisted of fish
and either berries or roots. Lunch was a light meal taken
about four o'clock in the afternoon. Rather late in the evening the natives ate their supper of fish or meat, and berries
or roots. Since dried fish was usually buttered with olachen
oil, they did not drink water with their meals, alleging that
oil and water do not mix and that to put both into the stomach at the same time would produce nausea. The men sat
cross-legged while eating; the women squatted on their
haunches, keeping their blankets carefully tucked about
their legs. After the meal shredded cedar bark was passed
around to serve as a towel on which to wipe the oil from their
hands.

There were a few foods that the Kwakiutl refused to eat.
They would not eat deer, believing that to do so would make
them forgetful. They were disgusted at the thought of eating dog, frogs, or snakes. Nor did they eat the sea gull or
porcupine—the former was considered too tough and the
latter unappetizing. Condiments were lacking from their
diet. They did not use honey, and their only sweets were
fruits. The only salt they had was contained in their sea
foods. Tobacco was formerly unknown, but since contact
with white culture smoking has been rapidly adopted. The
Kwakiutl enjoyed a native chewing gum—hemlock pitch,
which was refined by heating it over the fire and filtering
through a basket. Their only beverage was water drawn
from the mountain streams. Today they drink coffee and tea
and, when they can escape the surveillance of the white officials, they drink beer, whisky, and rum.

In former times the clothing of the Kwakiutl consisted of
a blanket and an apron. They never wore moccasins or shoes.
A belt was worn over the blanket, and the men wore fur
headbands to keep their hair back. Rain hats were occasionally worn. Since white contact, there has been a gradual
adoption of European clothing. The woolen blankets of the
whites first replaced those of native manufacture. Then the
men began to wear shirts and the women petticoats beneath

their blankets. Children, who had formerly gone naked and worn blankets only in cold weather, adopted shirts. Today the transition is nearly complete. Little girls usually wear dresses, sweaters, and often a pair of tennis shoes. Little boys are clad in overalls or pants, a shirt, often a cap, and sneakers. Women wear dresses, jackets or sweaters, silk or cotton stockings, and shoes; the men wear trousers, shirts, socks, shoes, a sweater or jacket, and almost always a hat or cap.

A few ornaments were worn. Both sexes delighted in earrings and nose ornaments of abalone shell. The women wore arm rings, wristlets, knee rings, and anklets of mountain-goat wool, yellow cedar bark, or, more recently, of copper and brass. The women used to bind their ankles tightly with cloth in order to make their legs more beautiful. The men wore their hair long and tied in a big knot behind; the women braided theirs on two sides. Strings of sea-otter teeth provided with tassels were used as hair ornaments. In daily life both men and women used to decorate their faces with red and black paint, putting tallow on the skin first so that the paint could be easily removed.

The language spoken by the Kwakiutl belongs to the Wakashan linguistic stock. Writing was formerly unknown. Since white contact they have learned to write their own language, but the letters of the English alphabet have been unsatisfactorily adapted to the sounds of the native speech so that the Indians have considerable difficulty both in reading and in writing their own language. Before the coming of the whites, the Kwakiutl did not shake hands or embrace upon meeting one another. They merely said *yo*, the native equivalent of "hello," and then began conversation. Husband and wife were no exception; there was no kiss or embrace of greeting or farewell in public although these might occur in private. It is interesting to note that the Indians now shake hands, but still do not embrace each other in public. They have taken over only part of the white man's custom of greeting. The reason for their selection of handshaking may derive from the fact that the Indians are regarded by the whites as an inferior caste so that, although white people often shake hands with Indians they never, no matter how good friends they may be, embrace them in public. The Kwakiutl have always lived in fishing villages, located close to the sea. Large, square communal dwellings with walls and gabled roofs of overlapping cedar planks, stood in rows with their main entrances facing the shore. In front of the houses, between them and the sea, ran a carefully leveled street. On the sea side of the street stood small shacks used by menstruating women, sick people, widows, and the infirm. On the beach, when not in use, canoes were hauled above high-water mark and, in summer, filled with water and covered with blankets or mats to prevent their cracking in the sun. On the beach, too, were the latrines: holes dug in the sand near enough the sea to be flushed out at high tide.

The dwelling was large enough to accommodate three or four families. Each family had its own bedroom compartment, its own provisions and furniture, and its own fireplace. All around the interior of the house, flush with the walls, was a platform about two feet high and four to five feet wide, upon which were built bedrooms in the form of miniature houses. Each of these rooms had a sliding door: a private family entrance through which none of the other members of the household could pass without special invitation. Within the bedrooms were beds of cedar branches covered with deerskin. Formerly the Kwakiutl used mountain-goat or bear skins for covering; more recently they have adopted blankets of white manufacture. The native pillows of skin filled with bird down were soon supplanted by trade kapok pillows.

In front of each bedroom was the family fireplace: a bare spot of earth with two or three stones serving as andirons. Beside it was a large wooden platform or seat upon which the entire family could recline. Above the fireplace stood a rough rack of poles upon which the housewife placed fish and other kinds of food to dry in the smoke of the fire. On the platform, along the side of the house next to the bedroom, she stored their boxes of provisions and their firewood.

Near the fire she generally kept a kelp bottle of olachen oil and a small food box in which she stored berries, roots, and dried salmon for daily use. Near the fire also were miscellaneous implements: a stone hammer and wooden wedges used for splitting firewood, tongs for handling hot stones and for broiling, cooking stones and boxes, mats, shredded cedar bark for towels, and a long pole for pushing the roof boards apart when the fire was going. Small buckets used as chamber vessels were kept near by; these, when filled, were dumped into a large box near the main entrance to the house. The urine thus collected was used for washing blankets. In the center of the house was another fireplace which was used whenever all the members of the household ate together or when guests from outside were invited for a feast.

The head of the household had his quarters in one of the rear corners of the house. Here, he and his wife lived with their unmarried children. In the other corners of the house lived the younger brothers of the head of the house and their families, or his sons if they were married. These were the people who had the most right to live in the household. Often, however, there would not be enough younger brothers and married sons to take up all the quarters available, in which case a sister of the household head or, perhaps, his wife's sister might be invited to live there, especially if her husband belonged to the same village.

Life in the communal dwelling lacked privacy. Quarrels between husband and wife were rarely concealed from the other families. There was constant intercommunication with the other members of the household. Often they would all breakfast together or share their evening meal. In the evening perhaps they would all sit around the central fire and chat, sing, or play games with the children. Later in the evening, however, each family retired to its own quarters, and all sexual activity was strictly a private matter. Moreover, parents usually waited until their children were sound asleep before indulging in sexual intercourse.

The number of houses in a village depended upon the number of tribes who lived there. Of the twenty-five tribes which formed the Kwakiutl nation, four were located at Fort Rupert. The natives aver that at Fort Rupert alone, at the time of white contact, there were over forty communal dwellings sheltering more than five hundred people. This was probably the largest of the Kwakiutl villages. The others generally consisted of one or at the most two tribes. When more than one tribe lived in the same locality, as at Fort Rupert, the tribal boundaries were well defined. Each tribe had its own block of land upon which its members constructed their communal dwellings. Thus, in effect, the village at Fort Rupert consisted of four well-defined tribal districts whose territories lay adjacent to one another.

Each tribe was composed of clans, varying in number from three to five. The right to live within the tribal district depended upon membership in one of its clans. A person obtained this membership by tracing his descent, in the paternal line, from the traditional founder of the clan. Young men whose fathers belonged to one of the clans in the tribe generally brought their wives to live in their own tribal district. A young woman went to live in her husband's tribal district, where her sons became members of their father's clan.

Within each clan there was a linear hierarchy of status positions, generally occupied by men. The position which a man held determined the order in which he received his gifts in a potlatch and, to a great extent, the prestige which was due him as a member of the clan. The man occupying the first position in a clan received his potlatch gifts before any of the other members of his clan and was regarded as the clan's head chief. The man in the second position received his gifts next and was regarded as next in importance to the clan chief. When a man retired from active participation in social life, he relinquished his position to his oldest son. It was possible for a man to occupy more than one position at the same time. He might, for example, inherit the first, third, and fifth positions in his clan. Under such circumstances, he would put his eldest son in the first, the next eldest son in the third, and his youngest son in the fifth position. Should a

man have no sons he would bestow his position upon his
younger brother or the latter's eldest son. Failing such a
relative, the position would go to his eldest daughter, who
would pass it on to her eldest son. In recent years many more
women have obtained clan positions than was formerly the
case because the rapid decline in population after contact
with the whites left too few men to occupy all the positions
of a clan.

When a woman did receive a clan position and passed it
on to her son, the rule of patrilineal descent in the clan was,
of course, violated since the son in such a case obtained his
position and clan membership from his mother. This did
not, however, disrupt the Kwakiutl social system. According
to the native kinship system a man's relatives were equally
important whether they were traced through his mother or
his father. This is clearly revealed in the kinship termi-
nology: a person called the parents of either his mother or
his father by the same term, *grandparent;* the siblings of
either his mother or his father, *uncle* and *aunt;* all his first
cousins, *brother* and *sister;* the children of either his son or
his daughter, *grandchild.*[1] Thus a person was always a member of a bilateral kinship group which cut across clan lines.
The close relationship which a man bore to his grandparents
made it quite possible for him to belong, should occasion ne-
cessitate, to the clan of his mother's father rather than to
that of his father's father.

This overlapping of kinship affiliation and clan membership is well illustrated by the way in which a man obtained
an ancestral crest. A crest was the dress and mask, or its
replica, which the clan ancestor wore when he visited the
earth. The founder of one clan, for example, made his first
appearance wearing a thunderbird dress and mask, the
founder of another wore the garb of a wolf, another that of a
whale, and another that of the sun. The right of a man to
refer to one of these crests as his own might be obtained
either from his father or his mother. If his father owned the

[1] These words are printed in italics since they represent native terms
which have no exact English equivalent.

sun crest and his mother the thunderbird crest, then he had the right to both crests even though the only clan to which he belonged was that of his father. This meant that, when he died, he might return either to the crest of his father or to the crest of his mother, i.e., he might go to live with the sun or with the thunderbird.

A function of the bilateral kindred extremely important in native life was that of providing hospitality to the traveler. If, for example, a man visited the village from which his mother came he would stay in the house of his *grandparent*, his mother's father, or, perhaps, that of his *uncle*, his mother's brother. They would treat him as a member of the family, affording him hospitality and protection in a strange village. There, too, he would probably find some of his cousins: *brothers* with whom he could hunt and fish and *sisters* who would wash and repair his clothing. In other villages he might find some more distant relative with whom he could visit and be sure of food, lodging, and protection. By way of contrast to the clan group, which shared a common locality,[2] the kindred extended beyond the community and bound members of different tribes and villages together.

The clans of each tribe were arranged in a linear hierarchy comparable to that of the status positions within the clan. This hierarchy ranked the clans in the tribe with respect to their general importance and dictated the order in which the clans, as units, received their potlatch gifts. When a potlatch was given to a tribe, the members of the highest clan of that tribe received their gifts first, after them came the members of the second clan, and so on. The person who occupied the first position in the first clan of the tribe was the most important man in the tribe and was regarded as the tribal chief. When more than one tribe occupied the same village, as at Fort Rupert, the several tribal chiefs formed

[2] Some clans in different tribes bear the same name. They were considered to have belonged, originally, to the same clan and claimed descent from the same clan ancestor. When they split and affiliated with a different tribe, however, they severed all connections and were not, thenceforth, regarded as sections of the same clan.

a tribal council, which acted upon matters that pertained to the village and decided upon the course of action to be taken by the members of the community.

The tribes, too, were arranged in a linear hierarchy within the nation. At the top of the ladder were the Fort Rupert tribes. First came the true Kwakiutl,[3] second, the Kweka or *Murderers*, third, the Walas Kwakiutl or *Great Kwakiutl*, and fourth, the Kumkutis or *Rich Side*. The other tribes, living in other villages, occupied positions lower down. Thus the Mamaleleqala at Village Island were fifth, the Nimkis sixth, the Tlowitsis or *Angry People* seventh, and the Tenaktak of Knight Inlet eighth. Then followed the Matilspe, the Tsawatenox of Kingcome Inlet, the Kwekwesotenox of Gilford Island, the Gwawa-enox of Drury Inlet, the Hakwamis of Wakeman Sound, the Nakwaktox of Blundon Harbor, the Newettee of Hope Island, the Nakomgilisala of Cape Scott, the Koskimo of Quatsino Sound, the Tlaskenox of Klaskino Inlet, and so on. The members of all twenty-five tribes referred to themselves as "those speaking the same language," or as Kwakiutl, taking the name of the first ranking tribe as descriptive of the entire nation.

The Kwakiutl nation as a whole was considered by its members to be higher in rank than any other Indian nation. This did not mean that they thought of themselves as stronger, braver, or wealthier, but, rather, to be looked up to as more "chiefly," and more respectable. If they saw some people from the north, they would say, "Oh, that's just the Gwetela, that's all," or some such phrase to signify that they were of little importance. Their contacts with the peoples to the north and south were characterized by a certain amount of trading and some sporadic warfare. Once in a while a war party from one of the other groups, the Haida of the Queen Charlotte Islands for instance, would raid a Kwakiutl village and carry off a few captives. If the raid were severe, it

---

[3] The attempt has been made, throughout this volume, to write the native names with the letters of the English alphabet. This does violence to the sounds actually uttered by the Kwakiutl, and the spelling of the names, therefore, is not an accurate phonetic transcription.

was necessary, in order to maintain the respect of the members of the community, to send a war party out in retaliation. But such raids were infrequent, and the superiority which the members of the Kwakiutl nation felt they possessed over their neighbors was seldom challenged.

The hierarchy of tribes within the nation, as well as that of the clans within each tribe and of positions within each clan, was of especial significance in the potlatch. The word "potlatch" comes from Chinook jargon, in which it means "to give." Giving was certainly one of the outstanding characteristics of the Kwakiutl potlatch. Depending upon the number of people invited to attend, a man might give away from a hundred to many thousands of blankets, or their equivalent, in a single potlatch. But a man did not distribute these blankets indiscriminately among his guests. The order in which he gave out the blankets and, to a great extent, the number which he gave to each person depended upon the hierarchy of tribes, clans, and positions within the clan. A brief outline of potlatch procedure will make this clear.

A man of the Kweka tribe giving a funeral potlatch for his father, for example, would, if the deceased were a chief, probably invite the Mamaleleqala, Nimkis, Tlowitsis, and Tenaktak tribes to come. The four tribes living at Fort Rupert would play host to the other four tribes. This pattern runs through all potlatches large or small. There always has to be the "other side." The Fort Rupert tribes were divided into groups which functioned in local potlatching. The first and second tribes formed one group, the third and fourth the other. Thus, if a Kweka chief gave a local potlatch, he would invite only the Walas Kwakiutl and the Kumkutis. Similarly, in villages composed of only one tribe there was a moiety division of the tribe, which provided the two sides necessary to a potlatch. Among the Nimkis, for example, the first two clans formed one of these divisions and the lower three clans the other, so that when a member of one of the first two clans gave a local potlatch he would give it to the members of the "other side," i.e., the third, fourth, and fifth clans.

In the potlatch the chief would distribute blankets to the men of the invited tribes in order of their rank. If the tribes outside Fort Rupert had been invited, the first gift would go to the man in the first position in the first clan of the Mamaleleqala, which is the tribe highest in rank after the Fort Rupert tribes. Rather fewer blankets would then go to the man in the second position of this same clan of the Mamaleleqala, and so on, until that clan was finished. Then the second clan of the Mamaleleqala was called, and these men received their gifts in order of their rank within the clan. When the Mamaleleqala tribe was finished, the first clan of the tribe next in order, the Nimkis, was called. After the Nimkis clans, the Tlowitsis clans were called in order and then, finally, the Tenaktak. The hierarchy of tribe, clan, and individual position thus dictated, in strict fashion, the order in which the blankets were distributed.

The number of blankets which a particular individual received, however, depended rather upon the position he held in his clan than upon the rank of his clan in the tribe, or upon the rank of his tribe in the national hierarchy. Men in comparable positions in different clans and in different tribes received gifts of approximately the same size. Thus the head chief of the first clan of the Nimkis, for example, would receive about the same number of blankets as the head chief of any of the other Nimkis clans or the head chiefs of the clans in any of the other tribes. Moreover, the number of blankets a man received was in good part determined by the number which he, or his predecessor in that position, in the past had given to the man now giving the potlatch. If he had previously given his host one hundred blankets in his own potlatch, he would expect his host to reciprocate and give him one hundred blankets at this time.

In preparation for giving a potlatch a man would lend his blankets to those who wished to borrow them. The loan was made with the expectation of return with interest which was roughly proportional to the time taken to return the blankets: a loan for a few months netted 25 per cent interest, a six months' loan brought 50 per cent interest, and a loan for a year or more brought 100 per cent interest. If, therefore, a man lent one thousand blankets he would collect two thousand blankets at the end of a year. If at the end of the allotted time the debtor could not repay the amount with full interest, he might borrow from someone else so as to pay his debt. If he happened to be one of those who were to receive blankets at the potlatch, he might borrow that much from the person who was going to give the potlatch and then pay his debt with those blankets. This made it necessary, of course, for him to relinquish his right to receive his gift at the potlatch. There was a great deal of incentive for a man to pay his debts and the required interest, for, should he fail to do so very often, no one would trust him. This would mean that he could neither borrow from others nor prevail upon them to accept his loans. Under such circumstances he would be deprived of the possibility of entering into the potlatch either as donor or as recipient.

The blankets for the potlatch were formerly of native manufacture: blankets of woven cedar bark or of skin. With the coming of the whites, however, the Hudson's Bay Company's trade blankets soon superseded the native blankets. They could be obtained at the trading post for their equivalent in mink or other pelts valuable to the whites. The monetary equivalent of these trade blankets was $1.50, and money often took the place of blankets in the potlatch. But when money was distributed in a potlatch, or lent for interest, it was regarded in terms of the blankets it represented. Three hundred dollars, for example, was always translated into its equivalent of two hundred blankets.

The potlatch did not always, however, involve the distribution of blankets or money. In one form of the potlatch, canoes, instead of blankets or money, were given away. The potlatch which took place upon the occasion of the marriage payment by the bride's family a few years after the wedding invariably involved the distribution of such household articles as provisions, wooden boxes, mats, baskets, and, more recently, canned goods, dishes, and washing machines. Another potlatch-like ceremony, the so-called grease feast, involved giving away boxes of olachen oil. Although somewhat different ceremonial marked these varied forms of the potlatch, they followed essentially the same pattern of property distribution.

For the Kwakiutl, the potlatch served to accomplish a number of different results. As might be suspected, it was often used in connection with the positions of individuals within the clan. A man who had a son whom he wished to place in one of the clan positions could do so only by means of the potlatch. If, for example, a man in the first position in a clan wished his son to be placed in this position, he would give a potlatch and announce at that time that his son was to be his heir and take the first position of his clan. At the same time he would bestow upon his son a name to signify that the boy now had a claim to that position and would assume it when he became old enough.

The potlatch could also be used as a technique to wrest a higher position from another member of the same clan. Thus a man in the third position of a clan who coveted the second position might give a huge potlatch and announce that he was changing his position from third to second place. The person in second place would probably contest this assertion and rise to announce that he intended to give a still larger potlatch to prove his right to retain his rank. If he did so, the challenger would have to retaliate with a still larger potlatch or else give up his attempt to improve his position. If he gave a potlatch which the defender could not match, he had the right to usurp the position and demote his rival. Such contests would go on for years and, during the rivalry, both men received their gifts together as though they both occupied the second position.

By similar means it was theoretically possible for one clan to supersede another or for one tribe to displace the tribe next above it. As a matter of fact, the Nimkis tribe made an unsuccessful attempt to take the fifth tribal position by displacing the Mamaleleqala. The Nimkis gave a number of potlatches to the Fort Rupert tribes and announced their intention of moving into fifth place. But the Mamaleleqala met the challenge and also gave potlatches to the Fort Rupert people. The latter, sitting in judgment over the two tribes, decided that the Nimkis had not yet earned the right to change their position.

The potlatch could also be the means of obtaining prestige, quite apart from a change in actual position. The person who gave great and numerous potlatches was, first of all, an important person in any potlatch given by another chief. He would have given so many gifts in potlatches of his own that, in return, he would receive substantial gifts in any potlatch that he attended. Moreover, no one could speak evil of the person who had given many large potlatches. Should he do so he himself would be subject to ridicule on the ground that, since he had not given as many potlatches, he could not possibly be as important as the man whom he was attempting to slander. Finally, in giving a potlatch, a man might change his name to one which carried more prestige. For example, he might change his name from Mountain to Great Mountain and thus assume somewhat more importance in the eyes of his fellows.

The potlatch was a means of avoiding anxiety about becoming poverty stricken: it functioned as a banking system for the investment of capital—a sort of old-age insurance. A chief who had distributed many blankets in the potlatches he had given could count upon a continuous return of blankets in the future. Since blankets formed the native currency he would never become destitute; the blankets he received could be exchanged for the goods and services he required. The same result could have been achieved by hoarding the blankets, but this would have removed them from circulation—a dangerous possibility for, if many chiefs had done so, they would soon have cornered the market and potlatching could not have continued. This circumstance did not arise, however, because there was more incentive for a chief to potlatch than to hoard his blankets: by distributing them he could gain prestige and yet know, at the same time, that they would be returned to him at some future date.

The potlatch also provided direct means of venting ag-

gression against another person. It was only in connection
with a potlatch that a copper could be broken and presented
to a person whom one wished to insult. Coppers were the
most valuable of the Kwakiutl possessions. Originally obtained from the Indians farther north, they were thin copper shields incised with designs. Their value was determined by the price paid when they were bought. If a man
had paid fifty thousand blankets for a copper, that was its
value, and should he wish to sell it he would expect that much
and more in return for it. A copper, therefore, was a certificate of expended wealth and one which could always be
turned into cash by its sale. If, however, a copper was bent
or broken during a potlatch ceremony it became practically
worthless. Therefore, when a man broke a copper in his potlatch and gave it to his enemy, the latter was placed in a difficult situation. Either he had to return a copper of equal
value in a potlatch of his own or else he had to submit to the
criticism of his fellows and forego the right to say anything
against a chief who had so forcibly demonstrated his supe-
rior wealth and power by throwing away a certificate for
fifty thousand blankets.

The breaking of coppers in a potlatch, however, was not
always done to spite an enemy and shame him before the
public. A man might destroy a copper to enhance his own
prestige rather than to lower that of his rival. In a grease
potlatch, for example, he might put one of his coppers on
the fire to make it "burn brighter" and thus let all the people
know how great a man he was, somewhat after the fashion
of the millionaire who lights his cigarette with a thousand
dollar bill. The destruction of coppers, either in vengeance
or as a means of increasing a man's prestige, actually had a
useful social function. Coppers, which could have been sold
to concentrate most of the actual wealth of the group in the
hands of a few men, disappeared; the money and blankets
which they represented remained in the hands of the lesser
chiefs.

The potlatch functioned in many instances to reward
people for effort expended. When a chief died, the other

tribes were summoned to come and bury him and to witness
the installation of his heir in the position of the deceased.
In return for attending the funeral, helping to bury the deceased, and witnessing the installation, they received their
gifts at the potlatch. Similarly, on the occasion of a change
of name, a change of position, a girl's first menstruation, or
a marriage, the invited guests were rewarded through the
potlatch for witnessing a change in the *status quo* which it
was important that everyone should know and remember.
Again, when a communal dwelling was built, other tribes
were generally invited to come and assist in its construction.
After the dwelling was built a housewarming potlatch was
given to the visiting tribes, recompensing them for their
time and effort; this reward by potlatch was in addition to
and quite apart from the specific payments which were made
to visiting young men for their labor in constructing the
house.

A great many potlatches took place in the winter time in
connection with the winter ceremonial. This ceremonial re-
volved about the initiation of the young men into secret societies. Every winter one of the chiefs would volunteer to be responsible for the ceremonial. This would generally be the year
when his son was eligible for entrance into one of the most
important of the secret societies. It would be in his communal
dwelling that the dances would take place, and it would be he
who would give a big potlatch at the close of the ceremonial.

During the winter ceremonial, the people were grouped
according to the secret societies to which they belonged. Of
these the most important were the Hamatsa or Cannibal society, the Grizzly Bear society, the Hamshamtses society—a
cannibal society distinguished from the Hamatsa by the absence of certain ritual characteristics, notably the absence of
whistles from their ceremonial paraphernalia—the Crazy
Man society, and the Warrior society. The rank of these
secret societies was revealed in the feasts and potlatches that
took place during the winter ceremonial; the Hamatsas received their food or gifts first, and the members of the other
societies received theirs later. Those who did not belong to any

secret society formed a group apart known as the *gwegwutsa*. These were people who had not yet been initiated into a society or who had retired from membership by initiating their sons in their places. Both *gwegwutsa* and members used different personal names from those employed in the summer. These winter ceremonial names were given a person by his father or mother, his wife's father or mother, or sometimes another relative. The *gwegwutsa* names were not associated with any special ceremonial; all other names, however, were assumed in connection with either a specific dance or an initiation rite.

Despite the change in names during the winter ceremonial and the change in the relative rank of individuals resulting from membership in secret societies, the difference between the winter and summer organizations was not so great as might be imagined. Members of different clans and different tribes were grouped together in the secret societies, to be sure, and to that extent the clan and tribal divisions so important at other times lost their significance during the winter ceremonial. But individual rankings within clans tended to carry over into the winter organization. Sons of chiefs were the most likely to rise high in the secret society hierarchy. Indeed, no one but the son of a chief ever became a Cannibal (Hamatsa). Moreover, the summer-time ranking of tribe and clan was strictly adhered to in one of the most important parts of the winter ceremonial. On this occasion each person who owned the right to have a certain dance performed would ask some one of his relatives to dance his dance, and the order in which these dances were presented depended directly upon the tribal, clan, and positional ranking in the summer organization, the members of the Kwakiutl clans displaying their dances first in order of rank, the Kwekas second, and so on.

These special dances were always performed with masks. In fact, the Indians inverted this relationship, saying that particular masks had their characteristic dances. Such masks were made to represent the bird, animal, or being whose characteristics the dancer assumed during the performance.

These dance masks, however, should not be confused with those representing crests. The Thunderbird mask, for example, represented a crest and was used only when someone died; it was never used as a dance mask. Many of the dances took place without any period of initiation preceding them. A chief would simply ask one of his young relatives to give the dance of one of his masks and, in return for the performance, would give that kinsman a name signifying his right to that particular dance. Other dances involved an initiation ceremony; these were the ones belonging to the secret societies. Thus, the first time anyone danced the Cannibal or Grizzly Bear dance, he had to undergo initiation into that secret society.

Initiation began with the seclusion of the neophyte in the woods for a number of days preceding his induction into the secret society. Actually, instead of going into the woods, he stayed in one of the back bedrooms of the communal dwelling in which the winter ceremonial was being held. While in seclusion, he was supposed to become wild, and the ceremonial which followed was designed to tame him just enough to render him acceptable as a member of the society. Part of the taming ritual for the Cannibal dancer, for example, taught the neophyte to stop eating human flesh, or, at least, to eat it with discretion. When the Cannibal came back from the woods, he was supposed to have become so "wild" that he craved human flesh. To demonstrate this, he attempted to bite pieces of flesh from the arm or leg of anyone he met. To cure him of this wild craving he was given hunks of flesh from a corpse. This he was supposed to eat and by so doing to become tame. As a matter of fact, he did not eat the flesh at all, but concealed it on his person or held it in his mouth until he could dispose of it without being seen.

The element of trickery ran all through the dancing and the initiation rites. The Kwakiutl winter ceremonial was more like the performance of a group of magicians than anything else. For example, the dancer who made a mistake in his steps, or in the words of his songs, was supposed to be killed. The punishment, however, was only an elaborate hoax; enraged Cannibals, Crazy Men, and Grizzly Bears pounced upon the dancer and pretended to murder him. The ways in which the pretense was carried out were often very effective, sometimes being so realistic as to convince the audience that the punishment had actually taken place. But the audience was reassured when, a day or two later, the dead dancer came back to life and participated in some other performance.

The tricks were the secret property of the members of the secret society which used them. To keep these secrets from becoming common knowledge, the members of each of these societies were forbidden to reveal to any non-members how the tricks were done. To aid in keeping the trickery from becoming known to outsiders, the back part of the communal dwelling in which the dancing and ceremonial took place was separated by a screen called the *mawitl*. In one of the bedrooms behind the screen the neophytes were secluded. Behind the screen, too, preparations were made for all the performances, and there no uninitiated person was permitted to go. About this matter the members of the secret societies were very serious; the penalty for trespassing upon this sacred part of the house was death, and, in such cases, the killing was not pretense.

The Kwakiutl winter ceremonial invariably smacked of blood and violence. Nearly every dance and initiation involved the simulation of murder, torture, or cannibalism. All the native talents for drama seem to have been devoted to the creation of bloody and violent scenes. This is particularly interesting since it was so unlike the situation in real life. Except in children's games the Kwakiutl were never even remotely bloodthirsty in their day-to-day relationships. Within village and tribe, physical strife of any kind was strictly discouraged and heavily punished, and murder was exceedingly rare. In attempts to advance one's own position, for example, physical violence was rigorously forbidden; it would not, indeed, have achieved the desired objective since even if a man were murdered his heir would automatically take his place. People contended with potlatches and with coppers; this was the only legitimate and honorable way to fight another Kwakiutl. And this channeling of aggressions through the potlatch had definite survival value: people spent their energies in amassing wealth rather than in brawls and violence.

Peace also reigned within the nation. Conflict between tribes took place in an orderly and sophisticated potlatch duel while the other tribes sat in judgment upon the outcome of the struggle. To be sure, the Kwakiutl were called upon many times to defend themselves against the sea raiders who swooped down upon their villages from the north, but they were not overeager for battle, and retaliatory raids were infrequent. They lacked a well-developed military organization, and their military tactics were rudimentary at best.

Why then did the Kwakiutl cling so tenaciously to the bloody and violent dramas that characterized their winter ceremonial? During the ceremonial, some of the Indians pretended to exhibit a violence and bloodthirstiness that at other times they did not reveal, while others witnessed these scenes and to that extent participated in the fierceness of the drama. Can it be that this aspect of the ceremonial pleased the natives just because their daily life demanded such strict control over aggression? Can it be that they derived pleasure from thus participating in acts of violence which they badly wanted to do yet dared not?

The suggestion that the Kwakiutl often actually hated their fellows, though they dared not openly attack them seems borne out by their interest in sorcery. Had their antagonisms not been suppressed, they would have had little use for sorcery and little reason to worry about the possibility of being bewitched. Yet sorcery was much practiced, and the fear of being bewitched was of common occurrence. Sorcery was a technique by means of which, it was believed, the health and life of another person could be destroyed. A number of different methods were known, of which the most effective method may be described. The sorcerer first obtained secretly some samples of the personal belongings of the person to be bewitched, e.g., a few of his hairs or nail clippings,

some earth which had been dampened with his urine or spittle,
and bits of his clothing. These the sorcerer put inside a human corpse or, if this could not be obtained, the body of a
frog, snake, or other dead animal. He then sealed up all the
openings in the body, sewing them together and covering
them with pitch, and placed the corpse in some secret spot
where the sun would shine on it or hung it to the branch of a
tree where the wind would blow it about. Whatever happened
to the corpse or its substitute would be revealed as a symp-
tom in the sorcerized person: when the sun struck the corpse
the person would have a high fever and would then have
chills at night; when the wind swayed it the person would
grow dizzy and feel faint. Finally, when the body decayed or
fell from its place in the tree, the victim would die. If, however, someone found the corpse before this happened, opened
it up carefully, and exposed its contents to the air or placed
them in water, the person would recover.

Not all the Indians knew the art of sorcery. There were
professional sorcerers who, for a fee, would contract to be-
witch the person whom his client wanted to kill. Any sorcerer, whether a professional or an amateur, would be very
secretive about his magic. If caught in the act of preparing
a corpse he might well be killed by those who discovered him.
Even if they spared him, they would make public the fact
that he had been caught in an act of sorcery and his behavior
would thenceforth be under grave suspicion. Any further
attempt on his part would almost inevitably prove fatal. Another reason for secrecy was the possibility that a person
who felt himself succumbing to the effects of sorcery might
employ countermagic against the person thought responsible for his condition. A suspected sorcerer might expect
that all the people who felt that they were being sorcerized
at the time would practice countermagic against him, and
this was a risk that no one cared to take.

In contrast to those who knew the art of causing sickness
and death by means of sorcery were those whose knowledge
of magic was primarily employed in curing disease and pre-
venting death. These doctors were summoned when the native

medical knowledge of drugs and potions failed to cure. They knew a number of magical techniques for combating mysterious illnesses, e.g., sucking out from the flesh objects which had presumably caused the sickness. For his services the doctor was paid, and he received his fee whether or not he was successful in his efforts. If he failed to produce a cure, he would blame the illness on sorcery, and, since he usually knew how to do so, he might offer to practice countermagic against the suspected sorcerer. This was a legitimate occasion for the use of sorcery and was not regarded as a punishable offense.

The Kwakiutl were not much concerned with theorizing about where their children came from; in general, they thought of babies as ancestors who had returned to this world. In accordance with this view, it was customary, when a person died, for those comforting the survivors to say, "After all, the departed one will come again, born to his niece or his granddaughter." Proofs of reincarnation were numerous: the baby might look like the deceased, he might have a birthmark where the ancestor had a scar, or, as an adult, he might evince a special skill such as wood carving which could only mean that he was an experienced wood carver reborn. The great number of births which seemed to follow this pattern reinforced the belief and insured its persistence.

The Kwakiutl were well aware of the rôle played by the father in reproduction. In fact, pregnancy was considered to be indisputable proof of sexual experience. The only effective contraceptive device was abstinence, although a few magical practices were thought to prevent conception for short periods. The sex of the child, it was believed, could be determined at the time of fertilization: if the parents wanted a boy they would put articles associated with male crafts beneath the bed, and if they wanted a girl they would substitute articles associated with female occupations. Neither barrenness nor sterility was considered disgraceful; they were merely unfortunate. If a man's wife did not bear children, he would probably separate from her and marry again.

If he were a chief, he might under such circumstances have two wives. A woman who thought her husband sterile might leave him and seek another husband, but, more often, she would commit adultery in the hope of becoming pregnant. Consequently the sterility of a man was seldom exposed.

The Kwakiutl woman reckoned the duration of her pregnancy to be ten moons from her last menstrual period. Early months of pregnancy were often marked by a feeling of lassitude and slight nausea. While carrying a child it was thought dangerous for her to see anything which might frighten her. Should she see a corpse or a dead animal, the baby might be stillborn; should she see a maimed or deformed person, or a person covered with sores, the baby might resemble the person she had seen. The husband, as well, avoided such sights. If either the woman or her husband accidentally saw something unpleasant, a technique was at hand whereby they could avoid the unfortunate consequences. A piece of cedar bark could be waved four times over the unpleasant object and then passed four times down the back of the woman. The bark was saved, and, should something be wrong with the baby after it was born, it could be cured by waving the bark over it four times. A pregnant woman was cautioned against certain foods; if, for example, she should eat salmon eggs or chew gum, their stickiness might be imparted to the fetus, causing it to adhere to her womb and thus rendering her delivery difficult. By somewhat similar reasoning she refrained from making baskets lest the navel cord become twisted around the child's neck. To insure an easy delivery she could carry out in pantomime an easy birth, taking four pebbles from the beach and letting them slip through her clothing onto the ground while expressing the hope, "May I be like these." Shortly before delivery it was thought she might further facilitate her delivery by opening her braids and drinking certain medicines.

Delivery generally took place in a hut apart from the communal dwelling. Three or four older women, who were experienced midwives, assisted at the birth. When a woman had her first baby, her mother usually came to help with the delivery. The husband seldom attended the birth; his task was to keep the midwives supplied with water and wood for the fire. He might stand around outside the delivery hut, going inside from time to time to see how things were progressing. No other persons were permitted to enter the hut, for childbirth was considered a private matter. When the baby was born one of the midwives tied and cut the cord, washed the infant in warm water, and wrapped it in soft cedar bark. If the afterbirth did not come out by itself, a midwife attempted to press it out with her hands. Since the blood expelled during the childbirth was considered poisonous, it was collected on cedar bark and buried with the afterbirth. The midwives washed the mother in warm water and then permitted her to lie down and rest. For four days after the birth the mother and her newly born child were secluded. During this period she kept very quiet and was waited upon by her mother or one of the midwives.

The birth of twins was considered to be a wonderful event. All twins were believed to be endowed with supernatural power, and their birth was surrounded with special ritual. Their parents found themselves encumbered with restrictions which were designed to protect them from danger. It was believed that twins could influence the weather and cure certain sicknesses as well. Stillborn children or mothers who died in childbirth were given a regular funeral. Badly deformed babies were destroyed at birth and buried in secret.

Four days after a child's birth the father gave a small potlatch and bestowed a name upon the child. At this time the baby was purified, the lobes of its ears were pierced, and it was put in its cradle for the first time. Another potlatch was given ten moons after birth. On this occasion the father gave the child its second name, straps were bound around its ankles and wrists, and its face was painted with ocher and its hair singed. These practices were believed to ward off sickness and pain.

The baby lived in its cradle continuously for a year or two, with its arms and legs so tightly bound that they could not move. Once a day, or oftener, the mother would take the baby out of its cradle, bathe it, rub it all over with fish oil, change its wrappings, and then put it back in the cradle. Whenever it was removed from the cradle it was massaged to change its features: the eyes were pulled upward and outward to make them large and the face smooth. The muscles of the forearm and the calves of the legs of girl babies were rubbed upward so that the limbs might become slender and graceful. The cradle usually hung suspended from the branch of a tree or a rafter in the house so that the mother could rock it whenever the child cried.

The mother took the greatest share in looking after her baby. If it were her first child, however, her own mother generally stayed with her for some time after the delivery, helping her with the baby and instructing her in its proper care. At night the baby slept in its cradle beside the mother. If the woman had an older daughter, the latter would do much of the routine work: bathing the baby, changing its wrappings, and the like. Any member of the household might rock the infant and sing it to sleep with lullabies.

A mother nursed her baby by holding the cradle in her arms. There was no nursing routine; she suckled her infant whenever she thought by its cries that it was hungry. Although the nursing mother attempted to regulate her diet by drinking soups and eating nourishing food, so that her milk would be abundant and wholesome, it sometimes happened that she would be unable to nurse her baby. In such a circumstance the child would be nursed by a relative— perhaps a sister or cousin of the mother. As the child grew older, supplementary feeding was gradually initiated in the form of premasticated food given by the mother, father, or grandparent. During the period of lactation, the mother was supposed to abstain from coitus lest she become pregnant while still nursing a small baby. This restriction is much less rigidly observed today than formerly, and babies are often born a year apart. This change has probably been facilitated by the introduction of the nursing bottle, a convenience which is being generally adopted. Weaning was generally initiated at between two and three years of age, al-

though it might be delayed even longer if the child were
sickly. It was accomplished by increasing the amount of
supplementary feeding and by punishing the child for suckling. The mother would put some bitter substance on her
nipples which, it is said, was very effective in discouraging
the child's attempts to nurse. After weaning, thumb sucking
was common but was discouraged by taking the finger out
of the mouth and giving the child some substitute such as
the muscular part of a dried horse clam. Today the pacifier
is in general use; it is tied with a string about the child's
neck so that he cannot drop it and can get it easily.

When it was old enough to talk, the mother or father
would take the child out of the house and down to the beach
to defecate. Somewhat earlier, it was taught to urinate in
the chamber vessel, and this is said to have been readily accomplished without punishment. The child was taught the
verb "to urinate" and learned first to tell his mother his want
and then to go by himself. Children were not punished for
wetting the bed; this, it was thought, would have had no
effect since children do not know what they are doing in
their sleep. They were, however, repeatedly asked to wake
up in the night if they wanted to use the chamber vessel.

Young children spent most of their time playing on the
beach and in the woods. Most of their games helped to equip
them for the life which their culture demanded of them as
adults. In their games, boys learned to hunt and fish while
girls practiced cooking and keeping house. Boys were taught
to be brave, to endure hardship and pain, and to act inde-
pendently without reliance on others. In particular, they
were taught the details of social organization; they learned to
know the names and positions of every person and the rank
of every clan and tribe. By watching the potlatch ceremonies
they learned the value of occupying high positions and were
told that the Indian is born only to obtain honor through
the potlatch. The boys also gave play potlatches of their own,
and in this they were generously encouraged by their elders.

When children were four or five years old, their parents
began to discipline them more severely, insisting upon more

and more conformance to adult behavior. If boys lounged about the fire, they were given a slap and told to sit up straight and to behave like gentlemen. Girls, lolling with their legs apart and their blankets carelessly placed, were strictly censured. Boys that fought with other members of their play group were ostracized for the time being and were permitted to join in the fun of the group only if they restrained their aggressive impulses. Aggression, in the form of striking, stealing, or lying, was severely punished, especially when directed toward the parents. Few restrictions, however, were placed upon sexual behavior. From early years, boys and girls were free to indulge in sex play among themselves. Their sexual practices took place in the woods and were seldom brought to the attention of their parents. For the boy, freedom to enjoy love affairs continued without interruption as he grew older. For the girl, however, the period of sexual freedom was brought to an end as she approached puberty. At the age of nine or ten, she found herself strictly chaperoned by her parents. She was then reaching the dangerous age when she might become pregnant, and, as a result, her parents watched her carefully and threatened her with dire consequences should she permit a lover to approach her. If a girl did become pregnant before she married, she would perform a secret abortion. Her mother would probably assist her, standing behind the girl and squeezing her abdomen downwards with both hands to expel the fetus. If the abortion failed, infanticide would be practiced, and the dead fetus would be buried secretly at night. It was considered imperative to avoid making the girl's plight known, for a girl disgraced by the birth of an illegitimate child would find it exceedingly difficult to find a husband.

When a girl reached puberty her father would give a potlatch, bestowing upon her a name taken from her mother's family and announcing that his daughter was now of a marriageable age. During her first menstrual period she was subjected to a rigid ritual. For four days she was required to rest quietly in a special shelter or, perhaps, in one of the household bedrooms. There were no very severe restrictions on her behavior during this period, although she was not permitted to sit near the fire and had to limit her eating and drinking. At the end of the four days she was placed in the charge of some elderly woman other than her own mother. She was washed at regular intervals and compelled to perform various acts in order to insure her health in future years. She wore a special hat to protect her eyes from the light, so that she would not become blind in later life; she drank water through the wing bone of an eagle so that she might never have too large an abdomen; and she wore a wide belt of mountain-goat wool across her breasts, furnished with holes for the nipples, to prevent her breasts from ever becoming too full. Finally, her hair and fingernails were cut, her eyebrows were trimmed, and she was given new clothing. At any time after this ceremony she might be given away in marriage.

Whenever thereafter a woman menstruated she remained in isolation until the flow of blood ceased. Menstrual blood was thought to be dangerous and was carefully collected in cedar bark and buried. Should a menstruating woman contaminate any of the fishing or hunting gear, fish and game would elude capture. Should she cook for her husband, some of the blood might get into the food and harm him. Should she make love to him, the blood would make him sick. The menstrual fluid was thought to be especially dangerous to sick people. While a woman remained in seclusion her mother, sister, or some other female member of the household would supply the food and water that she needed. After the flow ceased she washed herself carefully every day for four days, and was then permitted once more to mingle freely in the community. The malignant power which menstrual blood was believed to have for human beings extended to monsters; therefore when women were traveling they kept some menstrual blood in a bit of shredded bark to be used to poison a monster should one appear.

At about the time when a boy's voice changed, which the natives referred to as the boy's first monthly, his father would give a potlatch to announce the position that the lad would ultimately fill. At this time the father gave his son a name—his third—and announced this to all the tribes assembled for the potlatch. If the boy were his oldest son, the father would, at this time, assign him his own highest position. Since, however, an immature boy could not be expected to deal cogently with the proceeds of the potlatch, the father would continue to accept gifts in that position as he had in the past and invest them as he thought best. But it was understood that the son held the position in common with his father and that at some time in the future, the father would give another potlatch and surrender the position entirely. Should the father die before he gave this potlatch, his son would be the one to give the funeral potlatch and, at that time, assume sole right to the position.

Marriage took place immediately after puberty for girls and at about the age of twenty for men. Marriages were arranged by the parents; the boy and girl had little to say in the matter. This was always true of the children whose fathers occupied high positions. The son of a tribal chief was invariably forced, by his parents, to marry the daughter of some other tribal chief or, at the very least, a girl whose parents held an exceedingly high position. Apart from the preferences of the parents, there were only a few persons whom a man could not marry. Indeed, marriage was forbidden only when the union could be regarded as incestuous. A man could never marry his own mother or sister. Also forbidden to him were his half sister, his adopted sister, his father's sister, his mother's sister, and his sister's daughter. On the other hand, marriage with his stepmother was permissible if his father had separated from his wife or had died, and it was possible to marry, in exceptional circumstances, one's brother's daughter. Any other relative was marriageable. Equality in rank and position rather than degree of relationship was the important criterion in marriage.

When the parents of a boy had decided upon the girl they wanted him to marry, they sent a friend to talk with her parents. The friend asked the girl's father how many blankets he expected from the boy's father and then returned with the information that, for example, one thousand blankets were demanded. As soon after this as he could collect the required number of blankets, borrowing some if he did not have enough, the boy's father announced to the members of his tribe that the marriage was about to take place. At the same time, he sent a messenger to inform the girl's parents that he was ready with the payment. Then the tribe of the groom's father, together with the other tribes living in the same village, set forth in their canoes for the village where the girl and her family lived. When they arrived they sang, participated in contests, and pretended to fight with the members of the bride's village. Speeches were made by the visiting chiefs explaining that they wanted the girl for their wife and that this was a great honor for her and her people. The chiefs of the bride's village returned these speeches by pointing out that they were glad to have the bride married to such important people. The blankets were counted out and given to the girl's father. The latter, in return, counted out a much smaller number of blankets, which were given to the boy or to his father. These blankets symbolized his approval of the transaction. Actually, however, they functioned as a payment to the members of the boy's village who had accompanied him to witness the marriage, for shortly thereafter they were distributed among these people by the boy at a special potlatch. After the transfer of blankets the chiefs from the boy's group went over and took the girl, escorting her to her husband, for from this time on they were regarded as man and wife. That night the couple went either to the house of the groom's father or, if their village was too far away, to the house of the bride's father.

The parents of the bride now sought to amass as much wealth as possible. The young couple also accumulated property with the assistance of the groom's father and turned it over to the girl's parents. Three or four years after the wedding, when the bride's family had acquired enough wealth, they brought it in canoes to the groom's family. An important part of this property was a copper, referred to as the "mast of the canoe," which was given to the groom. The groom later distributed the property in a potlatch to those tribes who had come to witness the transaction. The amount thus paid by the bride's father was many times the amount originally received by him at the wedding; he attempted to return as much as he could for by his liberality he gained prestige and honor. This transaction was considered to cancel the debt contracted at the wedding, and the wife was thereafter free to separate from her husband should she so desire. Until this debt had been repaid by her father, however, she was under absolute obligation to remain with her husband.

After marriage, life took a serious turn for both man and woman. The husband worked hard during the greater part of the year to provide food, shelter, and transportation for his family. Furthermore, he strove to accumulate the wealth needed to give the feasts and potlatches expected of him. The wife spent her time keeping house, collecting roots, berries, and shellfish, cooking and preserving food, and making mats and baskets. When a baby was born, additional duties descended upon the couple. The mother took care of the child, nursed it, and later, taught it to take care of itself. The father gave the potlatch ceremonies that marked the stages in the child's social development and attempted to direct his child into an advantageous marriage.

The responsibilities and cares of married life, however, were occasionally lifted. Now and again, husband and wife took a trip to a neighboring tribe to attend a wedding or a funeral, visiting their relatives for a while. Even at home, friends dropped in from time to time for a casual meal, and all sat about the fire and told stories or played games with the children. In the winter time, moreover, there was the pleasure of attending the ceremonial feasts and dances.

Marriage did not demand sexual fidelity either of the man or of his wife. If philandering took place secretly and in accordance with the customary rules, no notice was taken of it. Only if a man flaunted his love affairs in public and thus shamed his wife would she censure his behavior. The husband might be slightly more strict about the love affairs of his wife, but he did little more than scold her privately so long as she did not openly disgrace him. A pregnancy resulting from an adulterous intrigue was rarely taken very seriously. Even if the husband knew that the child was not his, he would generally keep his knowledge to himself, not wishing to make the fact public by leaving his wife or forcing her to abort the child.

When a man's children grew up and married, his responsibilities began to taper off, and he spent most of his time playing with his grandchildren, attending feasts and potlatches, and talking over old times with friends of his own generation. As he grew more aged he depended more and more upon his married children for support. By this time he had relinquished his positions to his heirs, and they took care of him. His wife, too, gradually abandoned her household duties. She helped her daughters-in-law with the care of their children, tended to the drying of fish and berries, and gossiped with friends of her own age. Old age was not unpleasant for either a man or woman; old persons of both sexes were generally well treated.

When death came, the body was prepared for burial and taken out of the house through an opening in the wall. If the deceased person had been socially important, the survivors invited the other tribes to come and help with the funeral. The corpse was placed in a wooden coffin which was deposited either in a tree or in a small houselike shelter. For four days thereafter, it was improper to hold festivities of any kind. This period of mourning was followed by a ceremony during which the dead person was called upon to enter the community house where all the people were assembled. A man, dressed in a mask representing one of the clan ancestors of the deceased, entered the house and, after dancing around in solemn silence, went out through the door and disappeared. This signified that the deceased had at last departed to take up his abode with the ancestor of his clan. Then the heir to the highest position formerly held by the deceased person gave a potlatch at which he proclaimed his new name and position.

PREFACE TO CHARLEY'S STORY

Charles James Nowell now tells the story of his life. When he was born, seventy years ago, his native culture showed little evidence of white contact. Now that he is an old man, the great majority of Kwakiutl men and women have adopted white customs. Charley, however, remains a staunch supporter of Indian ways. He clings, even today, to native ideals. Despite the condemnation of the potlatch by missionary and Indian agent alike, Charley believes it to be a legitimate and honorable institution. He still gives credence to sorcery.

Charley comes of a high ranking family. His older brother, Owadi, was the head chief of the first clan of the Kweka tribe —a position formerly held by his father's brother and, before that, by his father's father. His mother's father was the younger brother of Tlakodlas, the head chief of the second clan in the Nimkis tribe. From his birth Charley was trained to take his place as an important chief in Kwakiutl society.

His older brother, who held a deep respect for white culture, felt that Charley should go to school. And so Charley attended the mission school at Alert Bay. While there, he learned to speak English. This has made it possible to take down the story of his life exactly as he told it. The story comes to the reader in Charley's own words. The following alterations, however, have been necessary: the narrative has been put as nearly as possible in chronological sequence; word order has been altered when necessary for purposes of clarity; many native terms and technical descriptions have been omitted; and, finally, false English aliases have been substituted for the real names of the girls with whom Charley had affairs. In all other respects the story has been repeated exactly as he told it. At various points in the narrative it has seemed desirable to introduce brief explanatory remarks; these have been put in footnotes so that they might easily be distinguished from the information given by Charley himself.

In Charley's story Kwakiutl society springs to life. He and his people are real: they laugh and cry, love and hate, live and die; they use the ways provided by their culture to achieve understandable goals; and, above all, they act in a sensible, intelligible, and human manner.

CHAPTER II

MY LIFE BEGINS

I WAS born at Fort Rupert in the year 1870. It was coming on to winter. Soon after I was born the Walas Kwakiutl lost forty men in front of Fort Rupert. They got upset in their canoe and all got drowned. When they found out that those people had died, my mother left me in my cradle, wrapped up, and went out to the beach with the others to find out if they could find any of the bodies. It was in the night time when all this happened, and my parents were living on the north end of the village.

On the fourth day after the time I was born, my father and mother called the people of Fort Rupert, that is, all but the Kwekas, to give them some blankets to give me my first name.[1] My first name was Tlalis—Stranded Whale.

The same day, the fourth after my birth, my father and mother gathered all the rotten stuff they could find—rotten wood, moss, the green stuff that grows on the outside of canoes, old rotten mats, and everything that was rotten. They brought these things into the house and set a fire on to that and put the cradle on top of the smoke four times, so that I will be mild and won't cry much. Then they went out and found water on the top of old stumps, and bathed me in that four times. This makes me meek, too. After that, once a day

[1] During the previous four days, Charley probably remained in rather strict isolation with his mother and other female relatives. This is a widespread primitive practice. Although the number of days varies slightly in different parts of the world, nearly all peoples isolate their babies for the first week after birth. The universality of this custom seems to indicate that primitive man has learned, through sad experience, that the infant is highly susceptible to infection during the time before the umbilicus heals. Such isolation delays the time when the baby is formally introduced to the adult members of the group. Here, four days after birth, Charley is presented to the adults of Fort Rupert and is given his first name. He has passed the first crisis and deserves recognition.

for four days, they do the same thing with the water, but
they only smoke me once.

On the same day, the fourth day after my birth, they put
me in my cradle. My arms were bound straight down and my
feet and legs, too, but my head was way down in a hollow in
the cradle. They have little sticks all whittled out flat to put
under me about three inches from the bottom of the cradle.
These sticks are made of yew wood. They say that if they
are made out of cedar, I would be laughing all the time. The
reason they use yew is because they want my backbone to
become as strong as the yew wood. Then there was cedar
bark, shredded very soft and fine, made up in fine layers for
me to lie on, and sometimes this was made of the yellow cedar
bark. There was the same kind of bark for the pad that goes
over my head, and it comes down in a peak over my eyes to
keep the light out, so I will be sleeping all the time.

After I was put in the cradle and after I was smoked,
they tied my cradle with a rope to a strong limb of a young
hemlock tree that is close to the house. The cradle was hung
on the rope inside the house right close to where my mother
is sitting. And they tied a rope on one end of this limb and
pulled it up and down every time I cry to make me go to
sleep. My mother called a lot of children to come and play
in the house and make a lot of noise while I am sleeping.
They say this makes the baby sleep afterwards without being disturbed by loud noises.

When I was put in my cradle, my mother didn't take me
outside the house. She took me out of the cradle in the mornings to bathe me, and, when I make a mess in my cradle, they
take me out and change me. My mother told me I used to
fuss about it when she tied me in the cradle. My mother
would wash me in warm urine and then rinse me thoroughly
in warm clean water. In the old days, they didn't have any
soap except the water they passed. After I am washed, my
mother rubs me all over with ratfish oil. When I have a cold
and my bowels is not moving, they rub me all over with olachen oil and wrap me up. The old people do this, too, and

they drink it for a cold, but it is too strong for a baby to drink. They say the oil just soaks through a baby.

From the time I am first put in my cradle, they be watching for the string to come off from the button of my belly. If you want your baby to be a canoemaker, they give it to a man to put on his wrist while he is making a canoe. They gave mine to my father, and he put it on his right wrist while singing. They say they took me out of my cradle and wrapped me up and put me inside a wooden drum. He began to hit the drum with his fists and began to sing. He put me in the drum and sing like this four times to make me like he was—a maker of songs. I could have been like him, and I was when I was a young man. I made winter dance songs and love songs, but we don't make them any more.

While I was in my cradle, I cried all the time. My parents wanted me to sleep. They got some boys with poles, in the evening, to catch a bat. They put it under my cradle. They say the bat sleeps all the time in the day, and that will make me sleep all the time during the day. Then they begin to wonder who was crying the way I was now crying. They think of a woman crying for a dead person, and asked this woman to come and pretend to cry. I was all covered up. They always do this when a baby cries too much, and they say it will stop him. But it didn't stop me.[2]

If a baby's skin gets yellow, they say that the parents of

[2] As will become clear later, Charley must have been born when his mother was well along in years. Because of her age, she may not have been able to give him an adequate supply of milk, hence his excessive crying. Moreover, a child strapped in a cradle can do very little besides cry when uncomfortable; it is the only act on his part which brings him food and other bodily satisfactions. Hence it will become the most successful response at his disposal, will persist and recur whenever he is uncomfortable, and will presumably be quite difficult to supplant with other habits when the child is finally taken from the cradle. It is probable that today, now that cradling is being abandoned, other acts such as reaching for the mother, crawling to her, and the like, will also bring results, so that crying will not be the only act which is rewarded. Should this be so, one would anticipate a corresponding decrease in the frequency of crying by children. Such methods as those described above, which were used to prevent Charley from crying, would not be in as great demand and would ultimately tend to disappear from the culture.

the baby have seen a frog. His parents go and find a frog and come in with the frog alive. They take the baby out of the cradle and cover him with something, and take the frog by the legs and pass it down near the back of the baby saying, "This is the cause of your sickness." They do this four times. If the baby doesn't get well, they do it the next day and so on until the fourth day. If the parents see a dead man or a dead woman, they take a rag and go to the dead person and wipe it on the face with a rag. And they say when a child has no breath and is like a dead person, they use this the same way on a child. When they hear crows crowing or any bird making a noise when a woman is pregnant, then the baby may make a noise like that. Anything they see or hear or smell while she is carrying, if it frightens them, the child will be like that.

At my tenth month my parents called all the young men to come. These men painted their faces with red paint and came to see my hair burned off. They used a flounder bone to hold my hair up like a comb and then burned it off. Before this my hair was not cut. My mother and father also put bands on my wrists and on my ankles. That shows that I am now ten months old. I had my ears pierced, too. They put ice on my ears so I wouldn't feel it and then put a needle through. They say that without having pierced ears, you wouldn't be welcome by the dead people when you die.

I used to have earrings when I was a boy. The last ones I had were gold. I sold mine after I got married. I wasn't allowed to wear them while I was in school. Mr. Hall didn't want me to wear them. Before my time, I am told, they used to pierce the nose and wear a shell ring in it. I never saw anybody with these rings in their noses, but I have seen my mother's brother had three holes on the ear and three earrings made out of abalone shells. The lowest was the biggest, and they get smaller going to the top. Some women were the same, and, when they die, they take off the small ones and put a big abalone shell about four inches square in the ear when they are buried. These abalone shells is like gold to the Indians. A big shell about three or four inches across used to be like ten dollars, but I don't see them use them any more nowadays.

After that I stayed in the cradle for about two years. All that time I was taken care of by my mother, and I got milk from her breasts. I don't know how long I was nursed, but I know I was hard to stop. My mother put bitter stuff on her breasts and sometimes a needle, so that, when I come to get on the breast, the needle cut me in my mouth. They say they tried everything with me to stop me. I know a relation of mine, a girl. We used to go and play, maybe on the beach and maybe in the back of the houses. We must have been about four or five years old and the same age, only she was a little younger. She used to say, "I'm getting hungry," and we used to go home together with her in her house, and she goes right up to her mother and pulls out her mother's breast and begins to feed on it. I remember that I wasn't nursing then, and I thought I ought to be if this girl was.[3]

When I was a boy and had to go to the toilet, they just called me to go with them. They had some places where holes were dug in the beach and flat rocks laid. That's where you'd sit and drop your mess in the hole, and you carry four sticks, maybe ten inches long, to wipe your bottom with. I, myself, used to use one stick dry and throw it into the hole and dip the second stick into the water and use it, and then dry my bottom with the other two. I guess why I did it that way, it was to be cleaner than if I used all dry. Before I know how to clean myself, I used to go out of doors and make a dump and then go inside and ask someone to clean me. Then I take the stick and throw it outside. I don't remember ever being punished for wetting the bed or making a mess in the house. When we go to the toilet, we face away from the water. The women face the water. They only make a small hole in the gravel and have their blankets covering

---

[3] This is Charley's earliest memory, and the incident must have been important to him. If the sight of another child suckling made him want the breast himself and thus envy his playmate, it is reasonable to suppose that he was not long weaned when this incident occurred. If this reasoning is correct, Charley was forced to forego the breast somewhere between the ages of three and four.

their backsides, spreading it on the side of the ground. Why they do that is that the men is looking toward the woods for any enemy, and their wives is looking for any canoes that would come. We used to pass water during the night in little boxes and don't go out. We have these small boxes we use and then go dump it in the big box that stands by the door. This was the only soap they used to have and it was a lot cheaper.

When I was a child, I was living in a community house with people living on the four corners of the house. They have their fires in the four corners. I and my parents were living on the back right-hand corner as you come in the door. My oldest brother was living in the other back corner with his wife, and he had no children then. My other brother, the one next to the eldest, was living with us. He wasn't married yet. On the front corner to the left was my brother's wife's mother. On the other place was a man called Poodlas. He was the husband of my aunt, my mother's sister. Her children were there, too; she had three boys and one girl. They were all older than I was.

Each person clears his land where he is going to build his house, and this way all the land gets cleared that belongs to the tribe. When they want to clear up a place, they make lots. My father and my brother built their house close to the fort, and another man built his next, and another man next to his and so on. There was just a little walk between the houses. These were the houses on the back—six of them. There was a road between them and the houses on the front where there were four big community houses and some smaller ones. These were all Kwekas. My brother and my father had to clear the land for their house themselves. They might have called in some friends from the Kwakiutl and Walas Kwakiutl to help them, but the other Kwekas was busy clearing their own land so they didn't call them. In those days, everybody was willing to help unless they had too much work of their own to do. When a house is finished, the owner of the house calls the whole Fort Ruperts to his feast or giving away of money or blankets. This is what we call warming up of the new house. This is always done when a new house is finished.

There was a well on back of one of the houses where the Kwekas get their water from. There was another well in back of the Fort—a big well that was made by the Hudson Bay Company. Should there not be enough water in our well, the people goes to the well of the Hudson Bay and gets their water from there. If anybody from one tribe should take part of the land belonging to another tribe, there would be quarreling about it. If they quarrel a long time, then one of them will give a potlatch, and then the other one would give a potlatch also, and, when that is finished, they don't remember what they have quarreled about. The chiefs of the two tribes would arrange not to have any more quarreling. If the Walas Kwakiutl is trying to get some of the Kwakiutl land where their houses has been, the chiefs begin to remember who cleared the land, and that person has the right to it as a member of that tribe. Within the tribe, the members of each clan can have their houses anywhere. The clans don't live together, and two clans don't live in one house. Only once in a while, when they are related, does a family from one clan live with families of another clan.

The best part of the house is in back. It is always the head man of the house that spends the most for the building of the house. It is the head man that gives the potlatch. The others is helping in the work and pays for the work that is done, and the lumber that goes into his part of the house where he is going to live. Each person is responsible for his corner of the house, and, if it needs repairing, it is up to him who lives there. If the center of the house needs repairing, they all help. We all lived in separate bedrooms. These bedrooms are private, and I never heard of anybody going into another one's bedroom, that lived in the same house, by mistake. Even in the old days, the bedrooms had doors that shut. If anybody wants my brother, and he is in his bedroom, they come into the house and call him from outside his bedroom. The door to the house is public to everybody. This is the one in the front of the house, and anybody can come in without knocking or hollering out. Sometimes there is a small door leading to the back ground, but this is only used by the members of the household.

The boards in the center of the roof of the house is short —maybe a fathom to a fathom and a half long—and these are moved to make a hole when the center fire is built. If the fire is big and the boards catch on fire, they are just pulled apart, and that stops the fire. If there is a fire in one corner of the house, everybody in the house helps to put it out, but it is that man's business to repair it. I never heard of anybody deliberately putting another man's house on fire. If he puts it on fire by accident, he wouldn't do anything. I know of a man who was giving a potlatch and was dancing at night, and he had a big fire in the center, and it wasn't his house either. During the night when they all went to sleep, this community house started to burn down, and only Likiosa, the owner of the house, was living in it. This house was burned down, and another house built like a white man's house, in two stories, also burned down. The owner of that house was Charley Wilson. This was at Fort Rupert, and, at that very time, Charley was visiting at Alert Bay. He tried and tried to get this man to pay for his house, but he couldn't make him pay for it, for it wasn't burned during the time he had his potlatch. It got burned down after he got through having a dance. He never paid for it, and Charley Wilson was out a house.

One in our house always gets up early and starts the fire and wake us up in the morning. Poodlas usually got up first and asked us to have breakfast at his place. He didn't have to; he just liked to get up early. He would get up and boil dried salmon, which was our main food, and serve it to us all with some olachen grease. After that, there will be something which we call "after-food." That might be rice or bread and molasses, which we got from Mr. Hunt who took the Fort after the Hudson Bay left.

Or, sometimes, it would be an Indian food—hemlock bark sap. To make this, we cut down the tree and take the bark off during the springtime. We put the bark laying on its back and scrape it and bring home the inner bark and steam it and make balls of it, pounding it until it is all come soft. After that, we put it on a cedar rack and dry it for the winter, and it keeps a long time. After it is dried, we store it away in Indian boxes. We take out one or two or three—as many as there are to eat—and then pour a little hot water on it and pound it with our hands until it gets soft. We spread it with our fingers and put it in the Indian dishes. Then we put olachen oil in and take it with the fingers of the right hand and eat it.

Sometimes we would have clover root as our after-food. We have sticks on the bottom of the saucepan and put this dried clover root on top of these sticks, and the water under the sticks boils. There is a cover on top to keep the steam in. It is only the steam that cooks it. They open the cover, which is made out of cloth, and take out a piece to see if it is soft enough to eat. Then it is done. They put olachen oil on it in an Indian dish. Then we pick it up and make balls out of it with the fingers of our right hand and put it in our mouths. Sometimes the children use both hands, but they soon learn to do it with only one. When there is a clover root feast for the whole village people, they have Indian boxes about three feet square which they use for cooking roots. They build a big fire in the center of the room and put stones on top of the wood until they are red hot. They pick the stones up with wooden tongs and put them in the boxes. Before this they have put earth on the bottom of the boxes to prevent them from burning. Then they dip the clover roots into water and put them on top of the stones. A bucket of water is poured over them, then the box is covered well with blankets. When cooked it is put into Indian dishes and grease put on top. Then they pass it around to the people, three men eating out of a dish.

Since the white people came here, the cattle eat this clover and the Indians can't get any more. In the olden days, the women had their own clover patches marked with sticks on the four corners, and, if one woman gets in another's patch, they fight over it. Sometimes they used to pick up sticks and hit each other with them, and their menfolks used to come sometimes, too, and butt in. I have seen fights like this many times when I was a boy. Clover patches are women's property, and it comes down to her daughter. If they have no daughter, the boy gets it, and then when he gets a wife the wife uses it. It is only this way with patches of roots. The berries don't belong to anybody.

Sometimes the after-food will be dried berries which we also boil. We put the berries in boxes and put stones in the fire—only particular kinds of stones that won't break—and, when they are red hot, we put just a little water in to keep it from burning and put in the hot stones and stir it until it all come to pieces. Then we have long stones which are flat on one end, and mash the berries right in a small box which we put the berries in to mash them. Then we leave it to cool and go out into the woods and get wild cabbage leaves and put those on the cedar racks. These racks are cedar poles tied together with a cedar-bark strip. We put the cabbage leaves on this, and then put crosspieces so that the berries will be made into cakes. Then we put the berry mash in these blocks and put them out in the sun to dry. At night we put them up close to the fire, and, when they are dry, we put these together very carefully and have long cedar bark stripped in narrow strips, and tie those ends. The long berry cakes we fold and put away in Indian boxes. These we take out whenever we want to use them for after-food.

We had potatoes, too, when I was a boy, but they couldn't be stored away in boxes. We dug a place in the earth of the floor and had it big enough for the potatoes we are going to store away under there and keep them from the frost. On the top, we put boards and mats over these.

The women have their own wooden boxes which they use for storing away food for the winter. Those kind of boxes they make are very big, sometimes three feet high and two and one-half feet square. These big ones they use for the olachen oil. The oil is put into kelp which has been dried and cleaned. When the kelp is filled with oil, they coil it inside the box like a rope. They stopper the kelp with rounded wood, and tie it tight so it don't leak. In our house we had a dozen of these big boxes that my mother used. We also had smaller boxes. These were for dried salmon. Another box we had, like the salmon boxes, for dried clams. Then there were smaller boxes for dried berries and others for clover root. All of these boxes were piled on top of each other at the side of our house—the biggest ones on the bottom and so on up. Each fire has its own boxes piled up on the side of the community house. When we have our meals in the wintertime, we open these boxes and take out what we want. In the summertime, we mostly eat the fresh things and keep filling the boxes up for the next winter.

It is not always Poodlas that gets the breakfast; sometimes my brother gets up first. Sometimes my brother gets up and makes a fire in the center of the house and calls some Kweka men to come and have breakfast with us. Maybe he calls all the Kweka men, and there must have been forty or fifty of them at that time. Sometimes he would call the whole of the Fort Rupert men.

At lunch time, we have dried salmon or dried clams in the wintertime. In summertime, we have everything: fresh salmon, halibut, flounder, cod, hair seals, clams, cockles, horse clams, fruits, and potatoes, but we don't eat all the different kinds of roots in the summertime. We eat all the different kinds of ducks, but we don't eat sea gulls, cormorants, and loons. They are too tough and too hard to pluck. I guess we would if we didn't have anything else to eat, but we always did. We eat eagles in the wintertime, when they get fat eating fish. We don't eat frogs, nor do we eat snakes. We are afraid of them and won't touch them unless we have to. Some of us run away from them, and some kill them. I know I kill them myself. There is a story of a man who died with a frog inside him, but I didn't know him.

We are afraid of snakes when they are breeding. They

say, if you see a snake in breeding time, the young ones comes in through your backsides. The person sometimes dies. The snakes eats all the guts out of him. You have to have strong medicine to kill that snake. The medicine grows on mountains, and it has long hairs on the root of it, and it is very bitter. You grind the root and mix it with oil and drink it. It is a poison. If you eat too much of it, it will kill you. It is a poison for everything. Every hunter has some of that in his canoe, and, if he sees a sea monster coming after him, he just scrapes some of that in the water. The monster goes away, and you are safe. When you drink that medicine, it kills the snake, if it doesn't kill you. You go out and dump it, and then you see the snake come out there. I knew some people that were sick with it, and they said they seen the snake come out all right.

Sometimes we have lunch in our own places, and sometimes one of the household will call us to eat with them, and sometimes somebody from another house will call all the men to go and eat. Nearly always, we have dried salmon to start with, and after that we drink water. Only when we have a big feast, we don't have dried salmon first.

We had only water to drink. We drink water before and after eating. This man Poodlas who lives in our house was the first man to drink coffee. All the Indians was talking about him and calling him "coffee-drinker." They all made fun of him for it, but he kept right on drinking coffee anyway. I had a cousin called Nulis who was the first man that drinks tea among the Fort Ruperts. They used to make fun of him and call him "tea-lover." The rest drink water before they eat, and after the dried salmon they drink water. We don't drink water while we eat. After we eat and are finished, then we drink all the water we want.

When I was young, my older brother was working in the Fort cooking for a white man, Mr. Hunt. This was George Hunt's father. That's why my older brother was the richest of all the Indians at Fort Rupert. Every payday he used to be paid with trade-in blankets. These were white with black stripes on each end. Our blankets is not much use to us

now since they enforced the Indian Act.[4] They bought some of
them during the war to send to the soldiers. The others we
just use for anything now, to cover the canoe, or anything
at all. When the people of Fort Rupert know that my
brother is paid, they come and borrow blankets from him.
They promise to pay double when he wants to collect them
after a year or maybe ten years or so after that. My brother
keeps on loaning until he has got enough to collect and give
a potlatch. Sometimes he would keep on loaning his earnings
out until he has enough to buy a copper. If a man that borrowed from my brother can't pay back, he borrows from another man and promises to pay him shortly after. He promises to give the other men one pair for every five he has
borrowed extra. If a man doesn't pay before he dies, his son
will have to pay it. If a man is slow in paying all the time,
he gets laughed at. Finally the chief would make a collection
of what the man owed to pay his debts. That makes this man
ashamed to think that the rest of the people know he is so
poor that he can't pay it back. And they wouldn't loan him
any blankets or money after that or invite him to feasts.

When I was very young, I used to sleep sometimes beside
my father. When I lie in bed beside him, he talked to me
about our ancestors. He told me about my grandfather and
his father and his father, and what they did, and about how
our ancestors knew about the flood. He told me the story of
one clan of the Kwekas: how the ancestor of this clan knew
there was going to be a flood, and how he built a house made
out of clay where he is going to live under the water while

4 The Indian Act to which Charley refers is as follows:
"Every Indian or other person who engages in, or assists in celebrating
or encourages either directly or indirectly another to celebrate any Indian
festival, dance or other ceremony of which the giving away or paying or
giving back of money, goods or articles of any sort forms a part, or is a
feature, whether such gift of money, goods or articles takes place before, at,
or after the celebration of the same, or who engages or assists in any celebration or dance of which the wounding or mutilation of the dead.or living
body of any human being or animal forms a part or is a feature, is guilty
of an offence and is liable on summary conviction to imprisonment for a
term not exceeding six months and not less than two months." Revised
Statutes of Canada, 1927, vol. II, chap. 98, no. 140, p. 2218.

the flood is on. This place is just ten miles from here. This is the only place where there is clay, and on both sides of it there is nothing but earth and gravel. They say this was the house that was built at the time. When the flood came, he went inside there and stayed. And my father told me about all the different men that first lived on the earth, and while I lie there, he also tells me about fairies and monsters—all kinds of stories which Dr. Boas has already taken down.

My father also tells me about the potlatches which has come down from our ancestors, how our great-grandfathers used to give potlatches, and so on down to his time. He told me to be careful not to quit the potlatch, but to look after my blankets when I grew up, and not to spend my earnings foolishly, but to keep them and loan them out so that I could collect them whenever I want to give a potlatch. "In giving potlatches," he says, "is the only good name you'll have when you grow up, but if you are careless and spend your money foolishly, then you'll be no more good. You'll be one of the common people without any rank." Those that has no standing and no place in the clans is the common people. They are not chiefs. In my time, they all had positions, but they was lower down. It is only the first four positions, when my father was talking to me, that was considered the chiefs, but now it is different.

He tells me about the people and where they stand. In the evening as I lay alongside of him he is talking how I can make a song for him and of the different ways of making a song for the head chief. The people that don't know the standing of all the men couldn't make songs, because, if they do and make a mistake regarding a man's position, he would be laughed at, because he put the man in a high position when he isn't or in a low position when he isn't. And, therefore, the man that makes the song has to know all the positions of the people so that the wording of the song will be just right for the man he makes the song for.

My father's father was Wadze of the Kweka tribe, and my father's mother was of the same tribe and clan as my father's father. They were cousins. My father was Malitsas, which means "the man who never lets you go hungry." He belongs to the Kweka tribe at Fort Rupert and the Kukwa-kum clan. He held the third seat in the Kweka tribe. My father's clan was the first clan of his tribe. My father had four older brothers and two older sisters.

He also told me about our tribe and how, in the beginning, the Kwakiutl tribe and the Kweka tribe was one. There was two brothers, and one killed the other, and then half of those people moved away from the Kwakiutl and became the Kwekas. Sometimes we call the Kwakiutls a name, which means they are the descendants of the one that was killed, and they don't like it either. We only do it when we are fighting them with potlatches. This is the story he told me:

The Kwakiutl were living ten miles from here, just across from the lighthouse, on Vancouver Island. The young men of the Mamtagila and the young men of the Kukwakum were having a game of throwing stones to get close to a post. They were two clans of the Kwakiutl. Which of the clan gets closest to the post counts one till they count up to ten. The side that counts up to ten wins the game. While they were doing it, they were arguing about the stones being near to the post so they measured them. Maxwa, the chief of the Mamtagila, got up and went to see which was closest, and he say that his young men's stone was the closest. Yakodlas, the chief of the Kukwakum, spoke to Maxwa and said: "Why do you go and interfere with the young men? You should only sit still and watch them. As chief of a clan that is what you should do. I don't go and interfere. I just sit still and watch. It looks to me that you don't have a chief's mind in you." Maxwa says: "Am I not a chief?" Yakodlas says: "If you are a chief, you wouldn't be doing what you are doing now. You seem to be only one of your young men that are playing." Maxwa took out his shell earrings and says: "I bet you these that my young men will win the game." Ya-kodlas took out his earrings of the same kind and says: "I'll go that, and I will raise with my blanket which is made of expensive fur." And Maxwa also took off his blanket and says: "I'll go that, and I'll raise you with this canoe." And so it went

on like that until they each had bet all that they had on the
game. So the both sides started the game anew. They all did
their best to win the game for their chiefs. One of Yakodlas'
young men had a small round stone—just like a ball—and he
was scolded by his clan for not using a flat one which will stick
in one place when he throws it, for every time he used this stone
it would roll away from the post they were throwing at. Finally
Yakodlas' boys count up to nine, and Maxwa's boys catch up
to that and also got nine. And so they were even, and one more
throw will win the game. Then they say, "We will go further on
for the last throw." So they went far away, and, when they
throw the stone, Maxwa's men put their stones only halfway.
Yakodlas' men was the same until this man with the round stone
threw his, and, when he threw that, it rolled and rolled until it
came close to the post. Yakodlas' young men won the game and
Yakodlas won his bet. He didn't want to take what he won
home. He put on his blanket and his earrings again and called
the Kukwakum clan and sang his song, and he gave a potlatch
to the Mamtagila. Maxwa also gave a potlatch, and so they
went on in that way. When the one give a feast, the other give
a feast; when the one give a potlatch, the other give a potlatch.
They begin to have hatred between them.

When they came to dry salmon at the Nimkis River, Maxwa
called the Kukwakum to his feast early in the morning. He
built a big fire there and put stones on top of the fire, which he
used for cooking clover roots. While the Kukwakum was eating
dry salmon, the Mamtagila went out one by one until there was
none of them left in the house. And that was the time one of Yakodlas' men sneezed with the left side of his nose. He says to his
clansmen: "There is something going to happen. I have sneezed
with the left side of my nose." Then he sneezed again. Then he
spoke to his people and says: "Do we not understand why all
these Mamtagila has all gone out? They are now getting ready
to smite our chief." Another man stood up and said: "You are
right [he was the wise man of that clan]; I was thinking of it
when I saw them all going out. We shall all rise now, and we
will go in two rows, and, when you get out of the door, you will
push all the people away that are ready out there. Then our

chief will come between us. But before he comes out, take out a
thick board from the wall, and some of the young men will hold
it on top of his head, for there might be someone on the roof
with a rock to throw on his head." When this was all done, they
went out, and they found people ready outside with spears and
with bows and with daggers. The strong young men pushed
them all away from the door. Yakodlas went out with a board
over his head holded up by some of his young men. There was
one man on the top of the house ready with a big rock to throw
down.

After that there was some salmon berries brought to Maxwa
by his Kingcome Inlet wife—canoes full of big boxes full of
salmon berries. Maxwa's messengers went around the houses at
night telling these people not to go anywhere because he is going to give a salmon berry feast. Before daylight, Yakodlas
got up and went away in his canoe. He stayed away all day
while Maxwa was waiting for him. When he came back, it was
time to go to bed, and another messenger came to him, asking
him not to go anywhere the next day. But instead, he got up
early in the morning and went away, for he knew that Maxwa
would try to do the same as he tried to do before. So he kept
on for so many days that they got afraid the salmon berries
will get spoiled, so Maxwa called the people and gave this
salmon berry feast and kept one of the boxes and poured it out
on the front of Yakodlas' house.

A canoe came from another tribe bringing his [Yakodlas']
wife, and they brought seals. Yakodlas sent messengers around
and told all the people not to go anywhere for Yakodlas is going to give a feast of seals. Instead of staying, Maxwa got in
his canoe and went to Turner Island and stayed there. When
Yakodlas gave this feast of seals, he got a pole and poked it
in the neck of a seal and put it up in front of Maxwa's house
and set a fire under it, and that seal was burning for many
days.

Then all the people moved and went to Turner Island for
the winter. Yakodlas called his clan together and say that he is
going to give a winter dance. And so his clan made ready for
that dance. He had a dance in which he danced all kinds of

dances. When this was finished, Maxwa also called his people, telling them that he also is going to have a dance. When he was through dancing it was time to go to Knight's Inlet for olachen grease. They all went there and Yakodlas gave a grease pot-latch which should always be done after the winter dance cere-monies. He made a platform on the rear of the house, high up, between the floor and the roof. When he had given all the grease around, the Kukwakum begin to sing their grease potlatch song, while the two young men was putting in hot stones in the grease outside to make it hot. When it was hot, they came and brought this box in full of grease and threw it into the fire, and the fire just hit the roof of the house and came down to where Maxwa was sitting and other people with him. Somehow Maxwa was saved from the fire, going through the boards at the rear of the house.

One fine day, at Knight's Inlet, Maxwa came along walking with his friends and came into Yakodlas' house. Yakodlas swept the seats and put new mats to where they were going to sit down, and Yakodlas says to Maxwa: "I am so glad you came, for I have been expecting you for a long time." Maxwa had a sweetheart on the front end of the house. While Yakodlas was talking to him, he had his dagger hidden in his right hand. "And now since you have come to see your sweetheart, I am glad," he says, "for now you will be a dead man." He took his dagger and tried to smite him on the head. But Maxwa came toward him fast, so the dagger passed his head. Maxwa got up and tried to run out of the house. The husband of his sweet-heart was working at the doorway with yew wedges splitting wood, and, while Maxwa was trying to make his escape, his sweetheart's husband saw him coming, and took the wedge he was using and hit him on the leg so he fell. Yakodlas run up to him and just took hold of him by the hair and struck him on the back of the head with his dagger and killed him. The news went around to all the different tribes, and they all came in ca-noes and began to ask who has killed Maxwa. "Did Copper-Maker kill Maxwa?" they say. Copper-Maker say in a loud voice, "No, not I." And they say, "Who killed him then?" And they ask another chief. He says, "No, I did not kill him." Then

they say, "Who has killed him then? Did Yakodlas kill him?"
And Yakodlas went up to the roof of the house holding his
dagger in his hand and says, "I killed him." And they all says,
that finishes that, because they all knew that Maxwa had tried
lots of time to kill Yakodlas and didn't make it. Those that
were on Maxwa's side was against Yakodlas, and those from
the Mamtagila that was on Yakodlas' side became their ene-
These Mamtagila that were on Yakodlas' side moved
y, and they are another tribe now. The Kukwakum split
from the Kwakiutl and became the first clan of the Kwekas,
which means "murderers."

My father was making songs for the potlatch. Nearly all
the good songs we have at Fort Rupert was made by him.
When he makes a song for one chief, the chief pays him five
pairs of blankets for one song. That is for a small potlatch,
and, if it is a big potlatch that is given to all the tribes, it
is ten to twenty pairs for the song. Indians used to come
from Cape Mudge and Campbell River even to take him
there and make a song for them. This was his work. What
he gets out of that, he loans it out the same as my older
brother.

My second brother was a hunter and trapper. He turned
in skins to the Hudson Bay, and he got blankets from them.
He used to trap with wooden deadfall traps. The Hudson
Bay paid only twenty-five cents for six skins, and only ten
cents for a small mink skin. They weighed the deerskins and
paid him by the pound. It took him $1.50 to get a blanket
from the Bay. Most of the Indians were trappers and hunters, and, before they had guns, they used spears and bows
and arrows and traps.

Poodlas was the first man that worked for the Hudson
Bay. He was cook for them. After this moved from Fort Rupert, Mr. Hunt took the Fort over and Poodlas cooked for
him. Then my brother took the job, and Poodlas hunted
again. While Poodlas was cooking for Mr. Hunt, my brother
used to go and help him packing water from the wells and
watching him and doing what he asked, and Poodlas used to

pay my brother one shirt a month, and anyway he was learning the way he cooked.

I was very young when my mother died. I only knew and remember when she called me to her bedside and told me she was going to leave me and told me to try to look after myself, so I don't get hurt and to listen to my brother and to do what he tells me. That is all I remember about my mother. I know she was out picking berries at the back of Fort Rupert. When she came back by the fireside, her face just swelled up. My mother told her sister she had seen the head of a snake which Wadze, my father's father, killed long before. She saw it up on a cedar tree and saw the teeth of the snake shining like glass, and, when she came home, she went toward the fire, and, for seeing that snake, that made her face feel swollen.

That big snake that Wadze killed was not one of the snakes we see around here. It was quite a big snake. It took him twice to chop the head of this snake with the ax he was hewing wood with, and that ax was awful sharp. This snake had legs on him—four legs—and had a long tail on him, and he just took a piece of cedar-tree bark and covered the head of this snake with it. He put it in a hollow place in the tree. That cedar bark rotted, and the head of the snake showed when my mother saw it. That night, when my mother went to sleep, a man came to her in her dreams and said: "You done a wrong thing. Why did you come close to the fire for? If you had sense enough, you would have gone right to the tree where you saw this head and take off some of your clothing and wipe the snake with that. Then you could keep the clothing and have power over everything you work at. But now that you have come close to the fire, you will never be well again. I am the one that killed Wadze. I am the one that smashed the canoe where the Walas Kwakiutl was traveling on. You will never get well again." She told her sister about this dream. My aunt told us all about it after my mother died. I think it was only four or five days after this dream that she died. I remember I felt very bad about her dying. I felt awful sad. I don't remember anybody trying to comfort me. I guess I was too young to remember, and I don't remember anything about her funeral.

But when I was young, I remember an old woman that was put in a big high box. She was the mother of the Tlowitsis chief and must have been over a hundred years old. Although she was the mother of the chief of the Tlowitsis, nobody cried for her. They simply pulled up her legs to her breast and put her hands outside her knees and set her in a box and put a lid on it. They put blankets around her and took her out on the island in front of the village and opened one of the little houses and put her in there. When the people that buried her in that house came back, the Fort Ruperts went to the chief of the Tlowitsis to comfort him, according to customs. When all the chiefs of the Fort Ruperts finished, the son of this woman that died got up and returned his speeches to the Fort Ruperts. He told them his mother has grown up to be a very, very old woman, and that she wasn't sick at all, but just slept and never woke up. "And," he says, "I got nothing to be sorry about. She has grown up to the end. It's not like as if she was young and sick. She was very old and has gone to the end of her life." Then he gave a potlatch for her.

My brother's first wife died when I was a little boy. I used to go with her in her father's house where my brother was living, when I was a little child. This was about the time when my mother died. I can just barely remember her. She died about the same time my mother did. I can't remember just when. Then my brother married his second wife and came to live in our house directly after my mother died. She looked after me as well as my mother would do and I looked upon her also as my own mother, although I knew she wasn't. Whenever they used to quarrel, and she would leave my brother's house and go to her own house, I would help her pack her things to her own house and go there every mealtime to have something to eat. I used to stay with her at daytime, and then come home at night. I go to her and tell her that I am hungry, and she cook for me. She used to tell me to stay with her nighttimes, but my brother wouldn't allow me to do that. I was willing to stay there. I wanted to, but my brother wouldn't let me. So I went home at night. Sometimes they would stay mad like this for four days, sometimes only a week. She was good to everybody, and so her nickname was "Aunty." She acted to everybody as an aunt does to a niece or nephew.

CHAPTER III

CHILDHOOD PLAY

THE first thing our older playfellows taught us to do was to go around to the different houses in the evening. We marched around, and this is the name of the game, "Marching Around." We go in a string, one boy after another. There used to be a lot of us. There must have been fifty boys in Fort Rupert at that time. We bent our backs and put our thumbs in our mouths, stretching our lips wide, stamping our feet, and singing, "Bend down, place of names." Then any of the household that has a feeling, tells the boys to sit down by the fire, and they give us something to eat—sometimes the fat of the mountain goat, sometimes dried berries, anything the boys like. We eat, and then go to another house. If we are lucky, they all give us something to eat, and, when we are full, we stop.

Another game like this we used to do at nighttime, close to bedtime. We used to go from house to house, feel what is in their house that we would like to eat. We call the name of a noble child, usually a girl, that is in the house. We say all this and knock on the outside of the house, calling out, "Turn over to your little box and get out the grub from your box." They will say, "Come in and sit down." They will get some kind of food and give it to us. Then we will go to another house. If one house don't call us in, we take sticks and beat them on the house, singing, "We don't think you are loved by anyone." When we get full, we go home and go to bed. When they go into my house, my parents would give them the food. If the boy's parents don't call us in, the boy usually goes home.

Sometimes they would make a big fire in one of the houses, and we would see who was the bravest, and who could face the hot fire. We would put a stick close to the fire and put a peg there. We go toward it without any hat and with our faces toward the fire and try to pick the peg up in our mouths. Those that couldn't do it, they go and sit down to watch. Those that could pick it up, move the peg nearer to the fire. Some boys can't pick it up, so they go and sit down. The others move it again until there is only one that picks it up. Maybe he gets his hair burned. He is the bravest. There is a second bravest and a third. All the people in the house say, "Aren't they brave?"[1]

Sometimes we burned hemlock twigs as big as our little finger and make charcoal out of it. We put one of these on our forearms. The charcoal was cut the same length for every boy. Then a man or boy goes around and puts a fire on top of this piece of charcoal on our arms. It burns, and it hurts, too. Some boys couldn't stand it and threw it off right away. Some boys with a strong heart keep it on until the fire is out and has burned a big hole in the skin. I still have scars on my arms where the charcoal burned out. This is done in the night, and after it they go home and get their blankets and come in and dance. Perhaps they pretend to be some of the Indians from up north, or, perhaps, West Coast Indians.

A brave boy will have scars right along in a line from that charcoal burning his arm. Then he goes to the other boys and says that he isn't afraid of anything and not like the

[1] This and subsequent games, which apparently function to toughen the youth, deserve special consideration. To a people such as the Kwakiutl, who occasionally had to defend themselves from hostile neighbors, it is perhaps not too surprising that a type of competitive ordeal should have become important. But there is probably more to it than that. It has been noted above that Kwakiutl babies learn only one response which they can use to gratify their cravings. This is crying, a response plainly not adapted to adult life in any society. People have to do something more constructive than cry, if the wheels of the social machinery are to revolve. Hence, in a society where babies are dependent upon crying to achieve what they want and have learned this technique alone, something has to be done to alter this habit. Games involving ordeals help to inhibit crying and tend to foster other types of activity, most of which will be useful in adult life. The punishment for being a crybaby is negative rather than positive. Crying just doesn't get one anywhere. The reward for being able to "take it" is definitely positive: the boy gets approval from adults and prestige among his fellows.

other boys. I don't think any boy would ever quarrel with such a boast. They have all tried this charcoal burning and know what it is and how it hurts. I have only a few scars, and I respect those boys that has more, because I know how those hurted me so long. The funny part of it is that our parents and the old people never stop us from doing any of these things, because they want us to be brave like they were in the olden days, when they was fighting and hunting all the time. If we wasn't brave and couldn't play all these games and be strong, they didn't think we was much good.

We used to have a stick and hold it. The others would try to get it from us. Each one has a lot of others pulling him from behind, and they see who has the strongest fingers. There is another thing that you do with the third finger, and hold to another's third finger. Both are held by others, and pulled to see who lets go first. Sometimes we would pull our fingers out of joint playing at this game.

There is another game that we used to like to play in the evening. It is started sitting down on the ground inside or sometimes outside the house. We sit with our hands together, and then we begin to sing this song. "Pretend to go to sleep. Pretend to go to sleep [snoring noises]. Pretend to wake up. Pretend to wake up." We sing this four times. Then the boss gets up holding the other boys by the hand, though they are still sitting down, and he looks around at them. This is now meaning it's on a fish trap, and he is looking at a fish trap—the kind that is made with a dam right on the salt water, and, when the tide goes out, the fish can't get out. And this one who stands up, he sings: "Get inside this trap, So-and-so." And then the boy whose name he calls, who is on his right side, gets up. Then he sings this again, and the boy on his left side gets up, and then they sing it until all of us gets up, and then we walk around singing: "Walk around. Walk around." And then we run around, singing: "Walk around fast. Walk around fast." And all these we sing four times. And then we go into a string and the circle breaks. And then we sing: "Going through. Going through." And while we are singing this, the first one goes under the

arm of the second, and then they both go under the arm ,of
the third and so on. And when it is all done to the last, they
all stretch out again in a line and sing another song: "Wind
up." And they turn around and wind themselves up, and,
when they are all in a bunch, then we sing: "Unwind." And
when we all get in a string, we join into singing: "That finishes it." Both boys and girls play this, and I remember we
used to have a lot of fun at it.

When I was four or five years old, we used to play with
other little boys. It was the time we used to be too little to
go and play with girls. The boys would pretend to marry
each other. We used to go and lay together and play with
each other's peckers, and this we call "a pecker to pecker."
The pecker of one boy goes together with the other boy's
pecker. I've heard about some that uses their hands while
they are alone, but I don't know who. I never did. I don't
know why. It is all right, if you want to. This is called "handling your pecker yourself." We were about three to five
then and were too small to take and ask the girls to go in
the woods. Although I used to play with the older boys, they
only used me as a play child.[2]

Then when I was about six, I see what the older ones are
doing, so I ask the girls to go into the woods and practice
on them. I begin to want a wife, I guess. We would build
branch houses and pretend that we were married. We used
to have younger kids that were supposed to be our children.
We used to have beds made out of moss and go to bed and
sometimes have our children between us. That is called "pretend to have wives." I played this all the time I was a child,
and the last time I remember playing this, I was twelve. The
girl I used to play with when I was twelve, I liked a lot, and,

2 Although Charley is somewhat vague about the exact age when he began these practices, it must have been soon after he left the cradle. Up to
this time, therefore, his sexual experiences must have been negligible. Apparently, however, it did not take him long to learn what his fellows expected of him. Whether or not handling his own genitals preceded this
mutual sex play and met with punishment, cannot be known with certainty,
but it seems clear that solitary masturbation was not as openly practiced
as mutual masturbation.

afterwards when I saw her, we remembered that we used to lay down together in the bush. Some were bigger than we were. When we really played man and wife, we didn't go and tell our parents. But they knew about it all right. If we got in love with each other, we want to really marry each other, but of course we can't—we are too young. Even when we get older, we have to marry someone else like I did. I remember that we see our parents and my brother what they do—how they sleep together, eat together, all those things, and we try to do them, too. In the woods with my girl, I was called the name of a chief, and the girl was called the name of a chief's wife. If our parents gave a feast, we'd pretend to do the same. She will cook for me, and we will eat together. Sometimes we call in other children to our house and feed them. This is something like learning how to act when we grow up.[3]

In the daytime, we play at war—the Kweka and the Kwakiutl, the Walas Kwakiutl, and the Kumkutis. They will go without anything in their hands. We will be standing in a row, and our enemy, the Kwakiutl, will be standing in a row as well. We don't use any weapons; we just fight with our bare hands to go and get slaves. This is what we call *askwane*. This is what we shout when we run toward our enemy. They also shout and run toward us. We hold each other and wrestle. If I am strong enough, I pick up a boy on my shoulders and carry him back to my side. That is a slave. When we all get back to our places, we count our slaves, and the Kwakiutl count theirs. Then we take one slave and say: "We will give you this one for one of yours. This makes it even." The

[3] Charley seems to regard this transition from another male to a female as the desired sex object to have been a definite step forward. He had become older, and heterosexual play symbolized his advance toward adult status. As will be seen later, homosexual behavior is looked upon by the Kwakiutl as infantile, and one who practices it is often severely ridiculed. This attitude helps to insure the perpetuation of the group. Homosexual relations do not produce offspring and, therefore, cannot be permitted to replace productive heterosexual relations. Charley is truly learning how to act as an adult. Pressure is being put upon him from all sides, forcing him to adopt more and more the type of behavior expected of him as a mature Kwakiutl man.

side with the most slaves, when they have been exchanged, wins. The older chiefs would come and watch us and tell us what to do, and when we got through with that kind of game, and it took maybe two hours, then there was another awful thing we do. We get nettles and we fight without any shirts. We go one by one and have these nettles in our hands and one of the other side and one of ours strike at each other with these stinging weeds. It is awful hot when they sting us. We will find a fellow with a snotty nose—that is our doctor. He blows his nose on his fingers and wipes the snot all over our bodies, and this stops the pain. Some of them wouldn't dare to do this. Others will have a strong heart and keep on until the other runs away. This one wins, and the old men would say: "Ah! there is a brave one." I used to do this game all right.

And when we get through with that, the old men would say to go and get long spruce twigs, and then we go to war with these. Hardly anybody could stand this game. We would whip each other. Anybody who could stand against that was brave. They cut right into your skin, and all of us was bleeding. I didn't like this game, and ran away from the other boys, but I had a nephew who could stand it though.

At the time we fish for olachen we would go to Knight's Inlet. There we would play different games. There are lots of ferns there that have big roots. We used to pull them up, roots and all, and hold the fern and throw it at each other. Sometimes it hurts and you get blinded with the sand and dirt from the roots. Everybody throws all together, and somebody usually gets hurt. In all these games, if they are alone, the Kwekas usually fight the Kwakiutl, but if two are against two, the Kwekas and the Kwakiutl go together.

Those, besides racing and jumping, are the games we used to play. There was another game like the others, only we played it with clamshells. There would be nothing but clamshells on the beach. We would go out and throw the shells at each other, and sometimes we would get a big cut on the head.

We had another bad game at Knight's Inlet. We would

have a bow and arrow with only a little point showing. They take the dried kelp which they use for the olachen oil and cut it in strips and tie it on the end of the arrows so it only leaves a little sharp end showing. We used to have wars with this. One tribe on one side, and one tribe on another. The Tenaktak especially used to come down through the woods and make war on us. Sometimes one of us would get hit in the head and the arrow would go in a quarter of an inch and the blood spurts out. Mostly the bigger boys play this when they are about fifteen to twenty. The younger boys would collect the arrows and sell them for a handkerchief. The older boys didn't shoot at the younger boys.

Sometimes we would go to the beach and pick up kelp. There would only be four of us in each bunch. We cut the kelp about ten inches long and put them in a pile, and the heads of the kelp we put behind the pile. The head part we call the chief. Each one has the same. This game is called "to spear each other." Now we have a way of seeing who will start. We throw a rock at each other, and the one who misses it, the other side starts first. Two of us are on one side, and two are on the other. We begin to spear these kelp with a three-and-one-half-foot spear which has an iron point. Most of the boys throw it wrong, only a few could spear the kelp good. The one who spears the chief wins the game. We take turns throwing, only after I spear a piece of kelp, I keep on spearing until I miss. Every piece I spear I take to my side and build my wall higher. We always try to spear the chief. He is the one we are after. That is why we don't get many pieces.

Sometimes we play another game. We use our hands, and it doesn't matter how many are on each side. There might be a dozen or more on one side. We have a ball about four inches thick. It is made of rags tied together. One player holds it and begins to shout like the name of the game. The rest shout with him, and then he throws it high up in the air. One boy catches it, and they all pile on him trying to get it away from him. The ones that are on his side have a signal—a certain thing that they all know. Maybe we pinch him three times, and then he knows we are on his side, and he slips us the ball and pretends to keep it. I get up, and when I can, I run to the mark with it. We keep on doing this until one side gets ten. The side wins that first gets ten.

We used to play another game with a round hoop made of twigs and tied with cedar bark. We have about ten and the other side about ten. We first roll them on the ground, and they try to get it with their sticks. We then say, "A—he—wa," and throw them in the air flatways, and the other side tries to get their sticks inside it. If there are two who get their sticks inside it, that is not good. If they could catch all those rings, they call for the bravest of the other side, and he will go forward using his blanket as a shield. They are all ready with their rings. He stands there and they throw their rings at him. If they don't make him run away, he gets the rings back.

One game that we used to play at the Nimkis River village is one we played with a stick. It is not a spear but it looks like one, only it has a round end. It is about three feet long. After fishing in daytime or getting wood we go into one of the houses where we dry fish. We sit in two lines facing each other, with a fire between us at one end. There will be the same number of boys on each side. Between the boys on each side there will be a springboard stuck in the ground of the floor. This is at about a forty-five degree angle, pointing toward the opposite line of boys. We have to be about fifteen feet apart, and we take the spear and throw it at the springboard which is about two inches wide, made out of some green wood that has lots of spring left in it. It comes back and every time the same fellow that throws it catches it, our side counts one. If he misses it, the other side takes it and one of them does the same until one side catches it ten times. Each one on our side will take his turn after one game is won and one side gets a count of ten. Some of the boys were very good and never missed it. I was never good at it. The side wins who wins the most games when all the boys have had their turns. All the young boys and even the young men used to play this. Sometimes we played it at

Fort Rupert, but they played it all the time amongst the Nimkis. While we were shooting, our side would cry out, "Go ahead; don't miss," and the other side would try to talk him out of it. "Miss, miss, miss, miss," they say, and then laugh a lot when we miss. The people in the house tried to chase us out, but we wouldn't go until we beat each other. We play with the Fort Ruperts on one side and the Nimkis on the other, but sometimes we play amongst ourselves at home, and the Nimkis play amongst themselves in case some other tribe comes that they are going to play against.

Another game at Knight's Inlet is played with a spear with two prongs in it. It has a line tied to it. We take some long grass and tie it around so that it looks like a seal. They throw this in the river, and that river used to run swift, and we boys stood on the bank to spear at it. If we don't lose it, we are lucky. If we do, the next tribe, the Mamaleleqala, they will spear at it. If they can get it, they are better than the Kwakiutl. Then the Tlowitsis try. If none of them get it, they call it the same for every tribe. We would go fish there in a boat and stay sometimes all winter, and have feasts and potlatches there.

In the summertime, we have bathing in the salt water, and we try out to see who has the longest breath. We would go one by one diving. Some could dive fast, but they would have shorter breath than the others. They used to see who could dive the furthest without coming up for air. I only knew one man who could dive real far. His name was Silver Salmon. He started from one point, swam around the bay, and came out to another point. He said he breathed under water, brought water into his mouth and breathed it out again. He said that everybody was afraid to do this, and that that was their trouble. I tried it, but I couldn't do it.

There is another game we used to play at Fort Rupert. There is a big low tide there—big enough to see all the sand way out. At low tide we used to get some of the girls to pull some of their hair out for us. We'd take sticks—about two to two and one-half feet long—and split them. Then we put some pegs in the split and bind them in tight. Then we take the hair and make nooses and tie them to these pegs right along the stick. We find a little bit of water and put the stick up close to the water and the other boys had theirs, too, all along where they find a little water in the hollows, and put this stick up close to it. You know those little sand birds that go in bunches when they fly or walk along the beach. Those birds we chase from where they are to come close to the snares and try to go over them. I come to the other side of the birds from my snare and walk slow toward them waving my arms easy-like and whistling a low sound. I whistle so they'll go slow, close to the sand and not fly while I am chasing them. And when they get into this snare, they get caught by their legs and when I catch one I take it out of the snare and tie a string to its leg and tie that to a log until I get more. The other boys does the same, and when we have finished we show how many we've caught. I go to one of the Kwakiutl boys with mine and take one of these poor things in my hand and throws this bird hard at him so that it kills the bird. We keep track of how many birds I throw at this one boy, and if he is not good enough to keep up with me, I have to go and get another boy and do it to him. That represents that he is no good at anything. He couldn't catch a bird or do anything else at all.

When I begin to play about, sometimes I get hurt. If I get hurt or hurted by somebody, my parents buy some calico from the store and tear it so that they make strips maybe one fathom long and give these strips around to all the Kwakiutl and the Walas Kwakiutl. This means that this is a bandage to my wound. Sometimes they call it a thing to wipe away the blood.

The first thing they taught me how to do was when my second brother used to take me fishing before I went to school. I used to take the paddle and steer while he is on the bow of the canoe with his fish spear which he used before the salmon gets up the river. The spear has two prongs, and the point has barbs and a line to hold these, and they are tied to the stick. When he spears a fish, the point goes right

through and comes off the spear. Sometimes he used to get
two fish and then he pulled the line to get the fish in. This
is the first thing he taught me how to do. Sometimes he
would let me try it, and sometimes a little later I went with
another boy and we tried it. I let him spear while I steered,
and then I tried spearing while he steered. This used to be
great fun for us boys. My brother made me a small spear
and then when I was big enough to use his, he let me use
that. When the fish come close to the river, we go and spear
them and take them home, and the women split them and
dry some of them, while we eat the others fresh. The salmon
we catch on the salt water, we don't keep many of, because
they don't keep long. This is because they are too fat. If
we get too many for our own use, we give some to the older
people that can't go out fishing. The fish are smoked and
dried.

Then we also go up the creek and hook the fish up there.
We have a pole with a hook on the end. We walk along the
bank and watch for the fish, and when we see him we hook
him and pull him out. We look only for the male fish. We
don't want the females because their bellies are thin after
they spawn. The males are bigger and keep better. We think
of that when the Government says we Indians are killing off
the fish. We don't take the females except in the salt water,
and there we don't get many. It is the seine and gill nets
that is killing off all the fish.

Every boy had bows and arrows. My brother made them
for me, and we used to go out in canoes bought by my brother
from the people that makes them. The Blundon Harbor, the
Newette, and Smith's Inlet Indians came to Fort Rupert to
sell their canoes. We made some at Fort Rupert, but not
many. We'd buy our paddles mostly from the Blundon
Harbor Indians. They are made of yew. We paid for a
small canoe, five pairs of blankets; maybe two pairs of blankets for a very small canoe. A real big canoe was ten to
twenty pairs. You couldn't get a canoe now for less than
two hundred pairs. I used a small canoe, and two of us boys

go together and chase the salt-water ducks while they are diving. I never got upset. We go to where they are diving and stop there and get out bows and arrows ready for them when they come up. All the boys' arrows is marked differently so they know which is theirs when they go to pick them up. They were marked in different ways. Mine was marked crossways with a hot iron, and another boy I knew, his was marked like mine only with two burns. The one that hits the duck gets it. Most often none of us hits it, but sometimes we do. On the salt water is where we learned to shoot our arrows. We hold the bow flatways and hold the arrow with the thumb and forefinger. I saw some Indians hold the bows the other way at the St. Louis Fair. It looked funny.

We also used to go into the woods with our bows and our arrows which have only a little point showing. We take them into the woods—all of us—and try to shoot little birds. And when we get one we throws it at another boy just like the sand birds. And every time we kill one, we make a mark on our bow for each one. Then we used to show our bows to each other and boast that we knows how to use our bows and arrows better if we have more notches. I feel pretty good when I have lots of marks. Those that don't have many feel pretty bad when they sees how many I have. We have to bring our birds to show if we really killed them, and everybody sees us make the marks. Whenever we wasn't playing any of these games, we was playing with our canoes in the water. We used to play a lot out there on the ocean.

If we have a real fight amongst ourselves and it's not a game, but we get real mad and pick up stones and sticks to kill the other fellow, then is only when they stop us. They let us jump and have races and race in our canoes, to teach us how to use the paddle, and to chase an enemy canoe, but if two are wrestling and one gets mad, then the other boys— the older ones—goes and stands between· the two that is fighting and stops them, and tells them they has to wrestle and not hit like that and not get mad. If a boy doesn't stop they send him away, and he can't play with the other boys.

That's his punishment—to stay by himself. We have a song for that that goes like this: "You may have to go away or you may come back." Some will stay away if he is too mad, but he won't stay very long. Mostly they come back pretty soon, because they don't like to keep away from the other boys that they is playing with.[4]

If we get mad at our parents or older brothers, they give us a licking. Some people never seem to give their children lickings, because they admire and love their children so much, that they say they couldn't punish or scold them. But this child gets worse and worse because he is not stopped by his parents or brothers and he is mostly the one that gets good lickings from the other boys, and gets sent away to play by himself.

My brothers always stopped me when I was doing wrong. They had to. A boy can't learn good if he isn't. Especially my eldest brother, who loved me so much that he looked after me better than my parents. If I do anything wrong he takes down my pants, if I have any on, and puts me on his lap, backside up, and slap my backside, which hurted me awful bad. He would do that for quite a while, and that pain will teach me to think of it, and I wouldn't do again for a long time what he didn't want me to do. He takes me in the house to do this. The most hurt to my feelings is he makes me stand up in front of him, when he finished slapping my butt, and uses kind words when he talks to me, and I see tears coming out of his eyes while he talks and tells me it hurted him most, and if he didn't love me so much he wouldn't care. But he does love me so much, he has to do this to show me the thing I done is not right. And the way he talked and the tears in his eyes hurted me, and I thought to myself I'll

---

[4] Here are set limits to aggression. To this point the whole function of the childhood games has been to foster certain aggressive acts. To fight, to compete and to win are encouraged. Crying babies are trained to become children who imperiously take what they want by force. But the angry child must exercise his power within the rules. Once he departs from them he finds himself punished. Thus children are taught to be aggressive, imperious, and power-demanding within the formal limits set by the rules of the games.

never do it again. That was worse punishment than the whipping.[5]

I never remember my mother punishing me—I was so young when she died. My aunt left everything of punishing me to my oldest brother. If I take anything out of the house that don't belong to me; if I go into the water with my clothing and keep it on wet all day instead of coming home and changing it, and if I stay out too long at night—and once I didn't come home at night, I stayed and slept with my chum all night—my oldest brother punished me, because he wanted me not to do these things. He wanted me to come home every night and sleep at home.

I remember a time a Hamatsa (Cannibal) came to me and Stephen Cook. He was told by our old people to go inside the bedroom where we was hiding, and to scare us. A Hamatsa of the Nimkis tribe, he was coming around to all the houses, and, when he comes around, they all go and hide themselves. And he was told that we was hiding in the bedroom. He came to us and got hold of Stephen Cook, who was also a little boy, and Stephen says, "Sir, I am your friend." And the Hamatsa let him go and came up to me. I didn't know what to say to him, and I was shaking and scared, because anybody the Hamatsa gets hold of, the

---

[5] This is an interesting procedure. Charley is probably pretty angry at his brother because of the restraints placed on his activity and the painful spanking with which the restrictions are sanctioned. What happens to this hostility? Charley says that after the spanking his brother speaks to him with "kind words" and impresses upon him that it is because he loves him that he punishes him. This probably conjures up for Charley visions of all the nice things his brother has done for him. Kind words and loving behavior are associated with the gratifying rôle of his brother and stimulate anew the love Charley has for his brother. These feelings are the direct antithesis of the hostile feelings engendered by the restraints and the punishment. The resulting conflict is painful, and Charley feels miserable. His anger toward his brother is suppressed—blocked in its expression by the love he bears his brother. Moreover, fear of still another spanking would help to prevent any expression of his resentment. Nevertheless, one would expect this hostility not simply to evaporate, but to find some indirect form of expression, and this, in fact, is what actually happened. Although he rarely expresses openly his antagonism toward his brother, it will shortly become clear that he spent a good portion of his time as a youth subtly harassing him.

Hamatsa is supposed to bite him. I was scared and said, "Sir, I am just a little boy." He went out laughing loud. He told them that my plea was so funny he couldn't scare me any more. Any time I was doing anything wrong after that, they would say, "Don't do that or the Hamatsa will come after you," and I would stop doing it right away. They knew I was so awful scared that time.

Once after I had seen my brother shave, I went and stole my brother's razor and went and shaved. This was when I had nothing growing on my face. After I done it, I go and tell the other boys I have been shaved. There was a thing I didn't know they do after shaving. I forgot to wipe it, and I cut his strap when I tried to sharpen the razor. I nearly cut the strap in half. He used that strap for strapping me with. When he asked me if I touched the razor, I tried to deny it, but I guess I looked guilty, and he says, "If you don't tell me, I'm going to beat you till you can't move." I told Mr. Hall about this when I went to school, and he told me about a captain on a ship that used to shave, and he had a monkey that used to imitate everything. The sailors didn't like the monkey, and one time a sailor went on deck and shaved and then put the razor on the wrong side and pretended to cut his head off with it. The monkey did the same and killed himself.

While I was in the bedroom of my brother, when I was very young, I saw a bottle of gin on top of a box. It was little more than half full. I had seen often my brother and his wife drinking from it. I took it and poured it in a glass that was standing alongside of it. I look at the glass and put my thumb on it at the place that he generally put his, and pour it up to there, and when I did this, I drunk it. I begin soon to feel funny. I begin to pinch my face, and I couldn't feel anything. I felt pretty good, too. I took the bottle again and take the same amount in the glass and drink it. This was while the people that came to invite the Fort Ruperts to their potlatch were in my brother's house. I hear them making speeches in a loud voice, and some of the old Kwekas were saying, "Yes, that's right; we know it is true." I begin

to think what are they talking about, and opened the bedroom door and stood in the doorway, and I begin to hear all
the old people say, "Yes, yes." And without knowing that
I spoke loud, I also said, "Yes, yes, that is true." Sometimes
I also say in a loud voice, "No, no." Then they look toward
where I was standing and begin to laugh. My brother says,
"Get inside the bedroom and shut the door." They didn't
know what was the matter with me. They thought I was
only making a joke, and when I went back into the bedroom,
that is the last I remember.

When I woke up I was lying by the fireside with a wooden
basin in front of me. They say this was for me to puke in,
and my brother says to me smiling, "You feel good?" I says,
"Yes." He says, "Will you have some more?" I says, "Yes."
He gives me more than half a glass full. I drank it, but I
couldn't drink it all. He says, "Drink it all." I did. It wasn't
long before I begin to puke. I thought I was going to lose
all my guts. I was sick for two days and couldn't eat. My
brother just smile at me and say, "You got what you want;
you got your medicine." He say I am too young to drink
that and that it is only a medicine that you should take a
little of. After I finished puking, he want to give me another
one, but I say no, I didn't want any. I begin to have a head-
ache and my stomach was out of order. I think that was the
first time my brother didn't punish me with a whipping, but
this way he did to me was the worst punishment I ever had.
From that time I never want to touch any liquor at all until
I went to work at River's Inlet at the Brunswick Cannery.

I remember once I took out my brother's big butcher
knife, which was so sharp, and used it to make a small boat.
I was cutting toward me and it slipped off the wood which
splitted and it cut my knee bad and opened it way up. I
have the scar yet, and it is a long one. I didn't dare to tell
him I cut my knee, so I tears a piece of my shirt and band-
ages it up and sit out all day watching the other boys play,
and when I tried to get up it was so painful I couldn't walk
and the other boys had to help me into the house.

My brother was working for Mr. Hunt at the time, and when I got into the house my father, who was blind, was the only one in the house. I picks up a big maul that we splits wood by hitting a wedge, and begin to split wood. Then I begins to yell and cry and tells my father that the big maul got on my knee and that it hurted awful bad. That was a big lie. I tried to fool him. My father comes feeling along and I takes off the bandage, and when he feels the cut, he feels his way out of the house to go where my brother is cooking. He gets near and keeps yelling to my brother that I got hurted splitting wood. My brother went and called the Indian agent, who was a kind of doctor, Mr. Blinkinsop. The Indian agent came and put some kind of medicine on it to hold it together, and put sticking plaster on it, and I had to lay in bed. The pain was bad.

My brother and his wife came home. I don't know where she was all day. I was on the bed and having something to eat in the bed. Three of my fellow boys came and asked how I was. I got scared because I know right away my brother is going to find out, and I am terrible scared right there in bed. My brother says to the boys: "Your friend has hurt himself. He was splitting wood and the maul slipped and he couldn't walk now, so he is in bed." One of the boys says: "What! He hurt his knee the second time?" My brother says: "Did he hurt his knee before?" The boy says: "Why, yes. He was making a boat with the big butcher knife, and it slipped and he cut his knee then. That was this morning." When my brother looked at me, I shut my eyes. My brother asked me: "Did you cut your knee?" I had to say yes. And then my brother says: "Where did you cut your knee with the knife?" I says: "Same place. And when I was splitting wood, the cut wasn't so bad until I hit it again with the maul, and that made it real bad." Then my brother went to where the knife was hid in the bedroom so I wouldn't touch it, and, when he saw the blood on it and came back, the Indian agent had come in to see how I was. My brother tells him I got cut first with a butcher knife and then second by a maul, but the Indian agent shakes his head and says: "There was no maul mark on that wound. It was a clean cut, and I knew right away it was a knife that done it."

Then my brother says to me: "You have told a lie and have tried to cover the thing you done wrong. [I never forget the exact words he used.] First you went into my bedroom and took away the knife that you know I don't let you have, and then you want to cover what you have done, and then you told a lie over and over and over again, and you deserve to be punished for these things bad, but I won't do it right now." He turns to the Indian agent, who was still there, and says to him: "When you think the wound is healed, that is the time I am going to punish him." The Indian agent says, "Good!" It was the most awful punishment I ever remember, because all the time it was healing I was thinking how awful the punishment was going to be. As it kept getting better, the punishment kept getting worse and worse. I was begging him all the time to punish me and get it over with.

It was about a month when the Indian agent finally said it was healed. Then my brother put me on his lap and takes his leather belt and puts it in two and begins to thrash me. I keep yelling all the time, "I'll never do it again." That was the last of it, and I never touched that butcher knife again nor anything else that belongs to anyone else. I used to say to myself, "He is a cruel brother." When I come to school, Mr. Hall ask me about those things and I tell him my brother was too cruel and mean to beat me for these things. Mr. Hall says he is kind, and if he let me do these things, I would be doing worse things right now and I would be in jail, and punished by the law for taking away other people's property. He says I should go to my brother and thank him for what he had done.

I've been telling my children and grandchildren about this. If my brother hadn't done these things, I don't think I'd be living now. All the other boys that was allowed to do these things is gone now—most of them dying by accident. That was the worst thing I ever did. After that I didn't dare do anything my brother tell me not to do. Any time I think of the thrashing I am going to have, I feel it already and don't do it. He never used to punish me the first time. He used to warn me that if I do it again I always get my thrashing. The most that hurts me though is his kind words, and I always think of those kind words and I use them for my children and grandchildren after I thrash them.

We used to do some dirty tricks, too. They used to have wedges made out of hard wood, and the old people didn't want to lose these. They had no axes. They only had a stone hammer. They put these wedges on the wood and then hit them with the hammer to split the wood. They used to leave the wedges where the wood is. We would dance around the fire, and some boys would slip out to look for the wedges and take them away and hide them. When the old folks come and ask for it, they have to pay whatever they ask to get them back. If they beat the boys that wouldn't get the wedges back, so they have to pay. Sometimes we see a house where there is an old man without any wood. We do the same tricks to get wood from another house and take it to this old man. Nobody would say anything about this to us.

You know, in the old days they used to have a big box close by the door where they used to pour the water from their chamber pots. They would keep it until it was very strong, and then rinse their blankets in it, and it makes the blankets clean. We would go around to the houses and sneak in and push these over. When they smell this, they get awful mad. Guess they would sure beat us if they caught us, but they never did. Some of the old people would be wise enough to keep the boxes in the light of the fire, so they could see the boys and chase them away. We just got long sticks then and pushed them over anyway. The next day they would just laugh about it and say, "They are just boys, and there is more of it to come anyway."[6]

[6] The boys enjoy these pranks probably because they know it annoys their elders. These are ways in which they can get even with the adults who have blocked their interests so often and have punished them so painfully. By permitting such tricks to be played upon them, the adults provide for the boys a comparatively harmless means of expressing their aggressions.

When the old people goes into the woods to get firewood, while I was a boy, and the firewood was all dead cedar, they go and chop it up in a big pile, and he, the man that cut it, would go back and tell the boys he has a big pile. And all the boys go there and packs the wood for all the men. We like to go and help. We would help anybody, it don't make any difference—especially when they are getting ready for the winter dances. All us young boys would pack the little logs, and the young men takes the bigger ones.

Some of the older people goes and fills up their canoes with driftwood, and comes in and all the boys would go and meet him and pack all the wood into his house. We never got no pay for that; we just had fun doing it. We feel it is a part of our game. None of us wears any shoes or any pants when we were boys. We just wear a shirt. So we walk out into the water and pick the wood out of the canoe. We had to wear pants when we go to school, and sometimes in the wintertime, but usually in winter we only wrapped a blanket around us.

When it is big tide in the wintertime, all the people goes to tow big logs. The big boys takes their axes and starts from one end of the houses and goes and cuts their wood log up, and some will have the maul and wedges to split it, and we, the younger boys, pack the wood into the houses. Some will cut other people's logs because there is so many young men. Nowadays they won't do it unless they is paid to do it. They see an old man working and won't even help him.

We dug wells in the old days where we used to get our water from at Fort Rupert, and from the water in the creeks in the wintertime. The water in the creek tastes good in the wintertime—nice and clear—when the water is rushing down from the snow, but it is awful in the summertime. We boys used to pack the water in pails—wooden ones if there wasn't metal ones bought from the store. We had great big boxes and square water pails—big ones made out of cedar. We brought in little buckets full and fill up the big one.

When we are playing in the woods or outside the house,

when we are boys, we have what we call "the boys' feast."
One boy will go to his house and ask his parents for some
kind of food, because he wants to give a feast to his playfellows. Some will be given a dried salmon or dried halibut
or anything we used to eat. We used to pretend to have seals
in our feast. The boy that gives the feast is not supposed
to eat any of it. They say if he does, the back of his head
will be full of sores. If he eats any of his own feast, there
will be another boy goes to him and slap the back of his
head, maybe ten or a dozen times, so that he won't have these
sores. And he slaps him good and hard, too. When they give
this feast, they have dried salmon and cut it and have it
like the back fin of the killer whale, and go around to where
the boys are sitting in a circle and point it at him and make
a noise like a killer whale until he gets to a boy who hasn't
given a feast yet, and says, "You," and gives it to him. This
boy runs home and gets something if he can, and when he
comes he is carrying what he brought and he talks and talks:
"I am a chief, and I am going to give a feast." Some of the
boys couldn't get anything and had to stay away. We call
that "never return," and when we finished and when we see
this boy who never returned, we clap our hands and make
fun of him and sing: "You stayed away. You never returned." And sometimes he is so ashamed he runs into his
house and hides. I always used to get something. My brother's wife and my mother's mother, who was very old, always
had some things to give us.

When I was a boy we used to give potlatches of small
canoes to imitate the potlatches of older people. I had
small canoes made for me just the shape of the big ones.
My second brother made some of them, and I paid other
older people tobacco and things to make some others for me.
When I have enough to give my potlatch, I go around to
all the boys of the other tribes at Fort Rupert. I call my
own tribe boys to come in front of my house and to count
these small canoes and put them in rows according to the
rank of the fathers of the boys. This imitates the real potlatch of canoes that the older men have. Then some of the

older boys of my own tribe make speeches like those of the men as they speak in their potlatches. In the potlatch I gave, they made speeches telling them I am giving away these little canoes, and that my name will be "Devil-fish" from now on.

Now when we have these boys' potlatches, we all get names of different kind of fishes or things like that. These are our names amongst the boys when we give these potlatches. This kind of potlatch is a play potlatch, and after the older boys that is taking the part of the chief speaks, then they begin to sing my song for this potlatch. The older boys gives this kind of play potlatch with boxes and shirts and other things, so that they have these different kinds of names. These are not real potlatches. I gave mine before I came to Alert Bay to school. The older women has the same kind of potlatch even when they are married. They used to give away dishes, spoons, boxes, and those things that belong to them, and they called it by the same name.

Our fathers and older brothers teach us to give these potlatches, and help us to do it, telling us all about what we should do to do it right. That is just like teaching us what we should do when we get grown up and give real potlatches. My older brothers were the ones who taught me, but they didn't come and watch us while we gave them. They only heard about it and how we did afterwards. When I come home, they tell me that is fine. They are the ones that started it—I wouldn't have done it if they hadn't started it—and they helped me all the time with my play potlatches.

If any of us has a quarrel between us, regarding our potlatch, then the other one that I have quarreled with would give his potlatch and try to make it bigger than mine. That is, he wants to get ahead of me. He wants to get in a higher place than me, even though we didn't have any real places in our clan yet. If he gives a bigger potlatch than me, I goes to my father's brother to help me give another potlatch that is bigger than his. For this we use little canoes and other things, until one of us has to quit. The other fellow's parents help him and so on back and forth till one couldn't do any more. The one that gives the most is supposed to be higher than the other. The other goes lower down. Every time we pretend to quarrel, or really do quarrel, if I give more than he does, I keep telling him he is lower than me. I never had any real bad quarrel when I was a boy, but I remember a bad one old Chief Whanock had when he was a boy. I seen him quarrel with another fellow, and it went on for a long time. I think Chief Whanock finally won. They were still quarreling when I came to school here at Alert Bay.

CHAPTER IV

AT SCHOOL IN ALERT BAY

WHEN I came here to Alert Bay, when I was six or seven, to school, it was pretty hard on me. Mr. Hall, the missionary, only stayed at Fort Rupert about a year, and we just went to where he was living to have school there, and, when he moved over here, he built this house and the day school. And after those was finished, he went to Fort Rupert and asked the boys and girls that went to school there to come over here. There wasn't very many of us came—two of old Mr. Hunt's daughters, one of George Hunt's daughters and myself, and the others came in later. I didn't want to go, but my brother says go and I go. That is all. He was the boss. You see my father got blind when he got old, so the time my mother died, my brother and his wife looked after me.

My grandfather, Tlakodlas, was here when I came to school in Alert Bay. Just before I was born, he gave a big potlatch close to Knight's Inlet. There is a beach there at the foot of a mountain, where the people used to wait for high tide to go up to the river. The potlatch was to his own people. He was my mother's mother's brother. The Nimkis and he got a copper and throwed it under the big rock and gave a name to that rock. He was a big chief, and he wanted that rock to be a memory unto him. Every time the people go by that place, they talk about the chief who done it. I used to come to Alert Bay and visit him, and, when I was at school, I used to visit him. He was Lagius' uncle on his father's side—his father's brother. Any time he used to come in with firewood, I remember packing that into his house for him. He lived in a community house with his wife and one son and Joe Harris, and his brothers lived with him.

When I first was brought by Mr. Hall and he built his

house here, it was hard. I cried for nearly a week. Mr. and Mrs. Hall did all they could to make me forget my feelings, but it was very hard to forget it, for I had never been away from my parents while they were living, and I never was away from my brother. Of course, my other brother never stayed home, so I didn't think of him much. He was down to Victoria at the time I was brought to Alert Bay. When he heard that I was brought to school, he quit working there to come to see me, and he brought clothing for me to wear in school. He stayed here a week, and went back to his work at Victoria.

While I was in school the first week, they tried to teach me how to write and spell, but I couldn't do anything for I didn't want to learn. I only wanted to get back to my home.[1]

When my brother was told I was crying all the time, he came to Alert Bay with his wife and stayed for some months and worked for the Indian agent, Mr. Blinkinsop. He lived with our grandfather, Tlakodlas, in a community house at the time. They came and see me in the mission house, and brought me a package of clothing. The Indian agent also came in to see the children in school, and took our measurements and ordered for the clothing. That made me feel better. The Indian agent says if I be a good boy in school he will buy me clothes every year. My brother and the Indian agent came together. Mr. Hall got all the children in a row and begin to make us spell the things that we have learned. Of course, I have learned some in Fort Rupert. He says to spell *yes* and *no* and all those little words and then he gets to the other side where I was and asked them to spell *said*. None of the others could spell it, but I says I can and I spelled it out *SAID*. The Indian agent and my brother clapped their hands. Oh, I felt proud, and from that time,

---

1 Charley's feeling of bitter loneliness probably indicates an emotional conflict. He obviously did not want to stay in Alert Bay, yet he feared the wrath of his brother should he return to Fort Rupert. Not knowing what to do, he resorted to the infantile response which had served him so well while he was in the cradle and spent most of his time crying.

about two months after I came, I tried to do better than all the others.[2]

When I came here first, I stayed right in the mission house where the girls stayed. I was the only boy here then. Two or three years after, Mr. Hall built another house for some bigger boys than us from Fort Rupert and other villages that came here to school. When the other boys came, I felt better, because I had some boys to play with.

When it was my fourth year, there was finally a dozen of us boys here at school. They all lived at the little house that was built for the boys, but I was still living at the mission house. I learned some bad words from the bigger boys in English, which I thought wasn't bad enough to make our teachers get mad, for I didn't know the meaning. Mrs. Hall told me to go and empty the mess in the toilet, me and another boy. In the toilet there was a box with handles. Mr. and Mrs. Hall had one on the next door of the toilet, and we had one in the other. We was looking for a pole, so we won't go too close to the box, and Mrs. Hall comes out and says: "Hurry up, what are you looking for?" Stephen Cook says: "We are looking for a pole to lift the box with." Mrs. Hall says: "Never mind the pole. Take hold of the handles and get it out on the beach." Stephen Cook says that we can't bear the smell if we get too close. She says: "It won't be long. Take your handkerchiefs and put them over your noses so you don't smell it." That's the time I spoke up and says: "You come and do it yourself, God damn you." She went right into the house and told Mr. Hall. He came out and called me into the house and told me to get into the front room. He went out again, and called all the boys in, and he told all of the boys and myself it wasn't right to swear at a lady, or even to anyone. He says: "That's why I want you all to see what punishment this boy is going to get."

2 Here is a reward in the school situation that Charley can understand—his brother's approval. Of importance, too, is the fact that Charley's older brother approves of school and Mr. Hall. Learning the white man's language thus becomes a part of what Charley—as an Indian—should learn.

This was about eight in the morning before we went to school. He got his walking stick, and told me to come out and stand in front of all the school children, and told me to hold out my right hand, palm up. I hold it out straight. He raised his walking stick and crashed down at my hand. I pull my hand away fast and the stick hit the floor and break it. He was awful mad. He still had part of the cane, and he says: "Now you've broken my cane. Put out your hand again." I put it out and when he was going to beat my hand, I pull it back again. The stick flew out of his hand and struck the floor.

He got mad and went out of the room, and Henry Beuhler says to me: "Look here, he is going to get another stick. You better run out while you have a chance." I did, but I run the wrong way. Mr. Hall caught me by the shirt collar and dragged me into the front room, and brought with him a broom handle. He says: "Now try and be a good boy and take your punishment." And he says this to me in our language. I didn't want to put out my hand, and just folded my arms and stood there. He got so mad he begin to strike me on my back hard. He was so mad he didn't know where to hit next. After a while he stopped and looked to see if I was crying, but I just smile at him. That makes his anger worse. He soon stops striking me and took me by the shoulder hard and took me upstairs to a room and locked me up.

At twelve o'clock the bell rang for lunch and I heard the dishes rattling, but they brought me nothing to eat. At six o'clock the bell rang again for supper, and still I stayed there. After supper all the boys went out. I heard Mr. Hall tell them to go out in front and play football. That is the time I begin to feel bad. I guess that is the reason he wanted them to play on the front so I could see and hear them. While the boys were playing, I went to the window to watch them, and the boys look at me. Some of them smile and Henry Beuhler says: "I thought you was brave. Why don't you jump through the window and get away." I thought that pretty good, because my grandfather was here, and Mr. Hall was afraid of him.

I opened the window and looked down and see the window below wasn't too far, and put my legs through the window first. I was holding on to the sill of the window and had my feet trying to catch on to something. There was nothing to put my feet on but the window, so I kick it in. Then a hand catches my wrist. "Here, come back." It was Mr. Hall. I pulled my hand away from him fast and jumped right down to the ground and just laid down and got a big cut on my elbow from the gravel. I got up and walked down to where the boys were playing, and when I get to them, Henry says, "Atta boy." I says, "Good by. I'm going to leave you." I walked away. Mr. Hall hollers after me and says, "Come back." I says, "Aday," which means "Yes, sir." He started to run after me, and I run, too. When he stopped running, I stopped.

At the time there was only a trail close to the beach. When I nearly got to my grandfather's house, I saw him packing out wood from his canoe, and I begin to run where he was. My grandfather says, "What's the matter?" "Mr. Hall's trying to lick me," I says. My grandfather dropped the wood and took only one and turned and faced Mr. Hall. My grandfather says: "What are you trying to do with my grandson? You better go back before I hit you with this stick." Mr. Hall turned around and went back. After Mr. Hall went home, Mrs. Hall came and asked my grandfather to tell me to go back. He got up and took hold of her and turned her around and pushed her out of the door and told her to go away from there. Mr. and Mrs. Hall went to the Indian agent and told him to come and get me back. We told him that he doesn't want Mr. Hall beating me up for nothing, for swearing don't amount to anything to us Indians. My grandfather says, "I won't let him go back to the mission house until Mr. Hall comes and apologizes, and says he is not going to do it again."

It took them a week before they made up their mind, and then they came back with the Indian agent. Mr. Hall tried to explain to my grandfather that a teacher should teach children to obey and go by all the rules of the school, and that if they don't the children have to be punished. My grandfather says, "I have never punished any of my children before I warned them and talked to them." Finally, they promised not to thrash me unless I do something very serious. They kept that promise. Whenever I did anything like disobeying or playing in school, Mr. Hall just called me into his office and talked to me kindly, telling me it hurts his feelings to know I am going to be disobedient and a bad boy, because if I don't try and be good now, I will be worse when I grow up. I felt bad the way he talked to me, and it hurted my feelings to know I was doing the wrong thing, when he explained to me, and that did good better than when he thrashed me.[3]

When he saw I begin to turn over a new leaf, after I tried my best to be obedient, he began to be the same way to the other boys. There is only one time he beat one of the boys after this. That was when Jimmy Provost took up a butcher knife, when we was having a scrap with him while sawing wood, and he threw the butcher knife at me and cut me on the leg. Jimmy was brought into the office, and Mr. Hall beat him. He was taken up to be locked up while all the boys remained in the office and Mr. Hall will talk to them and asking them not to fight with one another. Jimmy was crying and yelling when he got his beating, and Mr. Hall turned around to me and says: "Tlalis, why didn't you cry the time I beat you?" And Henry Beuhler says: "Aha! You think a fellow who is taught to be brave is going to cry at a little thing like that? We have been through worse than that," and he told Mr. Hall about our game, and that we are taught not to cry no matter how much things hurt.

My name at school was Charles James Nowell. I don't know how we got these names. There is a full-blooded Indian

[3] This was probably a turning point in Charley's life. In refusing to accept the discipline of white culture he found himself strongly supported by his grandfather—a powerful exponent of native customs and hearty enemy of English ways. In the struggle for control over the boy, two societies were competing—the white and the Indian. The Indian won. White discipline from now on held little terror for Charley, and he reverted to his native way of life.

called Hunt and another called Coon. Mr. Hall gave me my name when he baptized me. I got the name Nowell because a Sunday school teacher in England wanted Mr. Hall to give me his name, and they say that he was my godfather when I was baptized, and he used to send me presents every Christmas. One time when they were having a picnic in England, one of the boys got up while they were having all their fun and said: "Look here, we are having a good time and I wonder what our native brother is doing at Alert Bay. Maybe he is not like us having a picnic and having fun, and I hear he is learning how to play the concertina. I'm going around with my hat to all of you so that we will have a collection to pay for a concertina and send it to him." He went around with his straw hat and all the rest of the boys gave something and give it to Mr. Nowell and he bought a concertina and the remaining of the money that was collected was sent to me in care of Mr. Hall. And there was thirty-four dollars in cash together with this concertina, and when it came to me and Mr. Hall gave it to me, my, I thought I was the richest man in Alert Bay. I was about twelve then. I played the concertina and when I got my first boy, he spoiled the concertina. Mr. and Mrs. Hall ordered me clothing and other things with the rest of the money.

When I was a very young boy—when I was first at school here at Alert Bay—there was a woman here who was very sick. This was Moses Alfred's mother. She just wagged her head about without having any breath. She must have some pain somewhere because she just groans and wags her head back and forth. She came from Alert Bay, but she was in Fort Rupert at the time. Nobody seems to know what is the matter with her. There is no white doctor there at the time. Her relations went out to get some Indian medicine to treat her with, but that didn't do any good. She seems to be getting worse and worse all the time. One day, here at Alert Bay, a man went to the point of this Island toward Fort Rupert in his canoe to go and pick up some driftwood and put it in his canoe. While he was on the point there, he came to a tree standing close to the beach just above high-water

mark. He looked up to this tree and he saw something standing on one of the limbs of the tree. He took that down, according to what he told the people, and put it in the bow of
his canoe.

When he got home here at Alert Bay, he hollered out to
all the people that he found this thing at the point. He
brought it on shore in front of one of the community houses.
There used to be platforms outside the houses where we all
used to sit around on a fine day, and they begin to look at
this thing. It was a piece of wood tied up from end to end,
and on top of the string that is tied on it there was pitch.
People begin to open this, to untie the string, and to see
what it was tied up for. It was about ten to twelve inches
long and about two inches in diameter. While they were
working at it, a woman came out of the house and shouted
saying: "Don't handle it too hard. It may be the sick
woman who is dying in Fort Rupert that is making her so
sick." So the men got a pail of water and put this thing in
it. While they unties it, they keep this in the water and
handles it very careful. They opened it when all the strings
was off and found that it was a hollow stick. Inside they
found some snakeskin stuffed with some hair they think belonged to this woman for it was the same color, and some
dirt which they think was the dirt she passed her water on,
and other dirt that was on a small stick which they think
was her spit, and a small piece of rag they recognized as
from her clothes somewhere. They keep all these things in
the water when they get through looking at it.

They say that this same day in Fort Rupert this woman
was just rocking her head and sweating and hollering, and
yelling for the pains in her head, and she began to pull her
hair out. Then all of a sudden, she becomes cool and has
been well ever since, so they think this was the cause of her
sickness. They blame the thing on a man that wants to
marry her and she didn't want him. If anyone had seen him
doing it from the village, the young men would kill him,
murder him whenever they get a chance, or, if they catch
him at it, kill him right there where he is working at it, but

no one seen this man doing it, so they didn't kill him. When I look at this it seems to be real, that people could witchcraft and kill people that they want to die. They have often come to the Indian agent and tell him someone is being witchcrafted, but the Indian agent wouldn't believe it, but I do believe it, because I seen this one, and I seen the woman suffer and I seen her well after that thing was removed and put in water. The woman is still alive and we will get her to tell the story to you.

Statement of the "Witchcrafted" Woman

I was married to a man at Fort Rupert, and was there when I got sick. I was dying and my uncle came to see me from Alert Bay. I was unconscious then and didn't know anything, and then all of a sudden I was well. The time I got well I found out later was the same time the people at Alert Bay was putting that thing in water.

I was engaged to a man in Alert Bay. Then I married another man and went to Fort Rupert. This man I was engaged to first had a brother. I got sick not long after I got to Fort Rupert. I didn't know what was wrong with me. My breath would come short and I could hardly breathe. My head wouldn't stop dizzying. I didn't feel any pain—just my head spinning around, and my heart beating fast, and I go unconscious. When I come to, I feel fine and there is nothing ailing me. This always happens every night when the others go to sleep. Every night about the same time it happens to me, and just before I become unconscious, I usually see a snake stuck on the wall and it moves and comes toward me in my mind, and I see too the man I was engaged to. When the snake comes very near to me, I sweat all over and then I go unconscious.

The wife of the brother of the man I was first engaged to found out about them doing it in Alert Bay. Every night her husband pinched his wife's ear to see if she is awake. Pretty soon she decided to see what they are up to, and she stays awake, and when he pinches her ear, she pretends she is asleep. Then he pinches her arm and she still pretends she is asleep.

Then he gets up and goes out. She got up and looked through a knothole on the boards and then she saw what they were doing. They had a snake about two feet long and they put it, these two brothers, under the earth of the fire, and when it was steaming, they pour water on it. This is the time I was sweating. When the woman saw this, she went and told the uncle that I had in Alert Bay about it. Meantime, I was nearly dying, and they sent for my uncle. They put all the things in the canoe, and my coffin, and started off for Fort Rupert. When they got in the canoe, my eldest uncle got up in the canoe and says, "We are going to take these things to my niece in Fort Rupert, and when my niece dies, where will you live?" and he mentions the names of these two witchcrafters. This is the time they got scared that my uncle would kill them, and they went and put the snake in a hollow log and tied it to the tree on the point.

I didn't have no children at the time. Not so very long after I got well, those two witchcrafters turned around and witch-crafted my husband. He died from the very same kind of sickness I had. Nobody did nothing to the witchcrafters, because no one seen them witchcrafting my husband.

When I was at school in Alert Bay, Nigia and his wife was put in one dead body. While the Mamaleleqala were all at Knight's Inlet olachen fishing, he felt himself getting weak, and found himself getting thinner and losing weight. And his wife was the same. During the time, his body seems to be all dried. His wife died there. After his wife died, the news came to the people at Knight's Inlet that a dead man is found close to White Beach about ten miles south of here, and the dead man is facing the sun at noon between a rock. Some trees were growing on the front, which kept other people from seeing it when they passed. The people talked about it, and they say Nigia is the only man that is sick in the kind of way this would be, and so a canoe load of young men started off from Knight's Inlet and traveled in the night. When it is daylight they came to the place where this dead body was. In the meantime Nigia stayed in Knight's

Inlet and couldn't get out of his bed. He was so sick. They got this dead man out very carefully and put him into the salt water and begin to open the pitch that was sealing his mouth, and from the nose and from the ass-hole, and then they opened this man and took all the stuff out that was inside, and took those things up to Knight's Inlet. Before leaving the body, they washed the mouth and nose and the ass-hole thoroughly clean and then left the body in the water.

While they were at it Nigia felt chilly, and they knew at Knight's Inlet that they had got this dead man and put him into the water. They already know that this dead man has the stuff from Nigia inside him and told him right away that he is going to live. And when the people came to Knight's Inlet this stuff was put on a board in front of Nigia's house and everybody heard that they have brought this stuff and came down to see it, and they could tell which was from Mrs. Nigia's clothing and which was from her hair and which was from Nigia, and it was a piece of the collar of the shirt he wore. This he had already missed, seeing that a piece of it was cut off, and there was some manure and dirt he had pee'd on and some dirt they think he spit on. From that time he got well, but he was still a slim man with no flesh on him. But when that dead body was found it was too late for his wife. They say that if they had found this dead body before she died, she would also have been alive.

They think they know who did it. It was one of his own relations—his own uncle, but not a near uncle—a far uncle who was paid by another chief to do it. This chief was trying to get higher than Nigia, not to get his position, but just to get higher. They were giving potlatches and breaking coppers for each other. I never heard whether Nigia did anything to this chief or his far uncle for witchcrafting his wife and him or not. Of course his uncle didn't admit that he did it.

When a man is found out to be a witchcrafter, the head chief and the chiefs of each tribe would get together and decide what should be done with this man. This time it would only be the head chief of each tribe, because this is private and not to be talked about publicly. A man from the Walas Kwakiutl was a witchcrafter, and the head chiefs of the Fort Ruperts held a meeting. I was in school then. In the meeting they said: "We have known this man to witchcraft so many men now that he is not fit to be alive, and we want to get rid of him. We will get some of the young men to watch him when he goes to relieve himself, and when he goes out to pass water, and to get some of his clothing and some of his hair and spit. And when we get all that, we will collect blankets between us and we will pay this witchcrafter." "You, Ogwela," says Nekapenkem, "are supposed to be my enemy. As we are going to Alert Bay to a potlatch there, you go to this witchcrafter a day before we start off, paying him this amount of blankets that we have collected between us. Tell him that you want to get rid of me, for I am going to give a potlatch at Alert Bay when we get there, and that you want to get rid of me before I give this potlatch. Tell him to get it ready, and make me to drop dead before we get to Alert Bay, while we are traveling." So Ogwela went to this witchcrafter and told this witchcrafter what was told to him to say, saying: "You make Nekapenkem to die before we get to Alert Bay—just to drop down dead in the canoe. I am going to give you this amount of blankets to do it." Which was a big amount in those days—eighty blankets which he paid for Nekapenkem to be witchcrafted.

The next morning all the Fort Ruperts get ready to go, packing their stuff in their canoes, and they were waiting for this witchcrafter to come. He was working at it hard, and, when he got through with it, he put all the stuff in the iron barrel of a gun and drive a piece of wood in the end of it to keep the air in, and they found this afterwards. He put this iron about six inches under the fire and built a fire over it. When this gets hot, Nekapenkem was supposed to get ill and die while traveling toward Alert Bay. They had a fair wind coming down, and at evening while they were anchoring off the Nimkis River waiting for the last canoe to come, this witchcrafter dropped down in his canoe dead. When he found out himself ill, he told somebody that he was fooled by Ogwela, and he was the one that witchcrafted himself. "What can I do now?" he says. "We are away from Fort Rupert, and, before I get this thing out of the fire, I will be dead." Ogwela had given him his own hair and spit and things, saying it was from Nekapenkem.[4]

The witchcrafter that killed himself by mistake was paralyzed. There were a lot of them that was paralyzed there in Fort Rupert when I was a young fellow. Their ankles was dead. Their arms they could use. It was only their legs; their feet drops on the front when they lift them, and they have to pull their legs up high when they walk. They were all the same way that had it. There wasn't very many of the Nimkis that got it, but they used to have another kind of disease which other tribes didn't have. They had sores on their backsides. I remember my parents was talking about the time they came to visit Tlakodlas, and, while they were coming around the mouth of the river to the Nimkis village, my father says to my mother shaking the canoe: "Do you hear what I hear?" She says: "What is it?" He says: "I hear scratching. Your people must have a lot of sores on their backsides." My mother was turning around to him and try to club him with the paddle. They stayed here until the sockeye season was over. When they went back and went around Thomas Point, my mother turn around to my father and says: "You hear what I hear?" And he says: "What is it?" My mother says: "I hear some flopping feet. Your people must all be paralyzed." My father just sit down and laugh and laugh and laugh.

When I was at school in Alert Bay, I only had a holiday in the wintertime. The rest of the time I stay here in Alert Bay; I used to stay maybe four months, maybe not so long. Mr. Hall wasn't paid to teach us, I don't think. I think he was just paid as a minister. Any time my brother comes

---

[4] Here are vivid proofs, for Charley and the other Indians, that sorcery is effective. Moreover, he has no proof to the contrary. Brought up in a society which boasts no science to combat a belief in sorcery, Charley cannot help but be convinced that people can be bewitched. This explains, in part, how sorcery can be so effective as a means of social control, and, at the same time, such a satisfying outlet for aggression.

and wants to take me to Fort Rupert, Mr. Hall never refused, and I could stay there as long as my brother wanted me to stay.

I remember when I was in Fort Rupert during vacation, my second brother was playing *lahal*[5] with them against the Nimkis (my older brother never played—he did not like the game). They had their shirts to bet with, and the side that wins gets them both and so on with other things. The Nimkis chief, while he was playing, was cheating; after one from our sides points to his hand, he shifts the bone, he throws it in the other hand, and that's how he cheats. My brother and the other men on his side saw him do it, and they begin to quarrel. He got up and comes toward my brother, and my brother got up and stood against him. They begin to hold each other and wrestle. They were fighting for quite a while until our brother learned my second brother was fighting. As he was running toward them, he was holding this copper and banged the Nimkis man on the head with the copper, and it bended around his head. The man let my brother go and sat down.

When the owner of the copper, my brother, bends it over the chief's head, that shows he's not going to sell it but is giving it as an insult to the other chief. If he had a copper, he would get it and give it back to my brother but he didn't have any. He was going to buy a copper but he died before he had a chance to buy it. It's a disgrace to his family for keeping this copper that my brother gave him. If ever his daughters or sons or grandsons quarrel with anybody, all they say is: "You're not fit to quarrel with anyone. Owadi's copper is around your necks choking you."

Instead of bending the copper, my brother might have broke it. If I break a copper I can't sell it. I can only use it to fight with because a piece of it is gone. I might nail a piece on my copper to make it whole again but that is a dis-

---

[5] In the hand game, *lahal*, the players sit in two rows facing each other. A player on one side juggles a polished bone in his hands. When he is through moving the bone from one hand to the other, the players opposite guess which hand contains the bone.

grace to me and my family because then the piece I have
given to the other man isn't worth anything. The only reason
to break a copper is to save the rest of it to fight with—it
would be better to bend it like my brother did.

When my brother hit that Nimkis fellow over the head,
if he had gotten another copper, he could have given it to
my brother, and then my brother could have sold it, and he
could have sold my brother's, but they wouldn't get as much
for the coppers as they cost. If he had a more valuable copper, he could tear off a corner of it and give that to my
brother. Then he owns my brother's copper and can sell it.[6]

The only time I was very sick I had the whooping cough
for six months while I was at school in Alert Bay. I must
have been about fourteen or fifteen, and I was staying at
the missionary house because I was engaged to George
Hunt's eldest daughter, Maggie. This was my oldest brother's first choice for me. My brother and George Hunt came
and told Mr. Hall about it, and I used to go with her in a
white man's way, walking to the Bay and back together. I
begin to love her and she begin to love me. After we was engaged, all the children in the mission house got the measles.
She did, but I didn't. I wanted to, but I couldn't. We were
all kept in one big room at the mission house. I don't know
why I didn't get the measles. I used to go and lay down on
the bed with Mr. Cook who had the measles. This was about
the year after I was engaged to Maggie. When they all got
well of the measles, I had the whooping cough, and I was
the only one who had it in the mission house. When I begin
to cough, I just cough and cough until my breath goes out,
and I used to go unconscious. Blood used to run through my
nose. Maggie used to be right alongside of me, using rags
to wipe the blood off. Everybody thought I was going to die
of that. I was thin, and almost all my flesh is gone. When I

----

[6] This instance shows clearly one function of giving a copper: the symbolic act of giving a man a copper stops all physical combat, and, as a
result, none of the members of the society get hurt severely enough to interfere with their efficiency as workers. Indeed, the person to whom the copper is given is stimulated to redouble his productive efforts. Thus aggression is turned into a source of energy for socially useful labor.

get my conscious back, I see her face close to mine and her tears drop to my face while she was crying. I used to tell her not to cry, because I am not going to die. I says: "Maggie, don't you cry. I am not going to leave you. I am not going to die." And she was feeling awful bad, and she tells me her heart is breaking.

Before I could get up and out of bed, she got sick, holding her breast where her heart is. When I was allowed to get up by Mr. Hall, I was alongside of her all the time since she was in bed. She got worse and worse all the time, and died of that. It was her heart the doctor said. She was laying in one of the rooms on a table while two men was sent to Fort Rupert to tell George Hunt his daughter is dead. She was kept in that room for four days before George Hunt came, and during the time I used to get up in the night from the bedroom where the boys was to go down to the room where she was and stand by her crying. I was in a bad way at that time. I couldn't forget her for a long time. I loved her so much.

When I went out of school and went home to Fort Rupert, my brother spoke to George Hunt about me getting married to his second daughter, but it didn't go through. Something happened, I don't remember what, but anyway I didn't and I didn't care so much for her.

Sometime after Maggie died, I and Stephen Cook was sent up north to go to school. We stayed at the mission house where Bishop Ridley was. There was over twenty-four there —all boys. It was a kind of boardinghouse. We stayed there, slept there, and ate there. When we was there, we find that these boys are tough. They are fighting all the time, and they always want to tease us because we were strangers. One evening while we was having our supper, our cook, an Indian boy named Tlisk, he was mad with everybody, and he came along with a pot of stew to serve it out to all the boys. When he got to my plate, he bumped the pot against the side of my head. I took my elbow and jabbed it in his stomach, and he didn't give me any stew. He sat down and had his meal, and one of the other boys took the pot and came and gave me some of the stew. This cook boy was mad with us and talk and talk at us in his language. He was a humpback, and he look at me and talk at me. Finally, I says, "Shut up, you dirty humpback." He picked up his stew and threw it at me, and it got all over me and the other boys near me, and he took his tin mug and from where he sit—just across the table—he threw it at me hard. I put up my arm and the mug hit it. He was a short man, and I bent over the table and got hold of his shirt and pulled him right across the table, and picked him up and threw him right down the table, rattling all the dishes and spilling everything. All the boys cheered me and hollered out in fun. Bishop Ridley came running and says, "What's the matter?" It was the other boys that told him how it was started. The cook was fired, and after that I got acquainted with the other boys.[7]

We used to go out in the evenings and take a walk, and the girls from the village also comes out to take a walk in the street. We met two girls. I was with a boy called Peter Ryan. It was dark, and we stopped and we talked with these girls in their language that I didn't understand. He told me: "You go with this girl, and I will go with the other one." He was talking to this girl for me. I and she went into the brush, and I and the girl sat down, talking in English. The next day I received a letter from her saying that she couldn't go to sleep that night. She was thinking of all the things we talked about, and asked me to answer her letter and write it to her office. In my letter I told her not to go with anybody else, but just to go to the place where we was the night before. So we always go there every night, and she and I lay with each other and make love often. When I was there nearly three months, there was other girls writing to me, asking me to meet them in such and such a place. I didn't go, because I like the girl I met first, but I kept the letters. One time, they were taken away from my desk by one of the boys, and at that time I wrote again to the girl I first met telling her to go to the same place we always meet. This let-

---

[7] Charley becomes a member of the ingroup by doing something admirable in their eyes. Hitherto he has been an outsider—the butt of their jokes.

ter was taken away from the girl and was brought to Bishop Ridley by the stepfather of this girl. I was called into his office, and he told me that I wasn't doing right. I told him I loved this girl, and she also loved me. He says: "You couldn't love her, because you couldn't marry her. You have a brother that wants you to go home with him. If you marry her, you would stay here, and that means you would stay away from your own home. Besides that," he says, "I have several letters the other girls is writing you, that one of the boys brought me. You couldn't love them all, so I see you don't know what you are doing, and it will only make trouble if you stay here, so I will send you home." So we was both sent home, Stephen Cook and me, and we had only been there three months. I never seen the girl since. I came to Alert Bay—my brother had built a house here. I didn't go to school after that.[8]

Mr. and Mrs. Hall left here during the first war and went back to England. They both died there without coming back. Mrs. Hall was awful easy to get frightened. When she was here, any time it thunders, she lie on the floor putting her fingers to her ears, and if there is anybody shooting with a gun, she jumps right up and gets frightened. We think that the cause of her death at England is when she hears the bombs and cannon. Mr. Hall was the best missionary we ever had here. He used to go around from house to house every night and talk with the people and read parts of the Bible to them, and if they were eating he goes right amongst them and eats with them. He had a long beard, and the olachen oil used to drip down it. I don't know of any Indian food he didn't eat. He used a tablespoon for grease and every other Indian food he eats. He used to buy Indian food for all of us while we was at school. He used to order boxes of olachen grease for us, and he talked our language same as any Indian, so, when he preaches, the old Indians understood every word he says. The Indian agents under-

---

[8] Charley refuses to conform to puritan sex standards, and white discipline fails again. Indian culture wins, and Charley returns to his native way of life.

stand some of the Indian language but not all, and none of
them could talk it good. When one of the Indian agents first
came to Alert Bay, he came to visit us at Fort Rupert, and
he begin to talk to us about the potlatch and say he is going to stop it, for it is no good. I ask him how he knows. He
says: "I know all about it. I know more than you do." I
says: "You must be older than I am, because I have lived all
my life amongst them, and I still don't know everything
about it." He says: "I've been told." And, when I ask him
who tells him, it is always another white man.

CHAPTER V

GROWING UP

MAYBE I was twelve years old when my father took sick. He wanted to have a talk with me, so my brother came and took me out of school. My brother sent three of the boys to come and get me. He got one of the Hunt family to write a letter to Mr. Hall so I could go. Mr. Hall didn't seem to mind my going. He never even told me to come right back. I went to Fort Rupert, and, as soon as I get there, my father calls me to go to his bedside, and told me he is going to leave us, and told me to remember what he has taught me regarding potlatches. He told me to do the same as my brother does—that he is always loaning out blankets to other people, and that is the only way to get more blankets. "If you will spend your earnings foolishly, you will be no good. They will not look upon you as they are looking upon your brother. Most of all I want to say is, I know you have been to school, and I think the only way for you to remember the main positions and all the ancestors is for you to write them down, because it seems to me that everybody is forgetting all their ancestors and names. I have often heard people make mistakes. The first thing, you will write down our ancestors till now." So I did—all our ancestors right down to him. He then told me to write down the names we should use and told me about the positions in our clan, and told me who had that position and why we should use it. Then he begin to talk about the dances and the dance names, and, when he finish that, he lay down and slept. He lose his breath talking to me, and, when he lay down to sleep, he died. He was going to talk about our relatives, but before he finished his breath gave out, and he died.

What became of those papers I wrote I don't know. It was my brother that looked after it. It must have been burnt when they burnt all my brother's clothing, according to the custom of the Indians, that they have to take everything that a man used for clothing and burn it after the funeral. I was so busy when my brother died, I didn't have a chance to go and watch.

After my father died, they put him in a long coffin, and it was cedar boards nailed together, and they buried him in the ground in back of the porch. My brother had to pay Mr. Hunt one pair of blankets for a place to bury him in the graveyard. Four days after, my brother gave the potlatch, and that is the time he put me in my father's position in our clan—number three position.

When my father died I was old enough to have my position in my clan. My brother give a potlatch and announce my new name, Tlakodlas, which means "where you get your coppers from." After this two men are sent to go and invite me to a feast, and my brother gives them a blanket each. Then I go with these two men. I don't like to go—I would rather play than go to a feast. When the two men get to the front of the building where the feast is, one of them speaks to the people, saying that I have come to join the feast and that my seat should be open where I am going to sit. When I sit down, the chief of my clan gets up again, and tells the Kwekas to sit up and sing my brother's potlatch song. They begin to sing, and then after the singing, our chief announces that I am going to give a feast or a potlatch soon. After that, I am a man—not any more a child. They now have to remember me on every feast.

When I was in the third position in the first clan of the Kwekas, before I was married, a nephew of mine, Nulis, who was older than me and belonged to our clan, but his position was way lower, gave a potlatch after he sold a copper. When he was giving it to all the other tribes who came to Fort Rupert, he told the people of how we stand, and we are from one family in the olden days, that he has a right to be in one of our grandfather's positions, and that he wants to be put on the third position of our clan, and I was to be the fourth, which was a man called Likiosa who was a little older than me and was related to me, and we all just go down one so he can have my position. My brother wasn't at Fort Rupert. He was at Alert Bay working for the new Indian agent, Mr. Pidcock, and while he was talking to the people about this position, somebody told me to stand up and tell him I don't want him to come in front of me until my brother comes back, and agree to what he says.

When my brother comes back to Fort Rupert, there was another potlatch from other peoples to the Fort Ruperts, and this Nulis stood up and says, when the potlatch comes to my place, "Now give me my share on this position where I am now going to be." My brother stood up and told him he has heard about what he said, and that he doesn't agree with him. "If you had spoken to me beforehand," he says, "I might have agreed, but you have tried to steal the position away when I wasn't here, and so I am telling you by the face of all these people, that you are not going to get that position." Nulis says, "If you don't agree to that, then I'll be on the fourth position." Likiosa got up and says, "No, I'm not going to have you come in front of me." He then turned around to the Fort Ruperts and tells them to stand up and sing his potlatch song that he is going to give a potlatch. When we finish with this song, Nulis also told us to sing his song, that he is going to give another potlatch. They went on for so many years giving potlatches, Likiosa and Nulis. When they went to other potlatches, they were given gifts—both together, so they wouldn't quarrel in the potlatch. Finally Nulis won out and took the position away from Likiosa.[1]

When my brother wanted me to get my share, in anybody's potlatch, he gave a potlatch of blankets and told the people that this potlatch has been given away by his son. From now on I receive my gifts from the other people and use them for myself. That means that I am old enough to

---

[1] With his brother supporting him, Charley retains his position. Note, too, that Nulis is censured for even the slightest deviation from the customary procedure. Any tentatives in the direction of stealing a position are immediately punished. Nulis is forced to fight his way according to traditional rules and, when he does so, he wins an advancement.

look after them myself. That was when I was quite grown up but before I was married. Maybe I was eighteen or twenty. At this potlatch he announced my name, Tlakodlas, the same as the second, and put me in my position in the clan. My brother was the first, and I was the third. I took my father's position, and the rest of our family was way down about thirty or more after me. My next oldest brother was on that place that I took, and he died about a year before this. If he hadn't died, I would have been in the lower position that I was in when I was called to the feast.

When I was receiving gifts from potlatches, I had to look after that and not spend it foolishly. I had to loan some of it out to other people. My brother showed me how to do this. When I loan out money, they promise to pay double the amount when they pay it back, because that is the custom of the Indians, and any time I want to give a potlatch, I have to collect what I loaned out. In collecting it, I have to call my people into my house and have a meal there. That is the time I tell them I want to give a potlatch and want to collect what I loaned out. I loaned out to anybody, but I only call my own clan to collect it. They will send two men out to other houses to collect my money. They come back with the payment, and when they get it all in, then they begin to make speeches, and they begin to sing my own potlatch song. After singing, they say that I am going to give blankets away. I would do this as often as I could collect enough to give a potlatch.

When I was a little older than twenty, my brother gives a potlatch of his own to all the tribes in this agency. While they are in the community house, he tells them he is giving this potlatch to let them know that I am to take his place when he dies. He calls my name Husemdas instead of Tlakodlas. His name was Owadi. This was about the same time I gave my first big potlatch and invited all the tribes.

When I was quite a big boy, a chief of our tribe called all the chiefs of the Fort Ruperts and told them he was going to give a *tsitsika*. The winter ceremonial is called *tsitsika*, which means "everything is not real." When the winter comes, we always have this ceremonial. After they get through with drying dog salmon, they all go home to their own villages. He asked all the chiefs to decide when the whistle was going to be sounded which will make known to the other people that the ceremony is going to be held. This whistle of many wooden whistles was heard in back of the houses four times that night. At the fourth time the sound of this whistle came into the house of the chief, and then two men go around to the houses and tell the people to come to the chief's house, for the big birds that make this whistling has come into his house. All the people go in there— men, women, and children. The Kwekas will be in the back end of the house, and a big fire in the center of the house.

One man stands up and says: "We have come in here to meet the big birds that has come into this house, and we are now going to start with the first ceremony in this particular dance." The Kwekas all stand up. A man that knows the songs and the way the things are to be spoken starts to say, "Hi-i-i-i-i-i-i-i-i," in a long voice, and all the rest of the Kwekas say, "Hi-i-i-i, hi-hi-hi-hi." There is four different ways they go through. Before they begin to sing the songs, the women or children or men that is going to dance comes out. The women have their hair hanging on their faces, so the people won't recognize them, and those that are going to be taken away by the big birds come up behind the singers and stand up to show themselves. They are supposed to be taken away, but they really stay home. That is the first lie. The Kwekas shout out four times, "Wa!" Then they sing songs, and the chief stands up and tells the people that this Kweka chief is going to have this *tsitsika,* and asks the people to be ready to have a good time. Then they all go home.

Four days after that, we all went to the house of Omhede. He has the part of the dance to call all the people to his house to give to every person the red cedar bark which they wear in the ceremonial as a headband. When all the people get into the house, he says, "We will now call the one who has the most magic power." So some people bring her in.

She wears a big red bark band on her head, and the people are around her holding a ring of red bark, and she is in the middle. They go around the house four times with this woman and stop at the right side entrance. This woman was the niece of Omhede, the only man among the Kwekas that owned this part of the ceremony.

They also called for a man named Likiosa, who is the only one among the Kwekas that could cut this big ring of red cedar bark in half. He came in and went around the house four times, and at the fourth time he comes before this ring and trys to cut it. As he cuts it, the red bark begins to squeak and make a noise; the magic in this red bark is making the noise. Then they open the red bark, and the woman was shown in the middle. They put the bark on mats and cut it up in lengths to fit our heads. Then Omhede stands up and holds a rattle and red bark in his hand and says, "O-o-o-o-o-i," four times, using the rattle all the time. His face is painted with black charcoal, and he begin to sing his song by himself, shaking his rattle all the time. Then he stops still and everybody keeps quiet—even the children. The song is supposed to give more power to the red bark. Then the red bark is given around, first to the Hamatsas (Cannibals) and then to the other people—men, women, and children. The cedar bark has been beaten very fine so it becomes almost like wool, and this was given around to everybody. They wiped their faces with it, which means that they are wiping away all the ordinary human being. Then the fat of a mountain goat is cut to pieces and was given around to everybody and they put this fat on their faces. That is ready for them every time they are going to paint their faces with dried red or black powder. Then they pick up four dishes of eagle down, and they say, "Go and put it on everyone's head." Everybody now has their red bark around their head and they put the eagle down on their head. After that some of the chiefs make speeches, saying: "You will take care. Don't do anything against the rules of this ceremony. We are going to start on a narrow plank which means, if you do anything wrong, you will fall, that is, you will die, and so everybody has to be careful not to look around and not to do anything against the rules, so that we might go through the ceremony safely which is a very important thing. This is the only path you will walk in—not in any other. If you miss this path, there is death in doing it." That seems to be real, but it is only a thing that they use. Then the Cannibals sing their songs. After that they go home and go to bed.

The next night they all go into the Kweka chief's house. Sometimes it is this night and sometimes the fourth night after that. This is the first time all the masks that they use in the winter dance shows. First of all they call a man to carry a box and take it up to where the singers are. He goes around the house four times before he puts this box down amongst the singers. When he puts it down he presses it down and the box makes a squeaky noise, which means that the box has magic in it. After that they call another man that will come and begin to strike at this box. All the singers begin to strike it and beat the board. Then he beckons to them to stop beating the box. Then all the noises for the different masks are heard by all the people in the house. They make each noise that they make in the winter dance, and at the fourth time they beat the box, the screen behind the singers comes down and right on the back of the screen all kinds of masks is shown in one time—all the masks owned by all the Fort Ruperts. That means all these masks could be shown by anybody in Fort Rupert that wants to show them. After that the singers begin to sing to quiet these masks, so they won't show up without the consent of their owners. They have a special song for that saying that the masks are mad from the beating, and now they should be quiet.

That night there is about ten or more men goes around to every house and calls out everybody's name that are in the house and says that so-and-so is going to give a feast tomorrow morning. This is to stop anybody that might go away tomorrow morning from going, for everybody is called to this feast. Early in the morning they come along and say,

"We are calling you now to the feast of so-and-so." When they are all in the house, two young men from the Kwakiutl stand up and say, "Now we are turning around and we are the chiefs and the others that were chiefs have nothing to do with it. We are going to have all the fun we can have." They pretend to be fighting with the other boys who pretend to be crazy and pretend to be animals. The Grizzly Bears are chased by the boys to touch their backsides which is supposed not to be touched. The Grizzly Bears don't allow anybody to touch it, and if they turn their backsides toward the people they say, "I see that backside of yours," and the Bear goes and tries to hide it. Crazy Men—I was one of them at another winter ceremonial—could pick up stones and throw them at others and spears and anything we could get hold of to hit other people with if we were let to do it, but we don't bother the Hamatsas because they are the chiefs of all the Crazy Men and the Grizzly Bears and others. These Crazy Men don't let anybody say anything about their nose. If anybody touches it or talks about it, I get a stone or a spear and pretend to try to hit them with it. It seems that you really don't want your nose to be touched.

The Hamatsas are supposed to be cannibals that goes to other people and kills them to eat their flesh. In eating them, I don't think they were eating them, but just pretending. My old people was telling me that when the Hamatsas was eating the dead bodies, they wasn't eating them at all. They was pretending and putting the flesh in a basket concealed in their bodies. But they say that some of them did it, but these are the ones that didn't know any better. At the last time they was eating the dead flesh, they say two of the Hamatsas died right in the room, and that the corpse they ate was poisonous. Others of them got awful sick and nearly died too. When they get fierce they bit pieces out of the arms of those they come up against. When they bit a piece off another's arm, they have to give him something for it— maybe a canoe—maybe blankets or something the next day after he gets through dancing.

Sometimes the Crazy Men and Grizzly Bears and Hamatsas goes right into the houses and upsets things—especially the water buckets so they won't drink any water that day. And others guard the wells, and don't let anybody get near. Sometimes they pour water on the fires so they won't cook. "Let them starve," they say. Then somebody goes and gives them food and this quiets them down. Or singing songs will quiet them down so that they just walk around like other men.

This goes on for many days and many nights, sometimes right along during the winter. Every time there is nobody else gives a feast, the Kweka chief gives a feast, and any time nobody else gives a dance, he gives a dance. At the Kweka chief's fourth dance everybody dances during that night, dancing their own dances, starting from the head of the Kwakiutl, Peter Knox's granddaughter, then the head of the Walas Kwakiutl, and the second clan of the Kwakiutl, and then the head of the second clan of the Walas Kwakiutl, and so on, all except the Kwekas who has hired them to come and dance for them. Every time anyone comes in to dance, he or she is paid by the Kweka chief's wife. They come in through the door of the house and come in front of the singers and dance, and while she is dancing, she dances around and then goes out and then she gets clothing or something from the Kweka chief's wife.

At the Kweka chief's house, I did my dance—the Warrior dance. I had spruce twigs thrust through the flesh on my thighs by one of the men. He first put a sharp iron through. Then when they took the iron out he put the twig through and put a knot in the twig to hold it together, and the same way in two places on my back. That hurted a little bit, and then they tied a rope onto the twigs and tied it onto the frame of a double-headed snake mask. And they have three poles and lift me up by lifting the mask, and the ropes lifted me and take me along the beach toward the Kweka chief's house. All the time I say, "Hi-i-i-i-i-i-i-i-i, Hi-hi-hi-hi," and all those that has the same dance comes close around watching and make the same noise with me. They were the only ones supposed to come close. They all have their knives with them, cutting their foreheads. When we got to the front of the house, they put up a rope on the house and pulled me up to the roof, and all the singers were under me, holding up their hands while I was pulled up toward the roof of the house. When I got up to the roof, they pulled me to the back end, and put me through the hole in the roof and I was there hanging up till all the peoples came in. When they all came in, they lowered me down. But when I was hanging up there they all sing my song, and at the words "Cut with your knife," I cut my forehead and the blood came down all over me. I showed the knife to the people smiling, and then take the knife and cut, cut, cut my forehead still smiling to show the people how brave I am. When I am lowered down, they take off the frame and the rope is holded by several men, and they begin to pull while I am dancing while they sing my song. Then they begin to say, after the song is ended, shouting, "Go to war." And then they begin to pull the ropes and try to break the twigs out of my leg and back. Two strong men come on my both sides to hold me so that when my skin breaks, I don't fall. When they couldn't break my skin, they took my knife away from me and cut my skin, and when they have pulled the rope away, the Grizzly Bears they say, "Wo-o-o-o-o-o-o-o-o." Everybody was standing in the house at the time, and I go around the house after all the ropes is off and go back of the screen and stayed there, and in the night when they begin to dance again, they have small paddles all painted with red—that is the blood of the people I am supposed to have killed. Hanging around tied with white thread and a needle stuck in me all over, holding each one of these little paddles, holding a double-headed snake made out of yellow cedar wood in my hands all carved, and I come out and dance. That's all I have on when I dance that night. Hemlock branches is around my head. I go back again and I am finished my dance. All the time before this I was staying in the house for I was supposed to be out in the woods. I was just sitting down there, sometimes go to sleep. I eat because they bring me something all the time when they eat. I had to wait till nighttime to go to the beach

to the toilet so nobody see me. I had to go through the back
door and then go to where there is no houses. While I was
doing the dance, I didn't hardly feel any pain at all.

In my brother's winter dance, I was the Grizzly Bear. I
wore a grizzly-bear skin, and a mask carved like a bear.
That could be used at winter dance and at potlatches during
the summer. When that mask opens up, it becomes a double-
headed snake. The carved man's face inside is all dressed
up with abalone shells inside—abalone shells for the eye-
balls. This is used when it is opened in potlatches in the
summertime. When I danced, I didn't open it. This Grizzly
Bear mask is the only bear mask that can be used both winter and summer. The man inside it is the crest that shows in
the summertime. In the winter dance, I could have used another Bear mask as long as it didn't open and show the man
inside it. It is the same as any other Bear mask. I went with
all the people to watch them dance the night they all danced
together and I sat on the side. A Hamatsa came and pulled
me by the arm and took me outside. That means I am gone
into the woods.

The next morning the Hamatsas and the rest of the
people came and got me, and I was dressed up in my Bear's
clothing, and I came back to my brother's house and I go
around acting like a fierce bear, crawling on the ground and
pulling the earth and throwing it all over the place. Each
night for four nights I do this. During the daytime I stay
behind the screen, and in the meantime eat all the time.
When I go out and run around, I go into the other houses.
My brother told me once to go to a new canoe and break it
up, and so I did. It means I can do anything—break anything without any trouble, because I have a chief that backs
me, and as I go around the houses doing all these things, a
man comes with me and keeps track of everything I break.
I go into a house and pull down a cupboard and bust all the
dishes, and the owners never say a word because they know
it's going to be paid for. He pays for all those things right
after we get through the fourth night, and we are tamed
down. I had a lot of fun. I run after men and women and

they run away from me. When I'm tired, I sometimes let someone else go in my skin while I rest, because the boys want their Bear to go around all the time. In the old days, it was only the chief's sons that could be these things—Hamatsas, Grizzly Bears, Warriors, and Crazy Men.[2]

Another good dance is the Towidi—a woman that comes around the house slowly, and when she gets up to the front of the singers, she stands up and face the fire while all the people are sitting down and says, "Will some of you bring me a knife?"—that is to cut her head off. Nobody brings her one, and then she turns and says, "Bring me a hammer to crush in my head." Each time she says that she always turns around and face the singers, and the people ask each other who has the hammer, and nobody has it. Then she says, "Bring me a paddle to chop my head in two." And nobody has a paddle. Old ones but not new enough. And then she says: "Bring me a box, one of the Indian boxes, and put me inside it. Put the cover on and put the box and me into the fire and burn me up." They all try to find a box big enough, but none is big enough. And then the chief says to the singers, "Beat your board with your sticks, and let us see what she will do." And she go from one end of the house to the other pretending to try to catch something that she alone can see. When she catches it the chief says, "Stop beating that board." The chief listens but she don't say nothing so they beat it again. She does the same thing four times. Then when she catches something it whistles when she moves her hand and she throws it among the singers, and there at once there is a lot of whistling among the singers and then a big snake will come out that reaches to both sides of the house, and she come along with a wood made like a sword and there is a man on the center of this serpent—a man's face. And she comes there and strikes the man's head

[2] Here the function of the winter ceremonial as an outlet for pent-up aggressions becomes clear. But even here there are limits: the people who are bitten by the Cannibals and whose goods are damaged by the Grizzly Bears will be paid for their losses. It would probably be too dangerous to remove all restraints and permit the dancers complete freedom in their expressions of aggression.

with it and it splits and the two sides of the serpent spread apart, and then it comes together again and begins to go down and is supposed to go under the ground. Then the people begin to sing her song, and she goes around the house and back behind the screen and stays there. She does this only one night.

A girl, a chief's daughter, had a dance, a Towidi, and as she was brought to the front of the dance house from the woods, while she was dancing and everybody was watching, she turned the wrong way, and all the people start saying what she had done, and one of our chiefs stood and was talking about the thing she has done and says: "What shall we do with her? Shall we kill her?" Some of the Crazy Men came close to her with their axes and pretended they were going to kill her, and the Grizzly Bears came with their claws and stood around her, and she was just standing there pale. My brother says: "We better not kill her here. The best way is to tie a rock on her neck and take her out in the water and drown her." And so they shoved a canoe down to the water, and all the Grizzly Bears, the Crazy Men, and others went into this canoe, and while they were doing this, everybody was watching them, the clothing of this girl and the hemlock branches were taken off her and put on a boy her own size, while this girl was between a group of men that took her into the house without anybody seeing her.

The boy in the clothing of the girl was led to the canoe and got on to it still singing her song, and when they paddled out about twenty feet off shore, they tied her neck with a rope and tied it on a boom chain which they let down on the side of the canoe facing all the people. Then they left this "girl" and place her on the side of the canoe while she was still singing her song, and pushed her overboard. All the people in the canoe shout, "Woo-oo-oo-oo-oo-oo-oo, hi-hi." And all the people on shore that was watching, the relations of this girl, was told to sing their songs, but none of them could. They all say that their throat was blocked, and they couldn't make any sound, and there was four women wearing Wolf masks that sat down close to the water and begin to cry, because the thing seemed to be real. Nobody see how it was done. They had a rope on the other side of the canoe and when they pushed her overboard, the front side of the men on the other side was pulling this boy up and give him his own clothing and blankets, and then they came on shore and jump out of the canoe one by one until there was nobody in the canoe, and the people keep watching and see that the girl didn't come out. I was one of those people that took the girl into the house, and, when we got in there, her husband was in bed there crying to beat hell. It looked so real that everybody cried that didn't know how it was done. This is one of the reasons the winter ceremonial is called lies; it looks real, but it isn't true. I was a Grizzly Bear that time. Oh, she was scared! When she went to her husband, he asked her what happened to her. Her reply was: "I don't know. I don't remember when I went in the canoe, and, when I came here, I was so scared I went unconscious."

There was another Towidi who was asking for a box to be burned. They put her in the box while all the people saw her put in there in her blue blanket and tied the box, and then they put the box on the fire and poured on the olachen grease. The fire burned and the box burned, and she was still singing inside, and then the box go up in flames, and they can see her burning there in her blue blanket, and all her relatives just cry and cry. Although they know it is not real, it looks so real they can't help it. It was all a trick. There was a hole under the box with a tunnel leading out of the house, and the woman went out of the box and put a seal in her place wrapped in a blue blanket, and then someone sang into the fire through a kelp tube, her song. Oh, it looked real!

There was another one ask for a knife. That is the first thing that they ask for. They turn four times and ask for different kinds of tools to kill themselves with. The one that ask for the knife at the fourth time, a man came around with a knife, went around the house with it, took out some of the black charcoal from the fire, smashed it and put it all over his face, and, when he got to the front end of the house, he begin to speak to the people, and he says, "Take hold of her and lay her on a board." They brought a short board and laid the board on the ground, and he came around to her and took his knife and aimed for her neck four times, and, on the fourth time, he took hold of her hair and pulled her head back and cut it right off. Holding her by the hair, he turned around and put the head in his blanket, and went around looking fierce, and when he got to the front end of the house, close to the door, he sat down there and took this head and put it on the ground there facing the fire. And he went away from her and walked away from the head while the head was still standing on the ground there, and the mouth kept opening and the face twitching as if there was still life in that head, and the man came around and picked it up and put it under his blanket again, and he go to another side of the house, and put the head on a box, showing the people it is the same face as this woman has, and he went to the rear end of the house and put it down on the ground again, so the people on the front end will see it. And everybody with their mouths open—wide-eyed—because the head is still moving its face and then the fourth time he goes to the body of it and puts it back, and then they wrapped her up and put her on the place where she is going to be for four days. By the way the head acts it makes a noise and everybody thinks it is a real head, because it is the same looking as the head of this woman.

Here, too, they had a tunnel under the house, and the man that cut the head off is the only man that knows where the tunnel is. When he went there to set this mask down that he got away from the body, there was a man in there that takes up the board that covers the hole. When the killer puts the mask down, the woman that was supposed to be killed comes up and sets her head up. They say she had a hard time breathing because the boards were tight around her neck, and when the man goes to the top to take the head off, he only takes off the cedar branches that is on top of her head. While he is walking slow around the house she walks under the tunnel to where the box is and puts her head up there.

It looks awful real, and even if you know how it is done, it looks real. It was somebody else's body that the head was supposed to be cut off and when he was supposed to cut off the head, it is falling backwards behind the board so it can't be seen, and he holds up the mask and puts it in his blanket. On the fourth day she came to life again and came out and danced. The same way with the smashing of the head. It is all done in a similar way by tricks, and everybody thinks it is real. It looks real.

There was another good Towidi. She said that she had her magic power from the blackfish—the killer whale. While she was dancing, she begin to sink in the ground facing toward the people and kept on going down slowly still dancing the way the Towidi dances, and two men try to keep her from going down while the others are hunting around to find a rope. They find a halibut line and put a coil around her neck and tied it. Finally the woman went down and disappeared. While she went down, the rope begin to tear the ground going one way and another, and coming even among the people, and when it gets back to the rear end of the house, it goes through the fire, and the rope was burnt and the woman was gone, and they only had a short piece left. The next night she could be heard way out on the beach singing her song. The man gets up and says, "We better go and see." We went out and brought this woman in. It was cold that night. Before we came in, we pour a bucket of water over her and when she came in she could hardly sing she was shivering so. Her song was that she was taken around by this magic whale and she has seen all kinds of things all around the world—she couldn't remember them all there was so many. This is done by means of tunnels too.

CHAPTER VI

GIRLS

WHEN I got out of school I stayed in Fort Rupert for a long time. And then was when I began to go with girls again.

One thing you don't know is how we get a girl. What I do is tell some friend—maybe a man or maybe a woman. He goes and tells her I wants to see her. He sees her husband or father is out of sight when he does this. Then he says that I want to meet her in a certain place in the woods. If it is a woman who is telling her, maybe she tells the girl to come to her house, and I go and sneak into that house to see her. Sometimes when the husband is away from the village, we would make arrangements that I'll go and stay with her at night, and during the night I sneak in very carefully so no one sees me, and I get up before daylight to get out of the house, looking around on both ways from the house to see there is no one seeing me come out of the house. Sometimes someone sees me, and they go and tell somebody, because they think it is a good joke, and then it comes around to the woman's husband. Then there is liable to be trouble between the woman and her husband, and maybe she gets a licking from him.

I give these girls and women presents—sometimes blankets and sometimes money, maybe ten or maybe as much as fifty dollars at the beginning to start with them, and after that if she want anything she ask for it. How much she wants at the beginning, that is all arranged by my friend. A lot of them wouldn't come with me for less than fifty dollars.[1]

---

[1] Here is revealed a powerful incentive to acquire wealth. Without blankets or money Charley would have been seriously handicapped in his love affairs. Lending money and giving potlatches bring not only prestige but also the wherewithal to secure other and more basic gratifications.

I haven't any idea how many girls and women I spent money on like this. About two hundred, I guess. I think now there wouldn't have been so many after I was married, if I could have married the woman I wanted. Some of the girls I went with when I was young were married. A few weren't, and these were harder to get at, because they were so well watched, unless their parents wasn't alive. Some would be easy and wouldn't ask anything. Others would be hard, and it seems those are the ones I want most usually. But the only reason I paid fifty dollars for one and not for the other was her business; it doesn't matter to me.

Sometimes there would be two at a time, and sometimes three. I stop when she or I gets tired of each other, and sometimes there is trouble between us. I sometimes gets jealous of her going with someone else, or she gets jealous if she knows I am seeing another girl at the same time. Sometimes, too, she has trouble with her husband, and she won't see me any more. And sometimes if the husband is too good to me, I don't like to hurt his feelings if he finds out I am laying his wife. There were some girls from my own tribe I goes with, but not so many as from other tribes. There was none from my own clan. These is all relatives and friends, and I never had anything to do with them like this. I didn't want to, because they all call me brother or nephew or uncle or cousin. It's all right to marry close, but none of us would go with one of our cousins or aunt or niece unless they are from other tribes. And if I have a very good friend, I wouldn't go and interfere with his wife or the wife of his near relatives either.[2]

My best friend goes between me and the girls and comes back with the answer. They used to be strict in the olden

2 Two factors seem to be operating here. One is the extension of the incest taboo. Charley will not philander with his "cousin," "aunt," or "niece" because they are too closely related, even though it might be all right to marry them for reasons of prestige. The second factor is respect for the feelings of his close male friends. A friend might regard seduction of his wife as an unfriendly act, and, since Charley derives much pleasure from his masculine friendships, he refrains from doing anything to weaken these bonds.

days, though, and the parents wouldn't let the girl out of their sight. The only girls that isn't married that I can get is the ones that doesn't have any parents, and their brothers and uncles is away working. And another thing, the girls that I go to, I don't go to when her folks is awake. I go and hide myself in the corners of the community house till I know that everybody is asleep, and I walk from my hiding place then, very careful that I don't step on a stick that will break. When I get near to where she is lying, I could hardly breathe in case that would wake the people near her. When I get to her, I just touch her by the foot and shake her a little. She tries to stay awake, for she knows every time that I was coming, and I go and lay down with her, and I have to be very careful all the time I am lying with her. Oh, it is a hard time to go with a girl when she is watched! We couldn't talk; we would just whisper as low as we can.

I got caught once, at Fort Rupert. This girl was married, and left her husband. I went in to her one night while the others were asleep. While she was laying down in her bed, and we was loving each other, the old people—her grandparents—woke up. We must have made too much noise. The man got up and came right to her bedside and felt the woman. Then he put his hand over to me and says, "Who's there?" and he says, "Come on, get out of here." But we didn't speak; she just hugged me and holded me tight. He says to her, "Who is with you? What are you doing?" The woman says then, "You get away from here and don't bother us." Then this man felt all over the place, and found my hat on a box where I put it on the head of the bed, and took it away; then he felt all over the place by the bed and got my pants and shoes and shirt. I only had on an undershirt. Before daylight I got up and began to feel for my clothes. I couldn't find them, and so I didn't bother much to keep quiet. I telled the girl to help me find them. Finally she lit a lamp, and we see they is all gone. I had to go out with no shirt, shoes, pants, or hat.

I felt awful that time, because when I walked through that bridge on the little creek some men were up and ready to go out in their canoes and saw me. They hollered out, "Hello there! Who's there?" and I got so scared I just run in the house. My undershirt was so short I had to pull it down over my pecker. The next day we was invited to a feast, and all the men and women and children of the Fort Ruperts went. And while I was at the feast, the men that saw me spoke, and one said he saw a naked man who got so scared he ran into one of the houses. I felt so bad I slid down in my seat. He also says we ought to keep watch because some men from other places that don't know enough to wear clothes is coming into our village and prowling around. He says this just for fun. I looks at the woman, and she is looking at the ground, smiling. I never got any of my things back. They never found out really who it was, but they could guess all right.

When we are having a feast, the old people always talk about what they did with the girls, and they talked about my father being the worst one to go after girls. A girl that my father was in love with was kept in her room, and my father and his chums went together to this girl's room outside and talked through the knothole to her. They would kiss each other through the hole, which the girl took out from the board and put back when they are through talking. They say that they made so much noise in kissing that the parents of the girl say, "What's that?" and they say this girl had some excuse. One night, the girl couldn't come out, and my father was just talking through this hole. He told this girl, "Can we do something?" And the girl says, "How can we?" My father says, "Just put your backsides to this hole, and I'll put my pecker through it." It was a long time before she want to do it. My father says, "Hurry up; it won't take long." The girl gave in and says, "All right, try it." They saw my father put his pecker through the hole, and he have a hard time trying to catch hold of something with his hands. Then one of his chums comes and holds him while he was doing it. Finally my father's legs begin to shake, and he just drop down to the ground. Oh, they make me laugh when they tell me about this. He be there while they talk about this, simply laughing.

They say that my father had another hard time with this same woman. They try to find out how he could get to this woman, and while they were talking about it they saw a man making an Indian box. It was made nicely and carved outside, and my father bought the box. When it was finished, his chums came with my father and set my father inside this box and was going around the houses trying to sell it. They wanted an awful lot for it, so nobody would buy it. One of his chums went and told this girl my father has bought a box for her and told her to coax her father to buy this box for her. In her house they ask a low price for it, and this girl went up to the box right away and opened the box a little and kept one side of it open and told my father's chums to put the box at the head of the bed. The sun was still high up, and it seems to my father it was days and days while he was inside. When night came and the fire went out, this girl got up and took the lid off the box. My father told his chums the next day it was very hard on him; he was so cramped in the legs he had an awful time. They laughed about it for a long time.

Another time a woman in Fort Rupert whose husband was not feeling well says that she is expecting to have her monthly. So the woman made a bed outside of the bedrooms in the open room. This woman was laying with her head on one end and the sick man at the other. My father went in the house when the fire was out, and while he was going there the fire flared up and the sick man saw someone walking toward his wife. My father lay down with her, and the sick man lay still, listening. When he knows that my father was through, he got up and went toward his wife's bed and felt and says, "Who is this?" My father says, "It's me." The husband says, "What are you doing with my wife?" My father says, "Some one sent me to come and tell her that he wants to give her some blankets." And the husband says, "If you were sent, why were you doing this work with her?" My father says, "I never do it." He says, "Get up." My father gets up. He says, "I'm going to feel you, and if you are wet you are guilty." The man felt him and says, "You're wet." And he grabbed hold of his pecker and squeezes it. My father says, "Let go." He says, "I will not; you have been fooling around with my wife, and now I'm going to pull it off." He pull some more, and my father call out to all his cousins to come and help, and woke up everybody in the house. Then he kicks my father out without his blanket or anything. He says he never felt anything as sore as that.

At feasts between their own tribe they talk about all those things and make jokes, and sometimes they speak about other people's positions and how they stand. Sometimes they talk about the wars in the old days. But going around with women—that makes them laugh. If the women are there they don't seem to care—they laugh, too.[3]

When I first talk with one of these girls I just talk at first and then maybe we kiss. Maybe for a month I just talk to her, and then we hug each other, and then we kiss. That is the first thing we do. When I get the money she wants, I give it to my friend, and he takes the money to the girl and tells her I am going to come and see her that night. She wouldn't let me bring the money when I come, for fear I wouldn't bring it. She wouldn't think of backing out—not after she has the money. This is only the girls that you are fooling around with. It's not usually the girl you are going to get married with.

To have a baby without being married is a bad disgrace when I was young. It isn't so much now. I never knew of any when I was young. They say they used to kill the babies they was carrying. I never saw this done, but they say that they lay the girl on the floor and begin to step on the small of her back, so that she don't go on with carrying the baby,

[3] Seduction is permitted in the native culture. In these stories about his father Charley finds proof that love affairs are normal and even desirable. He is assured that no harm will come to him if he successfully seduces a girl. He has learned the value of imitating his elders, and this does not appear to be an exception. The native attitude sharply contrasts with the puritanical notions of Mr. Hall and Bishop Ridley, but here, once again, the Indian way of life wins out.

and the thing that is going to form a baby is busted. Sometimes they lift heavy things to spoil the forming of the baby. And, if they are too late, when the baby comes at first, they say that they take the afterbirth and put that on the face of the baby and that smothers it. It will be only the girl and her mother and perhaps some near relation that tends to her. Sometimes they just squeeze the neck of the baby and bury the baby secretly in the ground. They try to hide it from everybody, but maybe the relations tell somebody and it spreads. I don't know of any cases in the days when I was young.

I only knew well one of these men that wears women's clothing. There are others like that I knows, but they used men's clothing. They are mostly Quatsino Indians. I will tell you about the one I knew. This man, her name was Frances. The first time I saw her, he came to Fort Rupert and I was young. This was long before I was married. The Quatsino Indians came and camped at Fort Rupert on their way to Fraser River. I saw this man with woman's clothing, but she had a man's voice. We went to see the people in the house where they were staying, and she began to look at us, and she spoke to me and says, "You, young fellow, I'm going to have you for my sweetheart." She had long hair like a woman's. They didn't stay long, so I didn't get to know her then. When they came home from Fraser River, they called at Fort Rupert, and they stopped there for a couple of months. During the time, she called me to go and see her at the house where she was, and when I went there, she caught hold of me, and when I went there she throwed me right into her bed. My, she was strong—awful strong! She told me she want me to lie with her. Before that I was told that she was a man, and I was kind of scared to lie down with her, but I couldn't help it because she was so strong and hold me down. She opened her legs and pulled me in, taking hold of my pecker and putting it in. I didn't work; she done all the work. After I went out of the house, I told all the boys that she was a woman, and that I laid down with her, and all the boys went after her because she was free.

The next time I saw her, she went into my brother's house. She was selling baskets. I was lying down on my bed, and I called her to come to my bed and lie with me. She says, "Not this time; I've got my monthly." She used to go around with quite a lot of boys. Some of them say they think she was only using the bag for her balls. I tried to find out, and while I was laying with her, I feel for her privates, but she just take my hand and squeeze it until I couldn't move my hand. The other boys couldn't get their hand there to find out, either. I guess the Indian agent wrote to Victoria, telling the officials what she was doing. She was taken to Victoria, and the policeman took her clothes off and found she was a man, so they gave him a suit of clothes and cut off his hair and sent him back home. When I saw him again, he was a man. He was no more my sweetheart.

He went out in another sealing schooner the same time I did. At the Bering Sea he got sick and died. We happened to be close together. The people in the other schooner hollered out that somebody died. We went over to see who it was, and found out it was Francis. One of his own tribesmen says to me, "Let us find out what your sweetheart is—man or woman." He went up to him and take the blanket off his bed and saw he has a pecker and a pair of balls, and find there was a hole under the balls. He picked up a stick and opened it and saw there was a real hole there. He looked awful when he turned around. Some of the boys says, "It might be his ass." The other says, "No, it's another hole besides his ass-hole." Some of the others goes and looks, and says it is true. I didn't go myself. I didn't want to. He was wrapped up in canvas and throwed overboard. They put two bags of shot on the legs and put him on a plank, and the captain read out a funeral service and let the body down into the seas.

There were other men among the Koskimo and one from Blundon Harbor and one from Village Island who played the part of women but didn't dress like that. We call men like that "act like a woman." One was a man from Quatsino, and the way he acts when he works is the way women does

when they do anything. Playing ball he uses his arm like a
woman, and the way he walks is like a woman, and he chops
wood like a woman. Men swing their arms when they do
anything; women don't, and neither did he. This was the
man that helped me find out the woman who was bewitching
me. Every time I used to go and visit in Quatsino he used to
look after me—sew my clothes, wash them, mend them, just
like a woman. He had a lot of chums among our people
around here. Some of them says they used to lie in bed
with him, but I never did. He never gets married, and neither do most of them. Two of them that did get married,
died soon after. I don't know if it is because they got married or not. My chum go and pick berries with the women
and walk with them most of the time. They like him all right
and don't seem to be afraid of him. He acts toward me just
as if he were my girl-cousin, and cooks for me and everything a girl would do.

The other man from the same place is supposed to be the
wisest man in the Quatsinos. All the stories from the beginning of the world he knows, and he makes songs, but the way
his body acts is like a woman. He has earrings on his ears—
women's earrings—and all kinds of women's brooches on
both sides of his breast, and wore women's rings. One night
we were called by Charley Newman to come and have supper
at his home here in Alert Bay, and Spruce Martin was telling us a story about this same fellow. "At Quatsino canneries," he said, "I went there fish seining, and a lot of other
Indians went there to fish. One Saturday," he says, "everybody was not fishing, and in the evening toward dark, but
light enough for me to see the road, I was going toward the
toilet, and when I got to the toilet, I saw gum boots sticking
out of the door, but they were moving. I walked faster and I
looked into the door of the toilet and saw two more gum boots
sticking up. They didn't see me, and I says, '*Yo!*' The man
got up, pull up his pants and run out, and the other one sits
up, and I saw this was another man. He also got up and
pull up his pants. He was the song-maker of the Quatsinos,
and the fellow on top was the son of a Newettee chief." He

was amongst us at Charley Newman's feast. Everybody was laughing, but this man just hung his head down, he was so ashamed. Next day I heard he was sick and went to the hospital. The song writer act more like a woman than man, but he is always living with his wife. The other one was really sick, but he got well after a long time. They just tease him that he lies with men, and I guess it hurts him. This man felt like he was licked, and I guess that is what made him sick. Men who act like women I think get that way when they are growing up.

A Tenaktak man was the same. He wore pants and got married, but he was only married a year when they parted. They couldn't agree to each other. She was telling her second husband that this man never touched her at all—only by his hands. Another man from Village Island is the youngest son of a chief of the Mamaleleqalas. His elder brother got him to marry a woman, and they only lived together one month and then they parted. This woman also tells others this man never touched her.

There was another man I know that never go around with girls, but they only think that he is afraid of girls and that this is funny. I guess he was afraid. He didn't know what to say. He didn't do any more than answer what he was asked. He was from Alert Bay. He got married, though, and when he have his wife, he doesn't even ask his wife to cook for him when he gets hungry. When he has it cooked, he doesn't ask his wife to come and eat it with him. He had one son. I guess he was all right, but he didn't want to talk. He was a good worker. He worked all the time—built a nice house for his wife and their child to live in. He looked after them well, but hardly spoke to them. He gave a big potlatch. He is dead now.

Finally I learned to like one of the girls a lot. I became pretty crazy for her. This was the time I went to Frazer River without telling my brother. I told the woman I was going around with, who was going to Fraser River, that I'd go down there myself. So I came to Alert Bay and got on a boat that was going to Fraser River, and I got off not knowing where the girl was staying in the canneries. I had to swipe a canoe in New Westminster and got another boy my age, also from Fort Rupert, that knows the places and the canneries there, and we went down toward where the canneries were, and inquired where the Fort Rupert people are fishing at. They didn't know, they said, maybe in one of the other canneries, so we keep on going to cannery after cannery until we find another Indian from Fort Rupert, an old man, my aunt's husband, but not a near relation. He told me that the woman I want is gone down to a camp of that cannery where he was staying. He told me he couldn't get anybody to go with him as a partner in fishing. So I went to the manager of that cannery and asked him for a boat and net. I took this man to be my boat puller, and we went down to the camp where that woman was. I stayed with her there as my own wife in her tent.

Then when my brother found out I ran away, he want to find out where I am. He finally got there. I tell him I don't want to come back, so he got a boat and net for himself. We never fish with a net before. He got another man for his partner that knows how to fish, and he did pretty well. After fishing, I and my brother was ready to come home, and this woman I had been living with is going near Seattle to pick hops. There were lots of Indians that went there every year to pick hops. She had a brother and his wife, and they were all from the Tenaktak people. They got all their things in their canoe, and she called me to bid me good by. We went into an empty tent, and she begin to cry, saying she is sorry we are going to part. I also began to cry, and she says, "Well, I wish you would come with me." We were waiting for the boat to go up to New Westminster—me and my brother—and this woman's brother calls her and says he is leaving now, and she says to me, "Come along, let's go." I says, "All right," and we both went into the canoe and started off. This is the second time I ran away from my brother.

We went toward Seattle, and, when we got there, people came from the hop fields and tell us they have only just returned from there because the hops wasn't good. They were all burnt. We stayed at Seattle two or three days, and then returned to Vancouver. When we returned, my brother had gone to Seattle and went to the hop fields looking for me, so we missed him. When we get to Vancouver I was dead broke, and went over to North Vancouver in a small canoe to the sawmill, and asked the manager if he could give me a job. He told me if I could be a fireman in the sawmill. I says, "I never did it before, but I will try and do my best." He says there is another Indian there who has been working there for two years, and he will tell me what to do. I worked there for a week and we got paid on the evening of that Saturday. I told the bookkeeper I didn't like the job. It is too hot for me. He told me he'll put me to loading ships with lumber. I work there about two weeks, when a man that told the numbers of the lumber that fits in the ships—this man, a kind of a boss to us, he had his leg broken. The man of the sawmill came and asked me could I read the figures. He came to me with the figures on a board. He pat me on the back and says I'm on because I could read them easy. I was getting $2 a day loading, and now I get $7.50 a day, and all I do is roll the timber over, and see the mark and tell the others where to put it.

By the time my brother came back from Seattle and came to Victoria and got a boat there and came back to Alert Bay and didn't find me there, somebody that saw me working at the sawmill tells him where I was. He went back after me. He thinks I was his son, so he came and when he comes to the sawmill he tries to talk to me, but I wouldn't take any notice, because I was working at my job. At twelve the sawmill whistled and we went into the mess house, and he comes in to tell me he has been looking all over for me and wants me to come back. I told him my wages, and that I want to stay. He finally persuades me I better come with him, so he went to the manager and spoke to him. The manager says he couldn't let me go until this other man has his leg all well. My brother still wanted me to quit and tried another way. The man tells him all right, he will try and find someone else to take my place. The next day he finds one and I got paid off and went over to Vancouver. My brother wouldn't let me go anywhere out of his sight, though I tried to get away from him, and so we came back to Fort Rupert.

The woman that I was crazy over and went to Vancouver after, following her to the cannery, was a Tenaktak. Her name was Anna. At the potlatch at Cape Mudge she was in bed with a white man one night while her husband was gambling in another house. I saw her husband amongst the gamblers and thought I'd go and see her. I went to her house and went right up to the place where her bed was. It was late in the night, and when I got up to her bed, they were in the way of connecting together. I heard it and went right up to her and asked her who this man was. She never answered. I light a match and saw it was a white man, a logger. They had a bottle of whisky on the table close to her bed. I told her that I have been crazy for her for I thought she was a straight and good woman. "From this time I saw you with this man who is not your husband, I'll have nothing to do with you whatsoever, and I'll bid you good by, and I'll never touch you again." I had often told her if she goes with another man I'll never go see her again, and she knew I meant it. Next day I heard she had disappeared. She left her husband and went with this logger to his camp. I never had anything to do with her after that. Her husband knew all about me and her, but he felt good about it because I used to help them out.

That winter we young men of Fort Rupert went over to Quatsino. I never told my brother I was going. The Koskimo people were going out hunting for fur seals, and the captain of the sealing schooner wanted some more hunters, so I agreed with Charley Wilson to go. We went out that night on the schooner and sailed during the night. We had $30 apiece in advance from the captain. I gave it to a Koskimo woman I was fooling around with to go on with until I get back. That is the third time I ran away, and when I got back I found that my brother was a day late when he came after me.

I had a terrible time in the sealing schooner, for I was never out in rough water in a big boat before. I was seasick for two weeks and couldn't eat anything. The captain came down to the forecastle to see me and gave me some raw carrots to eat. He told me to eat as many as I could, and said it would stop me from puking. That stopped the seasickness, but I began to want to come home. I ask him how far out we had gone. He went down to his cabin and brought out a big chart and laid it on the desk and brought his instruments. He looks at the sun and hollers out "Time" to the mate. When he finished, the mate came up with the numbers, and he put a rule on the chart, which was about ten feet long. Where we were was about four inches, and he says we were going to the end of the map. I ask him how long it will take, and he says about two months. I lay back and groaned. He was right. It took us just two months and three days, and we were in Yokohama, Japan.

We waited there over three weeks for the Japanese to make us canoes. They were having war with China at the time, so all the carpenters were busy. During the time we were there I stayed with a Japanese girl, and all the boys had their Japanese girls. When the carpenter built us the canoes, we began to seal hunt. Charley Wilson was the hunter, and I steered the canoe. When we got through hunting there, we went inside to Hakodate. While we were going through the inlet, we ran against a sandbar during the night. It was foggy and raining that night, and our schooner got wrecked. The keel came off. We got into our canoes and heard the waves smashing on the beach, but the fog was so thick we couldn't see. When we got on shore, Charley Wilson and I went back to the schooner and take all our sealskins out and took them on shore. It was getting daylight, but the fog was still thick. Then the rest of the boys went back to the schooner and got their skins, and Charley and I went back and took some canned food and brought it on shore.

It was a nice sandy beach and we went back again and got the cannon so we can shoot it off if we see a schooner coming. I and Charley Wilson got the cannon, and then we went to the captain's cabin and got some clothing that he sells to us, and we saw some kegs of whisky and brought that in, too. When we got back in the canoe and just as we untied from the schooner, a big wave came and carried the schooner off the bank and into a deep place, and she sunk until only the top of the mast was showing. We went on shore and began to cook our breakfast. Before we ate anything, we saw a schooner way below us, sailing in, so the captain says some of us better get in that ship and go to the city. The boys loaded the cannon with powder and begin to shoot, while the captain's cook and four of us walked into a canoe to go out and meet the schooner. We were all soaking wet with the waves splashing us. The schooner turned back when they saw us, and they took us to the city, leaving the others on the beach. When we got there, the captain told us to stay on board and he will go and find a place for us to stay and will come back and get us off the boat.

One Indian man bought two bottles of whisky from the Japanese fellow that came out, and he took off his shirt and paid him with that. He tried to give us some whisky, but we wouldn't take it. I didn't want it because Mr. Hall had told me it was terrible bad for your health. This one Indian just finished it himself, and he got dead drunk. We didn't know what to do with him and where to go or what to do. The captain didn't come back all day, and it was toward evening when I told the two men who was with me we better go on shore and find him. So we beckoned to one of the Japanese in their skiffs to come and take us on shore, and I says to the Koskimo man, "We better take the drunk one." He says: "We better leave him here, the crazy man. We have enough trouble as it is." And I says, "No, we better take him." So the two of them took this man up and set him on the rail of the schooner and just let him drop like a dead man in the skiff. The Koskimo turns to me and says: "Why keep him? Let's throw him overboard." I says: "Let's get him on shore, and then let him turn into a Japanese and stay there all the rest of his life."

When we got on shore, we got a man that had a rickshaw,

and I put this drunken man in it and went with him and got another rickshaw for the other two. We got the Japanese to take us to a place to stay that night. We went to this rooming house, paid the landlady for the night, and had our meal. After we finished we took a walk and left the drunk behind asleep. We saw a sign saying, "All European People Are Welcome." We went over to the place and knock at the door and tell him we were Europeans, which means sailors there. He says, "Were you on the *Rosie Olsen*, that was wrecked?" We said, "Yes." He took us in and showed us some beds, where we were going to sleep. He got another man to go with us and fetch the drunken man. We brought him in, and as soon as we put him in the nice bed he began to pee. The man that I was with said, "That's why I don't want to have anything to do with this dog," and goes and grabs him with his fist right on his neck and wants to choke him. The white man told him not to do that, that he will change the bedding.

We went to sleep, and in the morning we was woke up by another man to go and have breakfast. We went downstairs and went next door, which was a restaurant, where there was about a dozen Japanese waitresses. We begin to eat. The drunken man was still in bed, so sick he didn't want to get up and eat. After breakfast we went back to the house where we slept and asked where we could find our captain. He says: "You go around until you get to Ninth St., and you will see a notice on a house reading 'European Councel,' and I think that is where you'll find him." So we went along and find the place. We inquire about our captain, and he says, "Are you from the *Rosie Olsen?*" and we said, "Yes." He says, "Where were you last night?" I told him where we stayed. He said, "We went to fetch you out of the schooner last night, but you were gone, but you found the right place anyway." I asked him again about our captain. Smiling, he says that our captain is not up yet; as soon as he got in here, he got drunk. He says we better stay there. He then arranges to get a steamboat to go out and get the rest of the crew from the beach where they were still.

About ten o'clock we was told to go to the boat, so we went out and started. It was foggy, and when the boat got close to land, the fog lifted a little and we whistled and whistled, but we only saw one man running about on the beach. He wasn't able to get the canoe down to the water alone, so we lowered one of the steamboat's boats and went on shore, and this man came and met us. It was Charley Wilson. I says, "Where is all the others?" He points to them lying on the beach, and there they were stretched out with sand in their noses and in their ears and in their mouths. They had drunk up the two kegs of whisky. Charley was the only one that didn't want to drink. We helped to pull all the canoes down. We put all the sealskins in and take them out to the boat. Then we come back and throw all the men in the canoes, and they were all pulled up to the boat. When we got back to the city, we had to get rickshaws for all of them. They were still so drunk they were like dead.

When we got there the captain came to us and say that there is people in Japan that wants to buy our skins. We says that is all right, and we sold them. He gave me all the money that the boys has earned and tells me not to give it to them right away, for they all just go and spend it on whisky. It was way more than $2,000 that I kept, and when they get sober, the men say, "What became of all the other things?" I say, "They are all left." They say, "Even our skins?" and I say, "Yes, you were so drunk we couldn't bring them, but Charley Wilson and I brought ours."

Then we was called into the office and they begin to ask all about what we had lost—clothes and all that. We told them, and they kept on writing it down. After it is all down, they give me a paper and told me to go to a store to get all our clothing and blankets and everything we had lost. All the stuff we lost was replaced. We went back and took the others to the store to get their clothes, and we was told we was to stay there almost a month before the ship leaves for Vancouver. Everybody felt good when they find they are not going to stay there. When we was there a week, our captain and the captain of another schooner came in and tell us

he would like us to go in his schooner to get seals for him in
Bering Sea. Our captain told us he was going to go, too, so
we agreed.

All the guns that we had brought with us from the wrecked
boat was taken from us by the customs at Japan. We had
to spear the seals in the Bering Sea. They don't allow us to
use guns, so every time a cutter comes around, he throws all
the skins on deck and sees if they are shot. In about an hour
another cutter comes and does the same. We were there
hunting about a month when it get nasty—raining and
blowing and fog. Almost as night it was so dark. The captain had no chance to look at the sun for a week to see where
we are. One morning the captain came and shouted, "It's
calm now and I see a lot of seals close to the schooner." So we
all went out and take our canoes down from the schooner, and
put our grub and compass in it and started off from the
schooner with our spears. Our canoe was soon full and we
skin them and leave all the fat off, and throw the meat over
and hunt some more. There were seals everywhere—lots of
them. We pick out only the small ones because they bring
the same price as the big ones and we can pack more in our
canoes.

I don't think we was two hours out when we hear our boat
begin to shoot with the cannon, and flags going up and down
for us to go back. The sun was out and when we look up we
see we wasn't six miles away from the island where the fur
seal breeds, and we should be sixty miles away from there.
We all turned back and throw our seals on deck. The captain was scared and we put every sail up—topsail and everything. The cutters were running in a steady string about
sixty miles around that island. When we started going out,
the wind came up and we was going full speed ahead. Finally we see the smoke of a cutter, and we sail away from
them. They begin to shoot and we still try to get away. The
wind blew more and more, and we got away from that one.
Another cutter came in front and the captain begin to curse.
They shoot at us and make two holes in our sail. Then, all at
once, the fog came down, and the captain turned back to

the island, and in about a half an hour turned back out again. The wind began to blow hard and the captain knows where to go. We never took our sails down until we get back to Quatsino, because the schooner is known by those cutters. It took us just nine months for all that trip from the time we left. When we got on shore at Quatsino, the captain paid us for our seals. My brother was right there. How he knew I was coming home, I don't know. I had over $600 clear from that trip. We spent the money from the other seals in Japan on Japanese girls and other things. The Japanese girls were all right, but two of the Indians got a dose from them. I was lucky. My brother took away the money from me, so I had to come home with him. That's the time he started to make arrangements for me to marry Lagius' daughter. He says that is the only thing to keep me quiet.[4]

I was thinking of the woman I went around with at Quatsino—the Koskimo woman that I gave the $30 to before going sealing. Her name was Lucy. She had brown hair and a round face. She was as tall as I and her eyes were black with long eyelashes, and she had a good smile. All her body was in a right shape, and she was clean. She had long hair that comes down to her hips; she had it plaited on both sides of her head, and tied on the ends with ribbon. The first time I saw her, I admired her, and when I went to talk with her, she talked back to me in a lovely low voice. She wasn't fat and she wasn't thin. She had rather large breasts. When she walks about she is straight. She is slim waisted. Her hands is medium and her feet the same. She was one of the most beautiful girls I ever knew. She was the most beautiful among the Quatsino Indians.

In a girl it is the smile, the shape of her eyes and nose and mouth, and her hair and her body that counts. Especially it is the way the eyes smile. Some have too big a nose

---

[4] Charley has been leading his brother a merry chase. He apparently resents the restraints put upon him by his brother but is not aware of his resentment. This is consistent with his early training. He dares not openly defy his brother; he has been punished for this too often. But he can annoy him by running away and repeatedly threatening to marry a girl of whom his brother did not approve.

and makes her ugly. A wide mouth makes a girl ugly, and a woman that never smiles is ugly. She should have long hair and be kept in good order. She shouldn't be too white nor too black, just a nice brown.

I was crazy after her. When she was at Quatsino village, I had to go through a ten-mile trail, not a road, almost like an animal trail from the back of the porch right through to near Quatsino. Then I take a canoe. After I came home from the sealing trip, I used to go over there and see her and come home for a little while and only stay at Fort Rupert one night, and then get up in the morning and start out again. When I get to the other end of the trail, I had to go to the village by canoe for about eight miles. She also loved me. Whenever I get to the village, she comes to meet me and wants me to stay in her house, although I have some other relations there I could stay with. I stay together with her in her house as man and wife. We wasn't ashamed of any of it. My brother would come over or send word for me to come back to Fort Rupert. I was willing to come back whenever he does this, but when we get back to Fort Rupert, I never used to sleep good, thinking of her all the time. And early in the mornings, before my brother gets up, I get up and run through the trail again. I run most of the time. It seems as if I want to catch something when I get over there. I always have her picture before me in my mind, smiling at me, and that makes me go faster in my walk.

One time one of our own people from the Kwekas came over to Quatsino village to invite them to come to his potlatch. My brother was with the man, and the Quatsino Indians say they are going to start in their canoes next day, going around Cape Scott. My brother got me to come back with him through the trail. We was expecting the Koskimo people to arrive in a week, and during the time it seemed to me as if it was months. When they arrived, I tried to get this woman and her parents to come and stay in our house, but they have already arranged to use another house, so I lived with her there. Her parents doesn't care, because they want me to marry her, and I want to marry her. They stayed there during the winter. At fishing time, we went up to River's Inlet to fish for sockeye. A tugboat came over to Fort Rupert to tow all the canoes up to River's Inlet. I went with her in her canoe, although my brother tried to get me to go in his. When we get through fishing, we came home in canoes, and I was with her and we came right past Fort Rupert to Alert Bay.

While we was in Alert Bay, my brother came to me together with Mr. Hall, and Mr. Hall tells me he wants me to work for him, and I promise him I would. That very afternoon, the woman and her parents say they are going home now to Quatsino. I bid them good by, for I have made up my mind to work for Mr. Hall. I was sitting on the beach in front of my brother's house here, and one man were coming down the road behind me and talk to me while I was watching the canoe disappear around the point. He says: "Well, I can imagine how you feel. I know how it is, for I went through that myself when I was a young man." When he said that, his words just break my heart, and I begin to cry.

Next morning when I was supposed to get ready to go to my work, I went instead to my cousin's husband and asked him to take me over to the other side—over by the Nimkis River—that I want to go to Fort Rupert and get something there. He says, "Let's have something to eat first." I says it won't take him long and I don't want to eat, so he took me over and landed me on the other side. I jumped out and begin to walk toward Fort Rupert. When I got to Port McNeil, I walked through the bush. I walk as fast as I can, sweating, and my clothes just soaked through. When I get ten miles from Fort Rupert, there is a river I have to get over and I just walked right through it. That cooled me down a little, and I started again. I get to Thomas Point and walk through the bush, taking a short cut. When I got to a place where they used to pick berries, I heard a woman who was picking berries hollering out to the others how far away are they. I went toward where they were and I saw the very woman who was in the same canoe with the woman I was crazy for. She hollered again without seeing me, and the woman I loved answered her. I recognized the voice and go and sit down watching her without her seeing me for a long time. She lay down on a patch of moss and begin to sing a love song, and I could see the tears running down her face, and I could tell she also was sore that she left me. She made a sob and called out my name saying: "Charley, Charley, come and see me. I want to see you. Oh, how I like to hug you and put my lips and press them to yours." This was part of the love song she was singing. I jumped down and hugged and kissed her. "Ahhhhhhh!" she says. The other women heard her scream and run to see her. When they see me they say: "Ah, ah, ah. How did you get here, you wonderful man?" I says, "I called down my Thunderbird dress and flew here."

When it was afternoon I jumped right in the canoe and went with them. It took us two weeks to go around Cape Scott camping. When the wind is too strong, we stop and camp, waiting until the wind is not so bad. I stayed there in Quatsino with her almost two months, then my brother came after me. But before he came, Mr. Hall came over to Quatsino to preach—he and an uncle of mine called Punqwit. The next day they got up early to go to Winter Harbor, and Mr. Hall asked my uncle where they can have breakfast. He told him that I was there and they can have breakfast there. Mr. Hall says, "Has he got a wife here?" My uncle says, "Yes." They came with a Koskimo man and have their breakfast and went away to Winter Harbor. At noon time they camped to have their dinner. My uncle was going to pack water and met Mr. Hall and the Koskimo man sitting close to the fire. While they were eating their lunch, my uncle says, "What's wrong?" and Mr. Hall says: "My stomach is awful sore. I can't stand it. It may be I ate some of Satan's food." He had found out from the Koskimo man that the woman I was living with wasn't my wife.

When Mr. Hall returned from Winter Harbor, my brother came after me. He was going to give a potlatch to the Fort Rupert people, so I came with him. We got to Fort

Rupert about noon, and I was watching the women washing their blankets in the creek, when suddenly I thought of
this woman I was crazy for. I couldn't stand it—I wanted
her so. I thought, "As soon as my brother gets through with
his potlatch, I go right back." Then I says: "No, I can't
wait that long. I'll go back right now." And I jumped up
from where I was sitting and walked toward the trail and
begin to run. It was low tide when I got through the trail,
and I had a hard time pulling the canoe down to the beach.
Finally it was almost dark when I got the canoe down. I
paddled with all my strength. I was almost mad, I wanted
to see the woman so bad. I got there and go into the house
of my relatives, and when she—my cousin—saw me coming,
she says, "Ah, ah! What are you doing here?" She says,
"There must be something wrong, or you wouldn't do this
thing." My cousin and her husband and others begin to talk
to each other, about how some women makes men crazy for
them, and say to me they think she is doing something to me.

She says to me, "You give her a drink of whisky, and
make her drunk." I tell her I can't buy it, and she says,
"We will take care of that." She sent her husband to buy a
square bottle of gin. A chum of mine was in the house, too.
He says, "We better call somebody to drink with her." He
says he will buy another bottle, so he did. I went with this
chum of mine into the woman's house and went right up to
her and kissed her. Oh, she was happy to see me, and I told
her, "I've brought a bottle of gin for you, and you are to
have somebody to drink with you." So Lucy sent the chum
of mine to call another woman and her husband. They drank
the bottle that I brought. When they finished, the man that
Lucy called went out and bought another, and they begins
to drink that. Soon they could hardly stand, and the man
and his wife went home, and my chum showed me where the
bottle he hid was, and he went home. So we went to bed—
this woman of mine and me. Pretty soon she tells me she
wants some more to drink. I says all right, and I got the
other bottle and filled the cup up. She sat up and drank it.

When she finished she just dropped down in her bed and didn't move any more.

Before I went to her, I was told by my cousin to take off everything she had and feel the top of her skirt. "If you feel anything like a lump on the top of it," she says, "cut that off and bring it to me." She had three skirts on, and the one next to her skin I felt a lump in about two inches long. I took out my knife and cut it off and told the woman's mother to lock the door and gave her the rest of the gin and told her to drink it, that I was going to the gambling game that was going on. I went to my cousin and gave this thing to her. She called her sister, who they say knows how to do this thing. They came and opened this cloth, and there was two little dolls lying inside—a man and a woman. The woman had long hair. We looked at it and says: "There was a lot of work in that. It must have taken her a long time." Both the dolls have eyes and mouth, eyebrows and nose, arms and legs. They was made of some kind of clay mixed with hair. They was hugging each other, and the woman was sticking out her tongue into the man's mouth, and this man was laying with the woman, with his pecker in her private parts, and it was all tied in hair together. They pulled it apart. They put the man in water which had my own hair, some from my head and some from around my pecker, and this woman had her own on hers, some from her head and some from her privates. They says there is some kind of an herb mixed with the clay too. When they do this, I throw hers in the fire. Mine they keeps in water.

When I see what she was doing to me, I begin to hate her. As soon as they took this apart, and I find out what she was doing to me, I realizes how it must have hurted my brother. I and my chum went to the place where they were gambling and asked them if they would take me in a canoe to the end of the trail. When they hear about what has happened, they all say they will go, and then they ask me if I'll go with them down to where the saloon was—about three miles down. The saloon was on an island and the owner was all alone there—a white man that knew me well. We went down there and they all collected their money. I was to buy a bottle for each boy—$2 apiece. I went up and woke him, and he says, "What do you want?" And I says, "I want some bottles." He puts on his pants and asks me why can't I come in the daytime. I counted the money down and says I want eighteen bottles of rye whisky, and he puts them in a sack. Some of the boys was waiting outside, and we took the sack and started off. They begin to drink when we started from the island. We went right to the end of the trail and got there before daylight. Then we made a big fire on the beach, and they begin to sing love songs and drink. They only drank half the bottles. Then we started through the trail. They all followed me to Fort Rupert—seventeen of them. It was still early in the morning, and we went into my brother's house, and my brother's wife begin to cook for the boys. My chum told my brother what happened, that we got what the woman was using to make me crazy. We left half the bottles on the trail for them to drink when they goes back, and after eating they started back to Quatsino. From that time on I had nothing to do with this woman. Whenever she sends people to come and ask me to come over, my hatred toward her was worse.[5]

When we went to stay at Village Island for some potlatches, I met the girl I really loved. Her name was Mary. It took her a long time before I give her the money she wanted, but after that she was always willing to meet me. I always kiss her when we first met and then again when we parted. I never used any love magic. That's just like witchcraft and sets the woman crazy. Only some men and women knows about it. I never knew how to do it and I didn't need it anyway, but we did have love songs, and I used to make a lot of these. A lot of us boys would walk along the front of these houses singing these songs at night. One that I made

[5] Charley has been so openly defiant of his brother that friends and relatives are criticizing him. The discovery of Lucy's guile permits him to blame her, instead of himself, for his behavior. He can now return to his brother without fear of censure and with a clear conscience.

myself I can remember. That was when this girl left Fort Rupert. It goes like this:

My love, oh my love.
How mean you are to leave me.
How I wish I could go with you and put my arms around you,
And how I want to kiss you.
Now I'm very sad that you've left me,
Very sad and I'm crying—crying all the time.
Wishing to see your face again.
How I wish I could lie beside you.
How long will it be before I see you again?
Will it be long or will it not be long?
I hope it won't be long.
Oh, how I wish to see your loving face again.
Please have pity on me and send me a comforting word or two,
So that I will smile once again,
For I have been crying, crying all the time.

I saw Mary many times after this, even after she got married, and when I got married we used to go with each other whenever we could. Just before I got married, she left her husband—he was one of her own tribe—because we thought we could get married. I nearly run away from them when my older brother wouldn't let me marry her. This was a chief's daughter, but they like to get Lagius' daughter, rather than this one, for me. Sometimes when he tell me to get up for breakfast I was so mad at him, I didn't get up till later. I used to go to her at night and stay with her, and we make plans and make plans what we are going to do. She is dead now but her daughters are still living.

CHAPTER VII

MARRIAGE

WHEN I was old enough to get a wife—I was about twenty-five—my brother looked for a girl in the same position that I and my brothers had. Without my consent, they picked a wife for me—Lagius' daughter. The one I want is prettier than the one they choose for me, but she was in a lower position than me, so they wouldn't let me marry her. I argued about it and was very angry with my brother, but I couldn't do anything. She was from the Mamaleleqala tribe. Her name was Mary. She was very beautiful. I used to go around with her when we were invited to her village for potlatches and feasts. She used to come to Fort Rupert, too, when her parents were invited to potlatches there. Sometimes they would stay a year. I remember once we were invited to the Mamaleleqala, and we stayed there two years. During this time I used to go around with her and make love with her. I loved her and she loved me. Anyway, my older brother made arrangements for my marriage. He gave Lagius, the head chief of the Nimkis, two hundred blankets to keep Lagius from letting others have his daughter.

Just before I got married to his daughter, Lagius come to a feast at Village Island. This was the first time his daughter had her monthly. She was with another girl in the bedroom inside the house where the feast was taking place, and she found out that she was having this monthly. She tells this girl to tell somebody outside to go and tell her father that she had the monthly for the first time. As soon as he found out, he got up and made a noise like the chief does—"Ha-ha-ha-ha-ha-ha"—when they are going to make a potlatch. All the people was asking what he was talking about, and he told all the Fort Ruperts to sit up. "My daughter has her monthly, and I am going to give potlatches." We

was on our way over to Harbledown Island. He says: "All
you young men get in the fastest canoe you have and go to
where I'm staying at Harbledown and get all my coppers,
for I am going to sell all my coppers for what my daughter
has done." We all walked out of the feast house, and he told
them all to wait in the house till we come back.

We went over to Harbledown and brought back four coppers—three that belonged to him and one that belonged to
his wife. He put two of them on the ground in the house and
put two of them on the back and called his daughter to come
out of the house and sit on the coppers, and lean her back
on the others. Then he says to the Fort Ruperts: "Sing the
song of the chief of my clan, which was sung when the first
Indian chief broke a copper at the time his daughter first
had her monthly." This must have been a long, long time
ago, and we begin to sing this song:

It has been a long time before your chief's name was mentioned,
For you are always breaking coppers.
You are a real fool;
You don't care what you do.
You lose your coppers, breaking them all the time. Now look out.
You are going to be sick. Go ahead and do it, you fool.

"Fool" means that he doesn't care and breaks too many
coppers.

When we finished singing he shows the two coppers he is
going to sell. He says anybody who wants them come and
take them. He says he is going to sell them cheap. The other
coppers was bought by other men. He picks up the broken
one that is his own and told the people that this is the blood
of his daughter, that he is going to give it to one of the
chiefs. While he was talking, nobody dared to talk. During
all this time his daughter was sitting on a platform in the
back of the house. Four images was standing below to hold
his daughter up. Slaves would have done this in the olden
days. There was two eagles on both sides of where she sits,
and she is wearing a beaded blanket with abalone shells on
it. Lagius stands holding this broken copper of his and then

he puts a mask on his face—a mask which is black with red on the mouth—and he makes a noise which represents a man of the woods, saying, "Oo-oo-oo-oo! Oo-oo-oo-oo!" When he took that mask off, he says, "Here, sir." All the chiefs, especially the Village Island chiefs, thought they was going to get it. They all lay on their backs just waiting. Then he says again, "Here, sir—Odzistales." The Mamaleleqala chief by that name thought it was him, but when Lagius sent his nephew to go and give it, the nephew turned around and says, "Which one?" Lagius says, "Tlowitsis." This man never dreamt he was going to get it. He never said a word. He was stunned and just lay there. The other one gets up and says: "Wa-a-a-a-a-a-a-a-a! Now will you stop your talking that you thought it was going to be me." This Tlowitsis fellow was quarreling with Lagius' wife's cousin. The other broken copper Lagius didn't use. He had it ready in case the Tlowitsis chief gave him one in return. Lagius' daughter was about fourteen or fifteen at the time—maybe a little younger—and after that I got married to her.

When my wife had her monthly first, they had a certain woman that come and bathe her at certain times and look after her while she was set up to stay in her own room. She bathe on the fourth day of her monthly, and four days after that she bathe again. Nobody else but that woman is supposed to be there, so I didn't see it. They have cloths to rub her down and put her face in a good shape after she bathes. At the fourth bathing at each fourth day, the woman took her tweezers and pulled some hair out of her eyebrows just to have the eyebrows in a good shape. They put tight bands on her head and her ankles, and she wore that but not very long. The old women wear them till they are very old, and even till they die. They say they used to be made out of skin, but what I saw was black cloth. They cut her hair, but not short—just small pieces of the undergrowth of her hair. She was sitting down and had an Indian hat with some kind of a string hanging down the back. She had to eat in a certain time and drink only so much water.

They were very strict with her and nobody was allowed

to go near her and talk to her, for if she talk she would become a chatterbox. And if she eats too much she will always be eating a lot, if she drinks more water she will be thirsty all the time, and if she is cold she will always be cold. She bathe only once every fourth day, only in the nighttime. Her fingernails was cut, too, by the same woman; she has new clothing to wear. When she comes out of the room, she sits amongst her parents with her clothing and blanket all clean. She has to sit up like a woman and is not allowed to look around by the instruction of the woman that looked after her. Anybody that comes and talks to her, she can't reply at once but take her time and not be in a rush in anything she does. When she goes out she has to use her blanket in a proper way and walk slow, and when she eats she has to take the food in her thumb and forefinger and eat carefully with her right hand, and when she drinks, take her cup and drink easy. She didn't do it long.

About a year later, my older brother gave this chief one thousand trade-in blankets. We got all the people of many tribes together to come and attend this marriage. The day before the marriage my brother got the head chief of every tribe to go and tell Lagius, the father of the girl I was to marry, that I was to marry her the next day. My brother paid each one of these men a pair of blankets.[1]

They go to the house where Lagius was staying, and they get up one by one and make a speech according to the rules of the Indian customs, asking his permission to let us get married the following day. After they finished, Lagius stood up before these chiefs and gave his consent. The next day the marriage was held. They all came in their canoes singing war songs and other songs to seem lively and let everyone know they are coming. When they all come in front of the house in canoes, the head chief of the Mamaleqala was asked by my brother to stand up and make a speech—the

---

[1] It is interesting to note how thoroughly the Kwakiutl reward every service, no matter how formal. For performing their obligations, clansmen and relatives are reinforced at every turn by payments in blankets or money which can be used to pay for gratifying goods and services.

marriage speech. He stands up and says: "Lagius, the Owadi [this is the name of our chief] clan has come to you to take your daughter to be their wife. We have all come together as we should when anybody wants to marry your daughter, and we have all come to witness it. We have come in our canoes, which could go around the whole world looking for a wife."

He sits down, and then the Tlowitsis chief also stands up and gives a speech. He mentions his first ancestor, called Numas. This Numas came to this world already an old man, and used to go all around to all the different tribes looking for a wife. The chief says that they are using his canoe—the one Numas used to go around on. He says that this Owadi clan has come to get your daughter for a wife, and the Owadi clan has found her to be equal with them. Then the Tenaktak chief gets up in his canoe. He uses a blanket over his arms outspread like a bird. He says that he is the Thunderbird and that he became a man. He says, "I have come to you in my Thunderbird dress to get your daughter to be married to the Owadi clan." Then the chief of the Matilspe gets up and makes a speech: "I am a bird that came down from the skies and became a man. I also have come to get your daughter to be married to the Owadi clan." That is the last of the tribes; the others were not invited to this marriage.

After they all finished, it goes back to the Mamaleleqala tribe. The chief of each of their clans gets up to finish all the speeches of these chiefs who has spoken. They correct and repeat everything that is said, so that there can be no mistake and everyone will hear them. Then they take up the blankets and begin to count them. Every time they count out one blanket they say, "Walk in with this." This means that I am walking into his house to take his daughter with these blankets. They keep on like this until they finish all the blankets. When this is all finished, Lagius and the rest of the Nimkis chiefs stand up in front of their house and tell the people that they have got their wife. He says, "Send all your young men to come and get her, and I will return some of the blankets for you to buy food for all the people you have asked to come and attend to the marriage."[2]

All this time I am sitting in the canoe with my older brother. Some of the young men brought her, and I took her in the canoe from her house to the one I was staying in at Village Island. Then everybody goes back to the places they are staying, and we are all invited to a potlatch. My older brother sends two men around to invite everybody to a feast—my wedding feast.

The next day the blankets I get from my wife's father were all given away to all the men. That represented the belongings of my wife which she takes away with her from her father to my home, and I give a potlatch with these at Village Island to the Mamaleqalas after my marriage.

After this potlatch, my brother's wife called all the women together to give a feast to them. They send two women to go to the bedroom where my wife is and call her to come out to the feast, for this is the first time she is going to eat in her husband's house. When they all come in, they give my wife the highest seat. They call the feast, "sitting together with a newly married girl that is going to have her first meal after her marriage."

They select a woman who has been good to her husband to take a piece of the food they are going to eat. She holds it in her fingers and tries to put it into my wife's mouth. They have to wait until my wife opens her mouth to eat. When she eats it, they sit down. Food is passed around to all the women, and they begin to eat. The wives of the chiefs, in order of rank, make speeches, telling the girl how she should be—that she is not to be proud, that she is not to go around with other men, that she must be good to her husband and not to go away from him but keep together with him as long

---

[2] This marriage ceremony seems to perform two major functions. First, since the marriage and the transfer of goods is witnessed by all concerned, there can be no mistake about the number of blankets received. This is of great importance when the time comes for Lagius to make his return payment. Second, the ceremony stresses the fact that Lagius is undertaking an obligation which concerns Charley's entire clan and, should he fail in his part of the bargain, he will have the clan to deal with as well as Charley.

as they are man and wife. The women that speak are the ones that are good to their husbands; they wouldn't let any woman that is not good to her husband make a speech. Every time she finishes, the woman says: "You will be like me. I have stayed with my husband all these years. I have never grumbled and never tried to go away from him, and now you will do the same." All these women that was asked to talk was paid by the parents of the man—sometimes blankets, sometimes money.

Girls couldn't go around with men until they were married, and it was a great disgrace, especially to a chief's daughter, if anyone touches them. It doesn't make any difference in the money, but the husband might not like the girl and might not stay with her. The man usually doesn't want her, and when he is asked why he tells them she is not a virgin, and they go and spread it all over the place. They says they know when a girl has been touched, because the private of the girl is already too wide. My wife was all right.

The first night some will come and get married and then take the girl back to the man's side, and others, if they are from far away, will spend that night in the girl's parents' house. If she is still in her own home, all the young men go to the house, and the groom is with them. They go into the house where the girl is, and the man goes into his wife's bed and lays down with her, while the others stay outside the bedroom singing love songs. They sing quite a long time while he is in there, until all the people in the house has gone to bed, and then we go home. If the girl goes to her husband's house, there is no love songs because she has already gone into her husband's house. That's the way it was with me.

After the potlatch and the feast all the Fort Ruperts went home. When we got back to Fort Rupert, we went to my wife's mother's house. She was a Kwakiutl. Lagius and his wife came back with us and lived there, and there was also his wife's father's brother and his wife, and Peter Pascero, who was a cousin of Mrs. Lagius, lived with us.

When your daughter is married to another man, the hunters will come in with the seal, and the father of the girl would buy seals from the hunters and give them to his son-in-law, and he will go and give a feast with it and with other kinds of Indian food. The man will buy it or get it himself and go and visit the son-in-law right when they are married, and afterwards, too, as long as the daughter is married to him, as often as he feels like it, especially when your daughter is married to another tribe. Every time your daughter comes to see you, she has to take back either food or blankets when she goes home to her husband. We call that "to go and visit her home." Therefore, the girl don't go so often to see her parents because she has to bring these things back to her husband. Nowadays they go all the time and don't bring anything back. Chief Lagius do this for me every time. My wife didn't go very often to see them, because we soon came to live with them, and her mother used to come often to Fort Rupert, because she had a right to come and stay there.

Any time I feel like giving á feast or a potlatch after I was married, I get my own money and give it to Lagius, and he give it back to me to give a feast or a potlatch. This is for the honor of my children, and most times he add some of his own money to it to make it more. And when I give the feast or potlatch, I say the money comes from him. After my child was born I did this, and every time a child of mine comes to the time when the baby begins to eat, I do this. Any time the child begins to play and gets hurt, I give money to Lagius and he gives it back to me, and I give it away to wipe the blood of the child's wounds. A good son-in-law would do this to the wife's father. I always did it for my wife's father's good name and my child's good name, and the way I do it nobody knows it except Lagius and myself, and everybody thinks it's all his money I am spending, except the others know that is what they should do themselves and that I probably do it that way. Some men wouldn't do it though. They think the father of your wife should do all these by himself.

When my wife and I got married, I wanted a boy, and I

made four small wooden wedges of yew wood and bow and arrows which men would use, and put them under our bed and kept them there. I wanted all boys.[3] We had all boys straight.

After about ten years, my wife wanted a girl, and without my knowing it took away these wedges and bows and arrows and got four small mats and four small baskets and put them there instead. When this baby girl come, I say: "That wedge is no good. That bow and arrow is no good. I'm going to make some new ones." I went to look under the bed, and they was gone, and there was mats and baskets instead. I said, "When did you put those things there?" And she said, "Before I carried." Then I said there must be something true about this, but I didn't change it, and we had girls right along while they was under there.[4]

While she was carrying, we was told to get up before anybody else gets up and open the door and go right down to the beach to relieve ourselves, and then it will be easy for her to have her birth. She go to a basket full of smooth stones that was in the house ready for her and picks out four of them, and when we was going to the beach she drops them outside her dress inside her blanket so that she will have a smooth, easy birth.

When the monthly stops we count ten moons, that is from wherever the moon is—maybe the first quarter, maybe the last, maybe the full moon, maybe the new moon. Only four parts of the moon was named. A woman will have her monthly the same quarter of the moon when it comes around again. If she doesn't have it then, she counts ten months—ten

[3] One of the distinct advantages in having male children derives from the Kwakiutl marriage transactions. As will be seen in the following chapter, the father of a girl is required to pay out more than he receives when she marries. The father of a boy is not thus handicapped. If he has boys first, and then girls, he is in strategic position. The returns from his sons' marriages help him in his obligations to his sons-in-law.

[4] This is a good illustration of how chance tends to perpetuate magical practices. Even if the device fails, however, Charley has an answer ready; he would simply assume that the wedges and bow were worn out and make another set.

moons—and that is when she will have her baby. The calendar in the old days goes by the birds and by the fish and by some of the ducks and also by the moon.

When I got married and we had a child I never thought of wiping anything I have seen, but when I see anything that is not good, I go right to it and handle it. That shows I didn't get scared of it. At the birth of our child, I and my wife go to the tub where it is to be washed and wash my eyes and her eyes and our ears and our noses, too, four times in that water. After we got back, the baby is washed in that, and we do that for four days after. They say that is why our children never had any sickness as babies.[5] We did this with all our children. They say that anything you see, hear, and smell the baby will copy it. Any animal laying on the ground dead with a wound in the head, or any kind of dead birds or dead people, and a woman crying when a dead person is lying in the house, and the smell of a dead animal or a dead person—all these is bad to the parents of a baby that is going to be born.

My wife's mother put our first two babies in a cradle. The blankets that the boys have has a hole in the center where the little pecker sticks out, so he won't wet himself. The girls have a hollow place where their backsides are, and the water goes to the bottom of the cradle where there is a hole for it to run out. If it is a girl, they often take everything out, the sticks and all, and wash it. They don't do it to the man-child, because cedar bark catches his mess and he pees right over the outside of the cradle. They didn't have to have any diapers; they saved money on that in the old days. If the baby is a girl and you want her to dance good, you put some pine under the sticks in the cradle and they run about on the bottom while the cradle rocks. When you want them to move their fingers swift, you take the worms from old fish or rotten meat and come and make the baby hold them on the hand and let them move there. You do that four times each day for four days. If you want her to know how to

---

[5] Charley's children that died young were killed through accidents; they did not succumb to disease.

make good mats, you give her belly-button cord to a woman that makes a good mat to have it on her wrist, while she is mat making, and anything you want you do like that.

When my first baby was born all I did was to get wood to warm the house. It is woman's job to look after the baby. They handle things like that better.

After my wife have a baby, I think she bleeds four to six days. She gets into a tub of hot water and covers herself up with blankets outside until she is sweating a lot. This she does four days after. That is to get the blood out that would remain in her womb. She did that for a week or two. It eases her body and eases the breasts to have the milk come freely. They have a broth from dried clams with olachen oil in it to make her breasts fill good with milk. We get the branches of a tree that has little red berries, and put that in the water and put it on her breasts, and that helps the milk to run; when the milk begin to run freely, she quit doing that. They have a blanket about ten inches wide tied around her waist tight every time she gets out of the hot water to keep her belly from getting swollen.

The first day of her baby's birth, she had a bed with a high pillow, and her mother wouldn't let her move at all. Her feet were stretched out straight, and she couldn't even go to the toilet the first day. After that when she wants to go to the toilet, she wasn't allowed to stand up straight. She walked with a walking stick stooped over. They wouldn't let her stand up straight at all; she might strain her stomach. The time I help her I used to make fun of her and when we get to the step outside, I say, "Be careful, old woman, can you see the step?" And how we used to laugh. I think she was nursing the baby the next day. They say there isn't any milk, but there is a medicine in her breasts that is good for the baby.

After a woman has given birth you can't lie with her. I waited ten months to one year after, so that our children would be two years apart—so that it won't make my wife have hard work looking after the children. The first child will be walking then. I was told by my wife's mother not to

go near my wife until one year after, but I didn't wait quite
that long. I don't think they wait even that long now, because women are getting children every year.

The older people say that going with a woman when she
is having her monthly causes sickness to the woman and
weakens your pecker. They are afraid of the blood that runs
onto you. They look upon this blood as a very poisonous
thing. If a woman has her monthly, they wouldn't dare let
her stay in a house where a sick person is; she will be put out
and stay in a tent. All your tools, your fishing and hunting
gear, shouldn't be in a house where a woman is who has her
monthly, because it will spoil them. She can't go in a canoe
then either. But when women travel, they keep a rag with
some of this blood on it in a bag, in case any monsters come
up and then they put that rag on the side of the canoe. I've
seen my wife's mother do that when we was going to Cape
Mudge. There came up a strong wind from a mountain tear-
ing the sails down and she imagined she saw something in
front of us and takes out her rag and hangs it on the side
of the canoe to make the sea monster go away.

Nenagwas was the name I gave to my first baby when he
was four days old. He was three months old when he died.
He was taken out of his cradle by his aunt, the younger sister of my wife, and she was walking about with him to stop
him from crying, and came close to the door of the bedroom
of the community house. When she came near the door, it
opened suddenly, and as she was swinging the baby in her
arms, the door hit the baby right on the head. Immediately
blood came out of the baby's ears and nose, and its eyes
turned red, and that night he died.[6]

My wife and I both saw it happen. When the baby died,
we all cried, and all the people come in to see what my wife

[6] This is an example of what can happen when a part of the culture of
a people is neglected. The baby was removed from the cradle and carried
in the arms—a novel and nontraditional procedure to which the habits of
the woman were not adjusted. Had the baby been carried in the cradle, it
would have been protected and would have received no more than a severe
jolt. As the cradle disappears from Kwakiutl culture, the number of infant deaths due to accident increases markedly. Another of Charley's ba-

and mother was crying about. There was not any doctor to take the baby to, and we didn't know what to do. They felt the baby's head which was swollen up and could be pressed down. The baby stopped crying immediately after he got hurt and was unconscious, just staring at one place. He never moved and never cried after that. It was before midnight he died. They say he has no more breath and feel that his heart don't beat any more. When a person is dying, they keep on feeling the feet. It gets cold on the feet and coming up, and then they say he is almost gone now; the cold is above his knees, and they watch over him and he begins to make a gasp like and then another gasp. Then there is a funny snoring noise like in the throat, and when that stops the lower mouth opens, drops down, and that is the time they feel the heart and they say he is gone. But they dare not say he is dead or gone; they simply say, "He is —" We don't finish it or say, "He is dead," but everybody in the house understands. Somebody goes out and tells people he sees, "His eyes are closed now." That is the polite way of saying, "He is dead." They don't want to say it the other way, for it might make the people who are relatives feel worse. They want to make it sound like he is just sleeping.

When my baby died, the women cry loud, and then all the other people begin to know he is dead. They all come into the house and sit down outside of the bedroom. Some will come right inside. My wife's relatives and mine helped bathe the baby and put new clothing on him, and wrapped him up in new blankets that very night, and when that was done, he was left in the room that night. This child of mine, they asked us, where are they going to put him that night? I told them he is going to be left in that room until tomorrow, but among other people if anybody dies in the house, he is not allowed to stay in the house, but is taken out and a tent put over him. That is the time they take him out of a hole

bies fell into boiling water at the age of a year. Still another fell off the cannery wharf before he was two. The Indians have no habits of watching over their infants. There was no need for such behavior in the past; the cradle automatically solved the problems of accident prevention.

in the wall or a window. I didn't agree with those other people that want to take my baby out.[7]

Next day I got two young men to go and dig the grave away from the graveyard behind the porch. He was put down away from the other graves, because they say that if we don't put it away from the other graves, and my wife have another baby, he will also die. By putting him away from the other graves, the child may return as another baby to my wife. If there had been boys from another tribe other than Fort Ruperts there, I would have got them to dig the grave, because I am going to give them a potlatch and not the Fort Ruperts, and I am going to pay them what I think is enough to pay them—besides the potlatch I am going to give. As it was, I got some boys from the Fort Ruperts that wasn't Kwekas.

When the grave is being dug, there is others that is making the coffin. The ones that make it will also be paid. These are young or grown-up men—any that knows how to do it. When the coffin is done, they come into the house and says that the coffin is ready, and that they want to put the child into the coffin. So they took the child away from my wife, who was still holding him on her lap, and the child was taken through the window of the bedroom at the back. The coffin was there in the back of the house. They put him on the ground, and one man held him on the feet and one on the head and get ready to put him in the coffin. They take him and swing him toward the coffin and back, till the fourth time they let him into the coffin. In the coffin with the baby they put a small bottle of water. That was all they put in there, because they haven't known yet what he likes to eat, because he haven't begun to eat. They would also put food in if he had begun to eat. The water is to represent milk from my wife. They put this right side of the body, and then

---

[7] To please his wife, who wants the baby with her, Charley deviates from native custom. Removing the corpse from the house may have developed as a means of minimizing contagion on occasions when death resulted from an infectious disease. The death of Charley's baby was accidental and therefore no dire results occur which would punish this departure from traditional custom.

they put on the cover. It had a line tied around it and tied at both ends. This was before handles was known to the Indians. The line is for them to hold the coffin while they carry it. They took him away and buried him. All the people in the village went, but I and my wife did not go. Then they all came back and went to their homes. That night they came to comfort me and my wife. After they finished, Lagius promised to give me so many blankets to wipe away the tears from my eyes.

On the fourth day after the baby was buried, I gave a potlatch. All the Fort Ruperts came in my house, and the Kwekas sang a lamenting song—four of them. When that is finished, some of the Kwekas got up and said: "We are finished with the singing, and we will turn over to forget about this. We will have a dance song and let one of our relatives dance to the song." This is what we call "to shake off sadness." After that, I gave the Kwakiutl and Walas Kwakiutl and Kumkutis some blankets. Then my brother says: "This is all through now. We are all comforted now, and we will forget about our child for a while, although we will never forget him, for he was the first child that is given us. Now you can do what you like. You can have potlatches and games." Before that, since the child died nobody in the village did anything. They were looking upon us to start and to tell them they could do anything they wanted to, and that used to be the rules of the Indians, but now they don't seem to care. It was at the potlatch, before I started giving away for the potlatch, that I paid those that dug the grave and those that made the coffin. One of our old people that speaks for me says: "We will start now to give the young men something to thank them for their kindness in doing their work. Although they don't expect anything, we will give them something for their kindness." I gave them $5 apiece for digging the grave, and the making of the coffin was $20—$5 apiece for the four of them.

The night the baby died we sat up all night, my wife holding the baby in her arms. Lagius and his wife, my brother and his wife were also there sitting up all night.

None of us sang any lamenting songs until early in the morning. They say it is not good to sing these mourning songs in the night. Everybody is supposed to bathe themselves on the fourth day after anybody has died. My wife and I bathed on the fourth day after our baby died, and Lagius and his wife, and my brother and his wife too. This was after the potlatch. Sometimes they don't give a potlatch on the fourth day, but they bathe anyway. Sometimes they won't be ready for the potlatch for a month or two till they get enough to give a potlatch, but on the time our baby died, we had the money on hand. When anybody dies in some other house, and they hear of the death, they take the water that is in their houses and pour it out, and then go and get fresh water. They say this water is the dead man's, that the dead man is in the water.

Sometime after our child died, while we was at Fort Rupert, Tlakodlas, my grandfather, died. There was a man before the Thunderbird; he was a steelhead salmon and became a man after the flood. While he was building his big community house he had all his posts ready and he was working at the beam he was going to put up, when suddenly came down a big bird—the Thunderbird—and sat on a rock in front of where the man was working on the beam. He turned around from his work to look at the noise that came down in front of him when he saw the big Thunderbird sitting on the rock, he said to him: "How I wish you was a man instead of a bird so you could help me put up this beam that I am working on, for I don't know how I am going to put it up." The Thunderbird put up its bird head and a human face showed. It said: "Why, I am a man. I have come down from the heavens when I saw you working and there was nobody to help you. I have come to help you." He put back his bird head and flew and picked up the beam with his claws and flew up with it until he come to the top of the posts and laid it on the post. Then he came down again and sat on the same place. The man say to the Thunderbird: "Brother, I thank you for coming down to help me. Now stay with me and you will be my brother. We will build you a house on

A Thunderbird Crest

the lower side of my house, and we will live together." The Thunderbird says: "This thing I will do. I will stay with you." He took off his bird clothing and said to the clothing: "You will go up to the heavens and stay there, but do not make thunder very often excepting when anybody dies that will come after me." So the Thunderbird dress flew up, and the man was left there. They lived close to Nimkis lake. From that time on, whenever anybody dies of that clan they say it used to thunder, and then they always know that some of their clan died.

While I was living at Fort Rupert there was a big thunder that came almost to the top of the houses and shook them, and my brother says early in the morning: "There must be something wrong with our clan at Nimkis, for it thundered awful last night." Before noon a canoe came with Nimkis people in it. The speaker in the canoe says: "We have come to you Kwakiutl, we have come to you Kweka, Walas Kwakiutl, and Kumkutis, to come and help us to bury our chief, Tlakodlas, who is dead. Other canoes has gone to the other tribes to ask them to come and help, for the great chief is dead and is too heavy for us Nimkis people to lift, and so we come to ask you to come and help us."

We all came to Alert Bay the same day, singing the songs that we use for dead people—for chiefs when they die—as we come around the point toward the houses. While we was coming, the Mamaleleqala and Tlowitsis came on, and they was also singing mourn songs. And the Alert Bay people was in front of the village singing mourn songs, too. We was called into Tlakodlas' house and had something to eat, and then we all went to bury him. Then we went back to his house and we begin again to sing mourn songs—the Kwakiutl first, and the chiefs of the Kwakiutl stood up and the head chief made a speech. The Mamaleleqalas the same and then the Tlowitsis, and after that the Nimkis sang their four songs.

Then Lagius stood up and thanked the people for coming to help bury their chief who has died. He says: "We don't know what we are going to do. We might be scattered all over the villages for a while till we get feeling better for the

loss of our chief. Our chief was a man that has power to
make a great wind blow us all over the place. When we get
over it, we may come together again." He says: "I am saying this for we feel that we will have no other chief that will
look after us the same as he has been looking after us. We
will have no more shield to protect us, for he was our shield.
He was our fort, and he was standing for us, and the fort
has broken down, and anything that you say against the
Nimkis people now, who is going to stand for them? Now
we will call him to come and see all you people, and we will
see which way he went." So he spoke out loud, saying:
"Come, chief, and see all your people who has been looking
up to you as their chief." He said this four times, and then
a whistle was heard in back of his house. Lagius called four
of his tribe to go out and meet the chief who is coming. So
they went out and came in again with a Thunderbird mask,
which one of the young men was wearing. He was coming
around the house and went out again.

Then his grandson was called by Lagius to come and
stand up. He was only about nine years old. Lagius said:
"I have already told you people that we are going to be scattered, and here now is the grandson of our chief. He is
young, while our chief was going on to old age; he is new,
and he will grow up to be the same as his grandfather. I
have taken back what I said; we will not scatter, for we have
our new chief here who will take his grandfather's place."
When he got through, one of the Fort Ruperts stood up
and thanked him for what he said, and says: "Why should
you scatter? You have been a big tribe while that chief was
living, and you will still be a big tribe for he has a grandson
to take his place. We Fort Ruperts, Mamaleleqalas, and
Tlowitsis are asking you to forget about the death of our
chief, and ask you to have a strong heart and one mind to
treat your young chief the same as you treated the old chief.
We other people will look upon him as we have looked upon
the old chief that has left us. Although he is young, he is
the grandson of that chief, and he will be treated the same
as a grown-up chief." He turned around to Willy Harris

and says: "From now and on, don't think that you are
young. You are grown up to be a chief now. You will walk
with all the chiefs and talk with all the chiefs, and whenever
the chiefs has a meeting you will be there. From now you are
no more young in our minds." Then Willy Harris was helped
by Lagius to give a potlatch, and it was announced that
until Willy Harris was old enough, Lagius would look after
his position.

Six months after our first baby was born we came to Alert
Bay because my wife wanted to stay with her parents, who
lived there. We lived at Lagius' house. My elder brother had
come to Alert Bay and had a house here. He was working
for the Indian agent, Mr. Pidcock. He cooked for him after
old Mr. Hunt died, and had better wages. I stayed at Lagius' house and was working sometimes in the sawmill. When
the Indian agent goes to visit all the other villages, I and
my brother went with him to help paddle and to look after the
canoe. We used to go from village to village and stay three
days and maybe more at each village. Sometimes we had to
camp in bad weather, and maybe we were stuck there a week
or more if we can't buck against the wind. This was the time
I started to work for Dr. Newcombe as his interpreter and
in collecting Indian curios. He used to give me $365 a year
as a bonus, besides the wages I was getting. I worked for
him for about thirty years until he died.

A year after my first baby died, Alfred was born. Alfred
was thought to have come back from the dead when he was
born, by the scar that was on his right temple, and they say
this was Nulis, my father's second oldest brother, who died
a long time ago. He had a scar in the same place as Alfred
had, and therefore they say this is Nulis, but I didn't name
him that. We gave him a child name when he was four days
old. This name was Wawalkine, which means, "the one that
is given to you when you have none."

CHAPTER VIII

LAGIUS GIVES ME A COPPER

WHEN Alfred was about three years old, Chief Lagius, my wife's father, bought a valuable copper.
He paid over fourteen thousand blankets[1] for it,
and gave it to me in payment for the blankets we give him
when I got married to his daughter. A man, when his daughter marries and he don't pay, it is a disgrace to him and the
daughter and her husband. He is saying to the son of the
daughter, "Your grandfather never gave any copper, or articles, or name to your father." I handed this copper over to
my brother, and he sold it and gave a potlatch with it years
after that.

I and my brother were helping him to buy this copper.
Lagius' share in paying for this copper was four thousand
blankets. Chief Lagius and his wife gathered about six hundred button blankets—blankets with buttons on them in
bird and whale designs—four hundred silver bracelets,
sixty dance headdresses, some boxes, brass bracelets, beads,
wooden bowls, boxes with sea-otter teeth in them, and gave
all these things to me. Those things they call *hawanaka*. This
means they have come to me with canoes full of stuff, and the
copper represents the mast of this canoe. I gave all that away
myself at a potlatch here at Alert Bay. In that potlatch Lagius gave me the copper, and I turned it over to my brother.
I called all the tribes together for the potlatch, and it took
me two days to give these things around. I only invited the
other tribes; the Fort Rupert tribes were left behind.

Lagius and me decide to give a potlatch so he could give
me the copper. It is according to the customs of the Indians
that the chief's daughter should have a copper given to her
husband by her parents, and also the goods that they

[1] The blankets used in this transaction were single blankets worth fifty
cents apiece.

brought. But before that he generally gives me some money or blankets to give a small potlatch, or he buys some food from the store and give it to me to give a small feast just for my own people. When I came to Alert Bay, he buys some food from the cannery store and give it to me, and I give a feast with it to the Alert Bay people. After that, every time we have a new baby, he give me money to give a potlatch to give a name to this new baby about four days after it is born, and the same when the baby begins to eat, and on his tenth month there has to be a feast or a potlatch and Lagius helps me out—either with his own money or the money I give to him.

This is the story of how Lagius bought the copper which he gave to me after I married his daughter. The name of the copper means, "to clean everything out of the house." Tlatlilitla, chief of the Tlowitsis, owned this copper. My brother and Lagius went to ask him to let Lagius have that copper, and say that they will give him one thousand dollars as the first payment, that is, the "pillow" of the copper. He agreed, and he called all the people to the front of the house in Alert Bay. All the different tribes was here at the time.

When all the people were gathered in front of Lagius' house, another chief, Odzistalis, spoke for the chief of the Tlowitsis, saying that the chief is now ready to get rid of his copper, which he has already bought, and say that he has seen the chief of another tribe, which he thinks is able to buy this copper. And he said, "I hand over my copper to Chief Lagius." He asked another chief to go and hand this copper over to Lagius. These were both Tlowitsis chiefs. When Lagius took hold of the copper, he says: "I have now received your copper, which you want to sell, and I'll only keep it one day, [that means one year] and then I'll buy it from you. I will give you a thousand dollars as a pillow till I pay the rest. I have been looking for a copper as big as this, for I have been awake every night, wanting to get a copper for my daughter's husband."

Then he counted out the thousand dollars, which the Tlowitsis chief took and said to all the people: "This money is ready to be loaned out. At the time Lagius will pay for my copper, I will collect this money, which is to be paid 100 per cent back to me, and then it will be paid back to Lagius." Lagius also stood up and say he has some money to loan out if anybody wants it, which is to be paid back in the same way. I also told the people that I have money to loan out. My brother also says he has money to loan out.

When Lagius or I or my brother loan out blankets, before we pay for the copper, we loan to anybody that wants them. Maybe they want to buy some food. Maybe they owe somebody else some money, and the owner of that money wants to collect from him; if he is unable to pay himself, he asks for the amount he is shy, to pay. Or maybe he wants to sleep with a girl and wants to get the money for that. So he goes to one of us and asks us for the money. He then uses it for whatever he wants. Then comes the time when we call in our money, because we are going to buy the copper. So we go to him and ask him to pay, and we collect what we had loaned.

One thing he can do is to go to Tlatli-litla and ask him for his share in the potlatch that this chief is going to give. He can only do this if he is not a Tlowitsis, because Tlatli-litla is not going to give the Tlowitsis anything in his potlatch. So he goes to him and gets his share and then pays one of us whom he owes, and when the potlatch is given he only gets a stick, which shows that he has been paid in advance what he is to get in the potlatch. If Tlatli-litla says that you want one hundred dollars but I'm only going to give you fifty dollars in my potlatch, then this man will go to another man that is loaning out money and say, "You loan me fifty dollars and I'll pay it back double." Or he may say, "I'll pay you 50 per cent or 25 per cent," depending on how long he is going to keep the money, and will point out when he is going to pay it.

Sometimes it happens that a man remembers something that was owed to his father or grandfather by another man's father or grandfather, and he goes to that man and asks him to loan him some money, and when that man comes to collect it, he says, "No, your grandfather owed my grandfather that

and never paid." They will argue about it if the man doesn't
know anything about it. I know a man from the Tenaktak
that always says he doesn't know anything about what his
father owes to somebody else. When he is asked to pay what
his father owed, he says, "Why should I pay what I don't
know anything about?" What can the other person say? But
everybody is afraid to loan him anything, and nobody will
borrow from him either. Nobody trusts him.[2]

When it was all collected, we told the Tlowitsis chief that
Lagius is ready to buy the copper. Tlatli-litla gave a feast
and called all the people of different tribes into Lagius'
house. While they were eating, Odzistalis, the other chief,
stood up and told the people that he is now going to ask Lagius to pay for the copper, for the time is up. Lagius says,
"I am all ready any day that you want me to pay for it."
Odzistalis says, "We want you to pay for that copper tomorrow." Lagius says, "You better not sleep tomorrow morning; you better get up early, because we will start early in
the morning."

The next morning, some men come along the houses and
say: "Wake up. Wake up. Come and watch the chief who is
going to buy the copper." When they all had their breakfast, they all come and sat down in the front of Lagius'
house. Lagius, at the same time, had a lot of young men to
take out the blankets from his house and pile it in rows—a
hundred blankets to each pile, starting from his house in both
ways, for his house was on the middle of the village. What
Tlatli-litla paid for his copper was four thousand blankets,
and this was all put down. The "pillow," which was now two
thousand dollars, was returned to us the morning that we
started to buy the copper. That made the four thousand
blankets that we could start with.

Odzistalis stood up and says: "I have now seen all the
blankets that we have been paid for the copper, and we are

---

[2] Here are sanctions that enforce payment of debts. One who does not pay
what he owes is economically ostracized. Unable to lend or to borrow, he
cannot participate in Kwakiutl social life. The principal means of obtaining
gratifications—sex, food, and social prestige—is all but taken from him.

not satisfied with the amount that we have seen. Knowing
that you are a chief and are willing to add more value to the
copper, we will ask a chief of the Mamaleleqalas to ask for
more," and he calls him up and he spoke and says: "I don't
see what I am going to say, for in my part I am satisfied with
all these blankets that are in a row, but for the sake of the
Chief Lagius' name we all realize that he wants to pay more.
So I am asking you, Chief Lagius, to pay more—whatever
you think is the right amount for my position." He was the
head chief of the Mamaleleqalas, and Lagius brought out
two hundred blankets and a copper worth a thousand blankets. He counted the blankets and says, "Now there is added
one thousand and two hundred blankets."

Then Nigia, the next Mamaleleqala chief, was called by
Odzistalis to speak. He got two hundred blankets and a
canoe worth four hundred blankets, but he stood up again
and said: "Thank you! Thank you! But you gave my chum
one thousand two hundred, and I expect to get one thousand
two hundred blankets, too," and he says: "I have brought out
this copper that I have paid for not long ago, and you all
know the value of it. Now you gain two thousand four hundred, which is double what your chum gained." Nigia stood
up and laughed and said, "Thank you; that is what I want."
Then the chief of the third clan was asked to get up, and he
asked for more in the same way. When he got through, Lagius got some more blankets and a canoe. The chief of the
fourth clan of the Mamaleleqalas was asked to stand up and
ask for more, and he gained two hundred blankets and a
canoe.

Then they started with the Tenaktak. They didn't ask the
Kwakiutl or Nimkis tribes because we was on the other side
—the buyers of the copper. They asked the head chief of the
Tenaktak to get up and ask for more, and he received two
hundred blankets and a canoe. Then the second chief of the
same tribe was asked to get up and ask for more, and he received two hundred blankets and a canoe, and so it went on
for every chief of every clan in the Tenaktak. Then the Matilspe, the Tsawatenox, the Kwekwesotenox, the Gwawa-

enox, the Hakwames. Each chief received two hundred blankets and a canoe.

Now Odzistalis got up and said, "All of you tribes have asked the chief for more, but Tlatli-litla isn't satisfied yet, and so we will return to the Mamaleleqalas." And one of them was asked to stand up, and he asked for some more. We sat down for a long time and talk together and say, "We don't know what he is thinking of; all the different chiefs has asked for more, and now he is starting it all over again." Finally my brother stood up and says: "I don't understand what you are trying to get at, for all the chiefs of different tribes have asked for more. We don't know how many more men you are going to ask to stand up. So the best way is for you to just tell us how many more blankets you want. If we could give you what you ask for, we will do it. If not, that is all there is to it. We won't give any more than what we can afford to give."

So the two chiefs of the Mamaleleqalas was asked to get up. Tlatli-litla told these chiefs how much more he wants, that he wants three thousand blankets more. They were afraid to tell us how much they want, and they stand up a long time talking. The one tells the other to do the talking, and Nigia says, "You do the talking." They are afraid, for it is a disgrace to them if they don't get what they ask for.

Finally Nigia begin to say: "This is not our own words. They are put into our mouths to speak by the owner of the copper. We have been afraid to tell you how much more he wants, for we know it is too much. This is the first time that such an amount has been asked for, but we feel, Chief Lagius and Chief Owadi, that there is nothing impossible for you to do. Nothing is too hard for you, so we will let you know what the chief says." He says, "There will be the boxes, and there will be the blankets that they wear when they give the potlatch, and there will be the belts and there will be the feather for the head, which all comes to three thousand blankets."[3]

All the people that was sitting down watching start a hum-

[3] In symbolic terms Lagius is being asked to contribute more blankets— some to represent the boxes, some the belts, and so on.

ming sound just like a bee, for they were all saying that it
was too much. My brother got up and said: "Now we know
what you want. So this is why you wanted to start over
again, because you want that much. You say that you want
three thousand blankets more. Ee-ee-ee-ee-ee-ee, Ee-ee-ee-ee-
ee-ee, where will we get that much? That is too much. The
best way for us to do is to return the copper to you, and I
will gather these blankets up and give a potlatch with it."
Saying that, Owadi walked home, leaving the people there
still talking.

The Tlowitsis people stood there looking down for a long
time. Lagius gets up and says: "Well, chiefs of your tribes,
we have heard the amount of blankets that you still want. I,
on my part, feel the same as Owadi feels. This has never happened in buying a copper before. I thought at first that I
wanted to get up and walk home, but what I think now is for
you to gather these blankets up and look after them your-
selves, and we will try and get some more blankets, although
it won't be three thousand—maybe half of that." The
Tlowitsis chief, Odzistalis, got up and says: "What you say,
Chief Lagius, makes things easier for us, because we were
frightened that you and Owadi talk together to say that you
will return our copper. That made us scared. But the way
you now speak, that makes us feel better, and we will gather
up the blankets and look after them ourselves." They gathered them up, and that was all for that day.

I went to my brother and asked him how many more blankets he has got. We walked in his house, and he begin to
count them. There was one thousand five hundred blankets
that he had. I told him that I'll give seven hundred and fifty
dollars. Lagius also has over a thousand blankets, besides
canoes and another copper, and my brother also had some
more canoes. All these together was worth over five thousand
blankets. I wrote it all down and showed it to Lagius. He got
up in his house and says, "Ah-h-h-h-h-h-h, Oo-oo-oo-oo-
oo-oo, Oo-oo-oo-oo," in a loud voice. He says: "Where will
Lagius be, if I fail to buy the copper? Where will I be tomorrow? I'll be going somewhere north or south for shame."

Then he went out of his house and speak in a loud voice, and tell everybody to be sure and get up early in the next morning and say, "Ah-h-h-h." And Odzistalis came out of the house where he was and says, "I have heard you, Lagius, and you are telling us to get up early in the morning." He says, "I will be bathing all night without going to sleep, and I'll be the first man to go and wake the people up." The next morning he was the one who woke up all the people and say that Lagius is going to give more. When they all finished their breakfasts, they all came to the outside of Lagius' house, and my brother says, "Now we will try again and give some more, but if you ask more than we can afford to give, that will be the last." And he called the young men to go and get the blankets from his house. They throw the rolls of blankets out of the window, and there was one thousand blankets.

When he finished that, I got my five hundred dollars that amounts to one thousand blankets, and Lagius also brought out one thousand blankets. Lagius says, "Wa-a-a-a-a-a, you have your three thousand blankets and everything you ask for—your belts and blankets and boxes and feathers is all covered now." Odzistalis got up and spoke: "I knew in the beginning that Owadi didn't mean what he says, and I knew that Lagius didn't agree with what Owadi said. That is why we kept quiet, for we knew those two chiefs was just fooling us and trying to scare us. Now we have our three thousand blankets and that is done. The copper is yours, Lagius, and you can do what you want with it. The copper is no more ours." And he says, "Wa-a-a-a-a-a-a-a."

My brother says: "You say 'Wa-a-a-a-a-a.' I'll see if I can find about five pairs of blankets in my house that is dropped down somewhere." He called the young men to follow him and brought out two hundred blankets, and he says: "Wa-a-a-a-a-a. That is finished." Odzistalis got up again and said: "I've already said Wa-a-a-a-a-a. Bring out that little image whose name is 'ready to throw.' "[4] So they brought it out and stood it in the middle of the road. "Now we will call our grandson," he says. "Let all the people look

[4] This was a little statue of a man about three feet high.

at him." He got Alfred, who was a little boy, and he cried
and didn't want to come. Tlatli-litla promised him fifty
cents an hour for standing there. So they put him on top of
the little statue. Then Tlatli-litla says: "All you Kwakiutls
look at your chief who is standing here now. He is now in the
midst of us all. Nimkis, look at your chief. He is now right
in our midst." And he turned to his own people and says,
"Tlowitsis, look at your chief." And they begin to sing the
oldest song they have.

Then Lagius got up and says, "Now, my grandson, you
will stand right in the midst of all the people that knows
you." Then he turned to the Alert Bays and asked the young
men to follow him, and my brother went toward his house and
called the Fort Rupert young men to follow him. I and my
wife went inside and got a hundred dollars. Lagius was talking on the back side of the road, and Owadi was talking on
the other side, and I had a man to talk for me on the front
side—all at the same time. The Tlowitsis people didn't know
which to listen to, and they was just looking around. When
we get through counting that, Lagius says, "Owadi, do you
feel that you are getting crazy like I am, to see who is standing in the midst of us?" And we all went in again, and kept
on doing that again and again, till we had finished all the five
thousand blankets we had. The people never said a thing;
they was just looking around. Then Lagius says: "Wa-a-
a-a-a. Now I know I have your copper. It is mine now. Now
I can do anything I like." And he brought it out and showed
it to the people. Then he turn around and says, "Owadi, I
don't want to keep this copper for myself. You better get up
early tomorrow morning and tell the people to get up early,
for I am going to give this copper to your brother."

When we bought it, Lagius' money and my money, my
brother keep track of how much we paid. We also keep track
of how much he paid. All the amount we paid for the copper
was 14,500 blankets. Lagius is the only loser. He paid four
times, besides all the things he gave, what I paid him when I
married his daughter—four thousand blankets for one thousand blankets. Three or four days after he sold the copper,

Tlatli-litla gave a potlatch to all the tribes except the Tlowitsis and distributed these blankets and money around.

The next day we all came together, and Lagius told all the people that the copper was on the back of my wife. It was tied on her back, and fifty ten-dollar bank notes was sewed on the blanket she was wearing. That money means it is the shoulder strap she is holding the copper with. The copper was given to me, and also the strap of five hundred dollars, and that day I gave the five hundred dollars away to all the other tribes, except to the Fort Ruperts. When he gave me the copper, Lagius got up and told all the people that he was giving it to me, and at the same time, he gave me a name, Hamdzidagame, which means, "you are the man that feeds other people." This name belonged to Mrs. Lagius' uncle, the chief of the Tlowitsis.

When I gave the potlatch with the strap from the copper, I changed my name to Hamdzidagame, which was the name Lagius gave me, and I gave Alfred the name Melide, which means "people are satisfied with olachen grease." At the same time, I put him in third position in my clan, where I was, and I went to the lower one—the ninth. From then on I received the gifts to him in potlatch myself and took care of him, but it was his position just the same. The same year, at Alert Bay, Johnny Whanuk also gave my brother, Owadi, articles for marriage, because my brother had married his sister. With these articles my brother gives a potlatch, calling all the same tribes that I called. At the same time he told all the people that Alfred's name will be "giving away of big coppers," and my brother put him in number one position in our clan, and my brother went down to his other position lower where he had another name. This was the sixth position in our clan, but he continued to get gifts for Alfred in the first position and take care of them until Alfred would be old enough to take them himself. If my brother had died before Alfred, then Alfred would have been the head chief.

In a marriage they have a box covered with a blanket, with red bark on it. When Lagius paid me the copper and all those things, he brought me a box, saying that masks are in there and all different kinds of dances. I can open the box when I give a winter dance and use his mask and dances. The masks all have their dances. I still have my box unopened, because I haven't given a winter ceremonial yet. Lagius also give me a little totem pole with all his crests on it. It was about seven feet long, and he always used it whenever he was giving a speech. I use it every time I give a speech. At the visit of King George at Vancouver some of our people went down. I wasn't feeling well and didn't go. Tom Johnson went with other people. He came to me to borrow my blanket and hat—a mask hat—and my totem-pole walking stick. He used that in Vancouver, and the stick was stolen from him there. A man wrote and say he saw this same stick in the States used by an Indian called Mathias from North Vancouver. The Indian agents are still trying to find out where this stick is.

At the time Lagius gave me this copper, he told all the people that he was going to give me different kinds of articles—that he was going to *hawanaka*, which means he is going to put things in a canoe for me to take back to Fort Rupert to my home. He brought out one beaded blanket, one button blanket, one silver bracelet, a headdress like the ones you see with ermine skins on the back, and other things. He says: "These are the kind I am going to give you, and you will call the people together and give them away. This copper will be the mast to your canoe." Then he went and collected all those things he promised me and gave them to me —dishes, pails, sticks with otter teeth in them, about six hundred of those. Any girl that doesn't have that kind, it is a disgrace to her; when she quarrels with other women, they say she has no teeth, and is not fit to quarrel with—she has no teeth to bite with. And he gave me some bracelets and a lot of those big beads—strings of them. I gave away all these things in a potlatch to all the tribes except the Fort Ruperts.

At my potlatch, I handed my copper over to my brother to sell, so he could give a potlatch. He took it and sold it for more than we paid for it. He sold it to a chief from the Nimkis tribe who was buying it for his daughter's husband.

When they come to buy it, my brother wanted more, but he and his daughter's husband says: "We haven't got any more. We will ask you to let us have our share in the potlatch in advance." They come and mention their relatives' names asking for their share. My brother gave each of this man's relatives one hundred blankets, and the Nimkis chief received one hundred blankets. When it comes to the one that the copper is being buyed for, my brother counted ten piles of one hundred blankets and says, "Those are for him." They counted all these blankets and paid them back to my brother to pay more for the copper. At the time my brother gave his potlatch he just had a stick and say, "So-and-so, you have already had your share." This man sold the copper to give a potlatch, and in his potlatch he give my brother a thousand blankets, remembering how much my brother gave him in his potlatch. My brother loaned these thousand blankets out to other people, always mentioning my name. He is going to collect later to pay for my copper, which he has already sold. My brother died before he paid me for the copper, but the stuff he loaned out is still out. If it weren't for the Indian Act, I could collect in my brother's place and pay myself. As it is, all that he loaned out is lost to me through the Indian Act.

When Tlatli-litla gave the potlatch with the blankets that we paid him for the copper, he used a crest which he got from the Kwekwesotenox—a big cradle ornamented with shells, ermine skins, and red bark about eight feet long. Early in the morning before daylight he called all the Kwekwesotenox into the house which he was using at the time of his potlatch. The Kwekwesotenox had about a hundred rattles—about three feet long, hollow inside, three to four inches in diameter and painted. They begin to rattle those, and Alfred was put into the cradle. Somebody else made the noise of a baby crying, and all the people are making the rattles go to stop him from crying. A man begin to sing a baby's lullaby. Then all the people standing on the front begin to sing it too.

All the people from different houses were awake, wondering what the noise was. Some women came in with only a

nightgown on to see what was happening, and they all want
to come to the house and stop the baby from crying. Some of
the people were so sleepy they didn't know what they were
doing, and just got up and came to the house. The Kwekwesotenox started over again, and after they got through they
got my wife to go and stand beside her uncle, Tlatli-litla.
The speaker, Odzistalis, told the three men that was standing behind the cradle to bring down the child, so Alfred was
lifted out of the cradle and was brought down. He had a
chief's headdress on him and shells hanging from the front
of him—four shells in a row. The speaker says, "Now we
have seen the baby of the chief's daughter." And he called
my wife's name. "We are all lucky to have a male baby
which you all see now standing here. This baby's name is
Yatlalasogwelaq." The name means that everybody has to
go and rock him. No position went with this name.

After they left Alert Bay, Tlatli-litla went home and came
back again and called all the tribes to go to his village, for
his wife is going to give him the articles to give away. At this
potlatch, when he received those articles from his wife, he
again put up this cradle and went through the same thing
that was done at Alert Bay with Alfred. When he was
through, his speaker, Odzistalis, stood up and says: "Now
you have seen that cradle there. The noble baby is sleeping
in that cradle, and nobody is allowed to come on the front of
this house and make any noise for four days, lest this baby
should be awakened and begin to cry. For if he does awaken
because somebody is making a noise outside, there will be
trouble."

The next day there was a potlatch on the other end of the
village, and there was a quarrel about positions by the Fort
Ruperts. There was a man half Mamaleleqala and half Fort
Rupert who wanted to change his position, but the chiefs of
Fort Rupert didn't want him to. The uncles of this man
brought out their coppers—coppers they had broken before,
and they only had the crosspieces of them—and says: "You
haven't allowed our chief and your chief, your nephew, to
change his position, and we are going to fight and put him

there. You, Whanuk, we hear you say that you don't want it. Now I am going to strike you with this copper to make you shut up." And he threw the copper on the ground saying, "You, Wilson, we have also heard that you are another one who don't want our nephew to change his position, and here is another copper for you, and I am giving it to you to make you shut up." They put these two coppers together and says to the young men to take these out to the deep water there and drown them. That means that they want to drown old Whanuk and Charley Wilson.

After this they went to the houses where they were staying. Tlatli-litla went into a Matilspe chief's house. I was amongst the people that was eating there. He came and stood at the place close to the fire and says: "I have come into your house to see you, for I know you have a big copper. Do you still keep that copper?" Maxwagila says, "Yes." Tlatli-litla says: "Bring it out to me. I want to see it." Maxwagila went into his bedroom and brought the copper out and handed it to him. Tlatli-litla looked at the copper, turning it over and over four times, looking at the back and the front of it. Then he says, "What is the name of this copper?" Maxwagila says, "The name of this copper is Dentalayu." This name means "people are quarreling about this copper," because it cost so much. Tlatli-litla says, "I will buy this from you." Maxwagila says, "That will be all right; take it away." And right on that place where Tlatli-litla stand, he begin to say right away, "Haw, haw, haw, haw." He goes around the house, and then he says: "I have told you not to make any noise in front of my house, where the baby is sleeping. You have wakened him up, and he is crying now. You have already been warned not to make any noise in front of my house. There is a sure thing that there will be trouble, and also that there is danger to the people that hears the noise and death to those people."

Then he went out and made a fire in his community house and all the people was called together. This was the second day of his potlatch, and they got this little statue that we mentioned before and put this statue on the rear end of the

house and then put this copper on top of it. He told the
people that he didn't want to do anything like breaking a
copper. "That was why I warned you not to come near my
house and wake the baby up, but since you have wakened him
up, today I am going to break this big copper for you two
that have been making the noise." And he cut half the top off
and another corner from the bottom and gave one part to
each of the Mamaleleqala chiefs that threw their coppers
into the water. Then he says: "Hap-hap-hap! I've eaten you.
You are all in my belly now."

This was a wonderful thing that he did. When we came to
Alert Bay about six months after that and all the people were
here to a potlatch, one of those Mamaleleqala chiefs died. He
wasn't sick at all—he just dropped down. The other one
went to Fraser River that summer, and he also died there
without being sick—just dropped down dead. They worried
too much about how they are going to get a copper big
enough to break for this chief that has broken a copper for
them, and that is why they died. They tried ever since Tlatli-
litla break this copper for them to get a copper from the
owners of other coppers, but they were too old to be trusted
with a copper, and were thought unable to buy any more
coppers.

About eight or ten years after this, Whanuk got a copper, and at his potlatch he told the young men here at Alert
Bay to take this copper out in front of the village and drown
it—all of it, the whole thing. This was long after the men
that drowned him with his copper had died, but he didn't
want to be spoken of as drowned by this copper. And about
seven years ago Charley Wilson gave a grease potlatch to all
the tribes, and he also got a copper and cut a piece of it and
throwed it into the water to drown it, the same as was done
to him, but he didn't mention the name of the man who
drowned him. He should have put the whole thing in the
water the same as Whanuk did. I don't see what he wants to
keep it for.

When Alfred was four or five, Tlatli-litla, chief of the
Tlowitsis, gave a flour potlatch—about two thousand sacks

of flour—and at this time he called Alfred his same name, giving his own name to him. He had a different name that he took at this potlatch; he gave his own to Alfred, and put Alfred on his position as chief of the Tlowitsis, because he was his grandnephew (grandson in our language) and he had no other children of his own. Mrs. Lagius' mother was a Tlowitsis and the sister of this chief's father.

A woman of the Tlowitsis tribe, who was getting old, wanted to put Alfred in her position, and she did at her potlatch. Her name was Hayugwis, and she gave her position to Alfred, and also her name. She was related to the chief of the Tlowitsis, and so to Alfred through Lagius' wife. This was sometime after the Tlowitsis chief put Alfred in his position.

Mrs. Lagius gave a potlatch when Alfred was about eight or nine years old. At that potlatch she gave him the name Maxwagila and put him in the number one position of the first clan of the Kwakiutl. This was her own position, and she continued to act in his place until he was old enough to take his gift himself. Lagius, when Alfred was about twelve, gave him a name and put him in his position in the Nimkis tribe. This was at Lagius' potlatch.

This boy Alfred, I thrashed him real bad only once. I told him I was going to if he did it once again, and when he did it again, I thrash him. He went away from here in a canoe that went to Fort Rupert, and we was looking for him all over the place, and we thought he dropped off one of the wharfs. I warned him, but he did it again. The next time he did it the same way with one of his relations, and somebody saw him went away, and we had to go after him and bring him back. When we got back here, I sent him upstairs to his room without any supper that night. In the morning I went up to him and gave him the thrashing I promised him. Before I give it to him, he promised never to do it again. I tell him he told me that before, so I give him the thrashing, and I tell him I give him more if he do it again. I find now that when I talk to them in a right way instead of scolding them, that they keep to what I say, and when I say anything they look at me, and, if there is something in my eyes that looks fierce, they say they is never going to do it again, and I says, if they do, they is going to get a thrashing. Alfred was only five years old then. Whenever I warned him after that, he never did anything else that was against my will.

When Alfred was about sixteen, he went to the potlatches himself. All of us gave a potlatch, at which we announced that we were through with Alfred, and that we wouldn't look after his goods in the potlatches any more. This was done by each of us when we wanted to give a potlatch.

I was about thirty when my brother built his big community house in Fort Rupert. He had the copper I gave him, and he was going to sell it to give a big potlatch. He sent out about six young men to look for a big cedar tree. Our grandfather, our mother's mother's brother, had a house with a big beam at the mouth of the Nimkis River. When my brother built a house he wanted to have a beam like that in his own house. When I was a small boy, I seen that beam on the top of the post. My brother got six men to go and look for a big tree. They cut it down at the entrance of Hardy Bay at this side of the hill.

The Fort Ruperts went there with the Koskimos to get this tree out to the water. They couldn't even move it, so we have to get the Nakwaktox to come over and help us. Still we couldn't get this tree out, so we hired the Alert Bay young men to go and help, and then we got it out. We had jack screws and put rollers on it to start and had skids all the way down, and when it started once, it goes right down into the water without stopping. We had cans of olachen grease which we used to oil the skids with. When it got out into the water, the Fort Ruperts, Nimkis, and Nakwaktox came home, and the Koskimos stayed behind with four canoes, to tow this log over to Fort Rupert. My brother gave a potlatch to these tribes the next day, and they rolled it up from the high-tide mark to dry land.

Then we begin to use axes and adzes to cut the sap off it, and those people that done it was paid for their work. Anyone that wants to earn some blankets comes along with his adz and works on the log. My brother put a blanket on the log, and when the men does all that's under the blanket he earns that pair of blankets. They also got logs from the woods at the same place for the posts. The people that dug the holes where the posts go, my brother paid five pair of blankets for each hole. They got the beam in place, and it was awful hard work. We jack up one end and put blocks under with boards on both sides, so it don't roll, pretty near the middle. Then we jack up the other end and put some more blocks under near the middle, so it will teeter. Then we gets on one end and pulls down and it moves easy, and the others put under some blocks, and so on, teetering back and forth until it is as high as the post, and then we roll it over on top of the posts.

When the beam is in place, my brother gives another potlatch, and all the other tribes came to Fort Rupert and helped with the building of the house. Of course, only the young men was working and the old ones only sitting down watching. When all the rafters and beams at the sides was put up, he gives another potlatch for them. Each rafter cost my brother five pairs of blankets, and when he had the roof up and the boards at the side, he gave a big potlatch. He had all the blankets in his house which paid for his copper. All the different tribes came in, and he gave also a feast and also a potlatch of bureaus, boxes, sewing machines, and everything like that. His wife gave dishes, glassware, and dresses to all the women. There was also canoes and boats with the bureaus and things he gave away when that house was finished. While he was giving these things away, we had dances. One I remember especially was a Hamatsa dance, and Ed Whanuk was the Hamatsa, who is our cousin, my mother's brother's son.

It took him more than a year to have this house done. We had that beam lying on the ground in the wintertime, and in the summer they put it up, and in that winter we had the big potlatch and the ceremonials at Fort Rupert. It was the biggest and the best-built house that I had ever seen.

CHAPTER IX

ADULT LIFE

WHEN we first come to Alert Bay, I start working in the sawmill. Whenever Dr. Newcombe comes, I stop working in the sawmill and go around to other villages with him. Sometimes we were away for a month and sometimes for a couple of months. When we come back, I go down to Victoria with him, and then we will put the names and story of all the things that he bought, and he write down a list of what he needs so I can find it when I come back. When I come home I find those things that he wants and buy them and put them in boxes and send them down. Sometimes somebody will be in the sawmill taking my place while I am working for Dr. Newcombe. I never know when he is going to call me. I'll find a letter in the post office, and he might ask me to come down to Victoria, or if he will be on the boat, he say, "I want you to go with me to Bella Coola," and I just go on the boat. Sometimes we would go to Quatsino.

It was Dr. Newcombe that took me and Bob Harris from here, and three men and two women from the West Coast[1] to the States. We went first to St. Louis to the Exposition. The men was doing some carvings there to sell; the women was doing baskets and mats. We had three or four Indian dances there. We used to make the people that came to see the dance pay so much to come in.

There is a good story about one thing in our dance at St. Louis. At the time all the big people of the Fair came to see us, we was given notice about a week beforehand that they were going to come. So we got everything ready—our dancing blankets, and a headdress with ermine skins on the back, and Bob Harris made everything ready for himself, because he was a Hamatsa. We kept Dr. Newcombe busy at that

1 These were probably Nootka Indians.

time, getting all the stuff that we wanted. There was a little
African pygmy that used to come and see us. He liked to
come because we always had bananas, and this little fellow
loved bananas. He didn't seem to want to eat anything else;
as soon as he come in, he look at the bananas hanging up and
say, "Huh—Banana!" Bob Harris wanted to make a little
man just like him, so I told him to come in every day and sit
down and eat bananas while Bob Harris was making a little
man with some bones and mutton flesh. He made it just like
him, and when it was finished it was put in an oven, and Bob
Harris looked after that while it was baking. Bob Harris
take it out and hold it up alongside of the little man, and the
little fellow would offer it a banana. Bob Harris was making
a whistle; he pinch the little fellow to make him squawk, until he made a whistle that sounded just like him. He made
the mouth of this thing to move; when he pinch the little
fellow, he watch how he open his mouth, and he put the whistle under the skirt of the little fellow he made, so that every
time he presses where the whistle was, he make the right
noise. He filled the inside with a tube of blood.

We went to the place where all the people was—they say
there was about twenty thousand people that came that
time. We was put to start first. We had a screen that was
painted in a square—about eight feet square. We told the
little fellow how it was going to be done, and not to tell his
friends about it or we won't give him any more bananas. We
had this baked mutton as a man inside the screen, where all
our dresses are. We begin with a Bella Bella dance; the
West Coast people all knew the songs, and they was singing
while Bob Harris and I was dancing. When we got nearly
through with one song, Bob Harris made a mistake in beating, and then he says, "Hap-hap-hap." I got behind the
screen and dressed as an Indian and came back and told the
people in English that the Cannibal is mad now, because
they made a mistake in beating the board, and we don't
know what he is going to do, because he is so fierce. The two
young men from West Coast came and held him—trying to
keep him from going toward the other people. Bob Harris

was struggling to get free from their hold. Finally he got away from them, and he ran around. When he got to where this little fellow was sitting, he picked him up and ran behind the screen and left him there. Then he took hold of this thing he made just like him and make it squeak and yell, and when he came out in front of the screen, it was yelling loud. Bob Harris came in front of us and set this little fellow in front of us and push his head down and bite the neck until out came the blood all over his face. All the little pygmies got up with their spears and was coming to kill Bob, and all the people in the audience thought sure he had bitten his neck off, but the guards just pushed them back and told them to sit down. The little pygmies just went home while Bob Harris was eating the mutton. I was the one that was cutting the flesh in strips while he was eating them, and crying, "Hap-hap." When he got through eating—some of us helped him because we were hungry—I looked around and saw there was no Indian in that place; they had all got frightened and went home.

I told the men in the hall that we have done a great thing that is only done in the wintertime, and that we are going home to our Indian house where we will try to bring him to life again. Dr. Newcombe never came near us, he was so scared at what Bob Harris had done. That was a murder, he said; that means he is going to be hanged. I told him to keep away from us. "You are a white man," I says, "and you better not come near us." I told the guards to go and put fire into our Indian house. While he was gone, we kept on singing songs, turning around as we go. People come with their kodaks taking our pictures; the guards couldn't keep them away.

It was evening when we get to our house and the house was already full of white people. Last of all the people that owned the Fair came in and sat in the front end of the house. All the ladies and gentlemen were sitting right on the ground with their silk dresses on—right on the dirt—because they were told by the guards that is the way the Indians sit. Dr.

Newcombe came over to us and want to have a talk with me.
I look at him with a strong fierce look on my face and told
him not to come near.

So we begin with one song and sing it, and Bob Harris
get up and go around the fire singing with the rattle in his
hand. Then he go to see the body that he had eaten and say,
"The bones are all stuck together now." I interpreted to all
the people in the house. Then we sang another song, and
then he got up and went around the house and went up to
where this little fellow was lying on a table. It was the little
pygmy himself, lying under a mat. He says, "He has flesh
on his bones now; the whole body is in good order." Then we
sang another song, and he went around again, lifted up the
mat, and felt. "He is quite warm now," he says. He came back
and we sang the last song. Then the West Coast men was
dancing over the dead man with their hands shaking while
we were singing. When we got through, Bob Harris went
around the house, still using his rattle, singing, and went
toward to where the little man was lying and lift up the mat.
He took the mat off, and took the little man up and sit him up
on the table, and he begin to look around stiff like as we told
him to do. Bob Harris took him down from the table and
took him around the house, holding him by the hand. And
all he say is, "Banana. Banana!"

Then they came back and sit down, and I got up and
spoke to all the people: "I am very glad to learn that our
friend here, Bob Harris, done this great thing. You all saw
him when he ate the flesh of this little man that is standing
by his side. This is the same man that was dead, and his
flesh was all eaten up. Now he has his flesh and his life back,
and now he is alive. And I am glad that there will be no law
that will come against us." Dr. Newcombe slapped his knee
and say in a loud voice, "Smart boys!" Then he got up and
made a long speech, telling the people about the Indians in
British Columbia and how they could do wonderful things.
When they all got out of the house, we took this little man
to his own people. When he got near their hut, they all got

up and ran away. They were scared, thinking he was only the dead that was eaten up, and he holler out to them, telling them that he is alive and not a ghost.

Bob Harris had a girl from the Mexican women whom he used to go and lay with. I had another girl in the same tent. Next day we went to see them. When we got into the tent they just rushed out and ran away. They didn't want us to come near them—a man-eater. Bob was called "man-eater" after that.

When we went in to sleep, Dr. Newcombe come in and ask us questions about it and try to find out how we did it. Although he brought the bones and the mutton, he didn't know how we did it. I guess he thought we wanted to eat the mutton right away. I tell him, "I don't know; nobody knows." I didn't let him know until he came back to Victoria how it was done. Then we told him all the story. He told Bob then he had thought he was going to be hanged.

After we stayed at St. Louis two months we was taken to Chicago—three of us, Bob Harris, Ateu from the West Coast, and myself. The others stayed at St. Louis. We went to the Museum there to put the masks in their right places. There was a bunch of statues looking like men from Fort Rupert—we could recognize them—which they didn't know what to do with because they was all naked. The Museum people was just about to go and dump them because they didn't think they should show them that way. So we found the Indian blankets—cedar bark—that the old people used to use and put them over them, and we put red bark on their heads and eagle down. There was also a row of people that was supposed to be the singers. We painted their faces in black and red—the same way as we paint ourselves at the winter dance. There were two Hamatsas (Cannibals) there which we also clothed with a bearskin, and neck rings and eagle down, and the Hamatsa head ring on his head. The women we made to sit around watching. When we got that finished, the head man of the Museum came in to see what we have done, and he says, "Well done." He wrote out a paper and put it on the door of the Museum, telling the people that there is a new thing for them to see in the Museum. He gave Bob $50 just for a present and gave me $75 and also the other man, the West Coast carver, who was looking after the West Coast masks. The next day they got me to stand inside the case—a big glass room—and explain the thing to the people that come, and to answer their questions. Some of the people would come up and shake hands with me, having money in their hands which they gave to me, besides what I was paid which was $7.50 a day.

Then we went to New York and stayed two months. We went to the Museum there and saw all the Indian stuff. But we didn't do anything; Dr. Newcombe just took us all over New York to see all the things there were.

When we came back to St. Louis, I found a letter from the Indian agent, telling me that my son Alfred was very sick and that he was taken down to Vancouver to see a doctor there. This doctor told my brother that he had diphtheria and wasn't allowed to get off the boat, so he was brought back to Alert Bay. Mrs. Captain Hughes, while the boat was at Vancouver, came to see Alfred and told my brother that her son was in the same way and had the diphtheria and the doctor told her to mix a brown sugar with butter and give to him three times a day or more, and she told my brother to do the same. My brother, Lagius, and Peter Edwards was with him, and they were not allowed to get off the boat as well. The next morning when he was taking this brown sugar and butter he felt much better, and before the boat left Vancouver the doctor came on board to see him. Alfred told him: "I'm all right now. What is the use of you coming to see me now? You never helped me any, only to tell me not to get off the boat. The Captain's wife is a good doctor—better than you." So they came back. He was all right when he got back to Alert Bay. When he was taken to Vancouver, this was the time the Indian agent wrote to me, saying that my brother and Lagius wishes me to come home right away. I gave the letter to Dr. Newcombe and told him I was leaving for home the next day. Dr. Newcombe wanted Bob Harris and the others to stay until the

end of the Fair, but they wouldn't. They wanted to come
with me, for none of them could speak English.

AFTER we came back to Alert Bay I used to go up to River's
Inlet and fish for the River's Inlet Cannery. When I first
went there, the manager told me to come back and hire some
Indians to go out fishing, and offered me so much for getting fishermen and fillers, and I worked for him quite a
while. My little education in English helped me in all the
jobs I got. When I go to River's Inlet, we go for six or seven
weeks, only just for the sockeye season. Mr. and Mrs. Lagius and my wife and children all go, and we stay in the
shacks that they built for the cannery people. The other
Indians go out fishing, but I have to stay in the cannery
and look after the women that are filling the cans.

In those days while I was hiring Indians for the cannery,
I was given authority by the manager to promise the Indians what I would do for them if they came to that cannery. I used to know beforehand what the price of the sockeye would be, and I would tell them that I'd give them gum
boots free or some raincoats or extra money, so that I'd get
the good fishermen for this cannery. I paid all their fares
up and back, too, and when I get to the cannery, I tell the
manager what I promised them. He get the bookkeeper to
write out all the promises and make me sign it, and then
it was sent to the head office. Before they start to fish, I call
all the fishermen. There were two men in a boat, and they get
fifteen dollars. When all the other canneries heard about it,
their fishermen begin to kick, and so they have to begin doing the same. Some time in January, I used to write to the
head office for advance money to give out to the fishermen.
That would be the time that everybody would be out of
money, and I go to my fishermen and tell them that I have
advance money if they want it. They all come to my house
to get what they want, and that is how I used to get all the
best fishermen.

WE used to go to feasts all the time—sometimes many times

in a week. Each man when he feels like it will call all his tribe, or maybe all the Fort Ruperts, to come and eat at his house. It used to be only the men and only those women that had positions that were called to go to the feasts, but nowadays all the women has their positions, because there aren't enough men alive to take the positions.

If I am giving a feast to the Kwekas nowadays, I call everybody—men, women, and children. When I was a boy this wasn't so. When I was a boy, my brother would only call those that has positions and are old enough to have positions and go to feasts. Whether you like a man or not, if you call a tribe, you have to call him. The younger men sit on the rear end of the house, and the old people on both sides. If it is dried salmon that we eat, the young men goes and roasts it by the fire and serves the food. The wife does the washing of dishes and shows the young men which dishes to use. After the salmon is roasted, the young men tears them up and puts them in the dishes. The wife of the one who is giving the feast doesn't eat with them; she does the work of picking up the dishes.

Sometimes my brother would ask all the Fort Ruperts to come, and then the Kwekas just come and look after things. All us Kwekas sit in the front end of the house. The young men of the Kwekas are the ones who cook the food; the old people just sit down and talk. The food will be served to the Kwakiutl, Walas Kwakiutl, and Kumkutis first, and the Kwekas last. All those that has positions are called to come to the feast. Such feasts are usually in the morning or in the evening, but not at noon because that is the time they are all busy working or fishing or hunting.

Those that is called to the feast sing their songs after they finish their first course—after dried salmon, for example—before they have their second meal. They sing the old songs of their grandfathers and great-grandfathers— potlatch songs. When there is a bigger feast than just dried salmon—if I have called all the Fort Ruperts together and I have bought about fifty boxes of biscuits and things like that—then there would be a feast song, and all those that

are invited sing their own feast songs. If it is a Kweka that
has called the other tribes, after the food is all served out
they will call upon the Kwekas to stand up and sing their
old songs, standing in a circle in one end of the house. They
will call the daughters of the man that gives the feast and
the baby—one of your grandchildren or perhaps your
youngest child, if you are giving a feast. You give this
child his first name—the four-days-old name—because that
is the time you would give a potlatch or give a feast to give
your child a name.

Sometimes we call just our own clan to feast. When I was a
boy, just men come to this feast. No woman without a position will be called, but a woman that has a position will be
called to that feast. And no child that hasn't been brought into
a feast like I was when I was a youth. I remember that Peter
Knox, when he was about six years old, used to be called to
the feasts, and I remember that he want to go out and play,
but they kept him in there. He was the youngest boy that I
have seen go and sit amongst the grown-up people; he was
called to come so young because he was the only child of
three chiefs. But every man has to be there whether you like
him or not. Even if you and he are fighting for a position,
you have to call him to the feast. I have heard of somebody
—I don't remember who—who was a chief of one of the
Kwakiutl tribes who had done something which the other
people didn't like, and so he wasn't called to any feasts or
to any dances. He is called by a name which means "he is not
liked by the people." Maybe everybody knew he was a witchcrafter, or maybe he speak evil against everybody, or maybe
the one he was quarreling with they all think is right and
he is wrong. That is the greatest punishment that they have
amongst the Indians for the wrong that they have done or
spoken. There isn't any way to get out of it, if they feel that
way about you. Giving a potlatch or anything won't help,
and nobody will loan you money or borrow money from you.
It will go on for a year or more until they forget about the
thing he did, and that is the time they will begin calling him
again.

Sometimes just the head chiefs feast together—the "chiefs' feast." This happens any time that one of the head chiefs wants to call the others to eat. The women, too, sometimes have feasts and just call the other women. There is another feast for the old men. One of the old people calls all the old men of the Fort Ruperts or of his own tribe to come and eat. They call that "the old people's feast." That is the feast I like to be in. I like to hear them talk about the old times, the old ways, the wars that we used to have, and all those things. They are about the best people to call. That is where you learn everything that they used to do in the old days.

Sometimes a man will come in my house and sit down to talk, and I will say I will go call his friends—all those that are about his age, his chums. That is important amongst the Indians. When a person comes into your house to see you, you wouldn't let him go out without giving him something to eat. If Billy McDuff comes and sits down in my house, I say I will go and call my wife to come and give him something to eat. Maybe I go and call his wife and then go and call the other men his age and their wives, and they all come to my house to eat. This is all by age, not by clan or by tribe. If Dan Crammer comes into my house, I call all those that are his age to come. If Billy McDuff comes, I only call the old people to come.

When I got married to my wife, I found out that my brother made a good pick. My wife and I lived happy together. I never had any trouble with her. She never scolded me, although I used to see my sweetheart all the time after I got married. Sometimes I stay away all night from her and go and stay with other girls in their homes. When I go home in the mornings, she just begins to cook something for me to eat and never say nothing. Some people goes to her and says they see me with a girl or a young married woman, and her answer always was, "He'll get over it." I used to go with others, but she never did. She was with her parents most of the time, and they were very strict with her. When I go with a married woman, I have to be careful, too.

I had one trouble here in Alert Bay. Before I go into the house where the woman is, I take off my shoes and hide them under the steps, for I had to go quietly in the house. In the morning when I went out, my shoes was gone, and I had to go home barefooted. Somebody must have seen me taking them off and take them away. About noon, while I was sawing wood, the man came and gave my shoes to my wife, and told her what I had done. When I came in, she says, "There are your shoes; where did you leave them?" I never answered except to say, "I don't know." She and her parents was laughing all the time. I had to get away from them. The man told her how I acted when I took off my shoes and how I act getting into the house.

There was one time my wife caught me herself. This was just before we had our first girl-child. There was a feast going on here at Alert Bay in front of the houses. All the people were sitting outside, and two young men was sent to go and call my wife to the feast. There was a woman washing her clothing near our house, and I thought to myself, "I guess I go with this woman." So I go behind the house and went to the woman and called her into our house and told her to hurry up for I am going to the feast. She came in, and we laid in the bed. While I was doing the work, my wife returned. She had forgotten something. She tried to open the door and I had locked it. She came around to the window and looked in and saw us right there and called me by my name that my children call me—Ossitlal—just looking through the window. I never answered. She says, "What are you doing?" but I kept on doing it, and she called me again. The men that was going to the feast was standing close and heard her. She stayed right there until I got through. I opened the door and went out, and she came in.

I walk as fast as I can, and when I get to the feast I go to a place close to my chum. My wife was coming around, and they sit close to me. She never spoke to me; she just sit down smiling. I guess the people were telling the others what happened. My cousin, Ned Harris, shouted, "Ossitlal, what are you doing?"—just what my wife had said—and kept on saying it. I just slipped down and lay down in my seat. I kept expecting my wife to slap me on the face, but she didn't do it; she just simply start smiling. When anything was done during the feast, everybody kept shouting, "Ossitlal, what are you doing?" Every time they talk about me, they say I am just the way my father used to be. One of the chiefs of Fort Rupert begin to wonder why they are asking me the question, and he says, "What is this that you are asking him?" He wants the men to tell him what I had done. Ned Harris says, "His wife caught him in his house with another woman, and she looked through the window." And everybody laughed. Gosh! it was awful. When we went home after the feast, some boys outside the house kept hollering, asking me what I am doing. My wife told this woman that they had been asking me the same question at the feast, and she just laughed. She didn't seem to care. My wife likes this woman because she always comes and helps her, and she didn't say nothing to her.

It is always me that goes and asks my wife if I can touch her, and I sometimes get refused if she is tired and don't feel like it or is sleepy or isn't feeling well.

When we lie with girl friends we lie on our sides. This is the Indian fashion. When we get tired of one side, we roll over and try the other side. We kiss each other, but we don't rub each other's hair or bodies—just hold each other while we are moving. I never do anything else. I never play with her breasts or her hair or anything. I just tell her how much I love her and how hard it is for me to stay away from her, that I am crazy for her and that I want her. Then we go to do the work. Maybe I whisper some love songs to her, and maybe she likes that and sings some to me. If it is a woman I see all the time, I only work once in a night, but if it is a woman I have a hard time to see, we do it twice—once when I come, and once when I leave in the morning.

I HAD nightmares when I was younger. I'll tell you about one I had when I was married. I was in bed with my wife, and the children was grown up and in another room. In my dream I see a door open and a big hand reach in from the door and caught hold of me on my face—cold. I tried to holler out and couldn't. For a long time I struggled, and when I got my hands from under the blankets I tried to get this hand. I got hold of it and took it off, and I was looking at it—a big hand it was. I told my wife, "Quick, get up and put on the light; I am holding a big hand." I thought the only way is for me to throw it on the floor. I threw it, and it was the table and I threw it on there. It was my own hand that I threw, and did it hurt! I says, "Oh!" She says, "What is the matter?" I says, "It is my own hand." Next morning I couldn't use my fingers at all—I threw it so hard. When I was a boy I used to have the same thing. It was always a hand clutching my face so I couldn't holler out, till I wake and see it was a nightmare. Sometimes I would see a black thing come down from the ceiling and come close to my face. When I try to push and strike it, it goes away, and I go after it and climb on something to catch it until it disappears in the ceiling. One time when I was first married a person that I didn't know came into the door holding a frog in his hand. He says, "You see this?" I says, "What is this?" He says, "Here, look at it," and he threw the frog right in bed with me. I wake my wife up, and we hunt through the blankets looking for the frog. She tells me I am crazy after I tell her I dreamed that. She thought I seen a real one.

My brother had a real one. He was sleeping in his room, and a man came over with a salmon. The salmon was moving —still alive. He threw it at my brother, and it went under his blanket. He was dreaming that, and in the morning he felt something beside him and found a herring. It must have been a rat or something that brought it there, but he says it was real, that he saw the man. This was long before I dreamed about the frog. When I was young, everybody try to find out the meaning of their dreams, but I never bothered about it.

IF there is a man and a wife and a baby, they all sleep in the bedroom. The baby maybe sleeps with them in the same bed, for they dare not put him aside. Being a baby, he is easy to get at by ghosts, and so they wouldn't leave that baby sleeping in that room while they are out sitting by the fire. I knew better than that when we had our first baby. We had him in a rocking cradle close to our beds. At night, if we want to go to another house carrying this baby with us, we get a charcoal from the fire and smash it and put it on the nose of the baby to scare the ghosts away, and also carry burned wood with grease poured on it.

A man and his wife sleep together, but when we had a baby I had another bedstead and slept at one end of the bedroom and my wife at the other end. Our baby was with my wife while the baby was taking my wife's breast. When she found out she is going to have another baby, I took the baby and he comes and sleeps with me. When the second baby is born, he sleeps with the mother while feeding on her breast, and then when they grew up a little more, we fix a place for them to sleep together. If they want to go and sleep with their grandparents in the same house, in a different room, they can. Even if they are boy and girl, they sleep together until they are pretty old.

After Alfred we had three more boys and then four girls. All the boys but Alfred died young. The girls grew up to be married.

My wife nursed Alfred ten months, and every baby that we have ten months, because that was the doctor's advice. My wife got feeding bottles when our babies were ten months old; she had half a dozen of them and gave them milk that way. My baby Alfred must have been about three years old when he stopped taking the nursing bottle. I was going over to Fort Rupert to visit my brother, and he wanted to go with me, because he liked to be with me more than with his mother, so I took him up. But I didn't take no feeding bottles, so he had to stop. He stayed there over two weeks. When we come back, he don't want no more of the feeding bottles.

I bought a little chair made like a toilet and a chamber

goes under it, and let him go without diapers. He must have been two years old then. Every once in a while his mother put him in this little chair and keep on telling him to pee or to relieve himself. The baby seems to understand and pee or relieve himself once in a while. Later, when he is crawling on the floor, he goes himself up to this little toilet of his and sits on it, saying the same as what his mother said, "tsi, tsi." I don't think she ever punished him for going somewhere else, but sometimes she scolded him. I'm the only one that do the punishing; all my wife used to tell him is, "Your daddy don't want you to do that." I don't remember him wetting the floor. He used to wet the bed, but pretty soon he learned to wake up in the night and call out he wanted to "tsi, tsi."

The only child we had trouble with was Jane, the first girl. She cried and cried all the time—day and night. She started doing this when she was six months old. I used to be up nearly every night, and my wife would get up too. We do everything to stop her. One day I took her to my brother's house. They have another girl the same age, and she begin to cry and his wife took this child and feed her on her breast. She begin to suck the breast, and when this finished she went off to sleep and slept all that night. My brother says, "Leave her here tonight." When she woke up again she begin to cry, and my brother's wife feed her on the breast again, and she go to sleep again. Then we found out it was my wife's breast wasn't full enough for this baby. I took my wife to my brother's house and got her to squeeze her breast into a glass, and I told my brother's wife to do the same. We compared the milk, and my wife's milk was just watery, while my brother's wife's milk was thick. So we find out that is why Jane was crying—she was hungry all the time. I came to the cannery and got a case of Eagle Brand milk and some more feeding bottles, and we begin to feed Jane on these bottles. From that time, we never had any trouble feeding her.

The younger sisters all lived on feeding bottles. When my

wife stop nursing, the milk just dry up. She used to have trouble at the time the baby stops because the breasts get big and very painful, but after a while it just dries up without her doing anything. Only she had some cloth to put over it while the milk is dropping.

I knew an old woman who had a grandson, and the mother of the grandson died at childbirth. This old woman took the child over and used to give the child seal fat to suck, and, after he sucks the seal fat, she makes him suck her breast without any milk in there. She did that for a number of days, and then begin to have milk, and she fed that baby until it was old enough to eat. That boy is fishing today— a big boy. Everybody thought that was wonderful, but the old woman say it was easy and a lot of them did it in the old days.

SOME Indian women are sick when they are with a child, but my wife never was. The weak women are always sick. Alfred Nelson's wife is always sick when she is having a baby. Every time she is going to have a baby she is always in bed. Sometimes you would think she would die, and then, when she has the baby, she gets all right after that.

When my wife had her first miscarriage, we were at Hope Cannery. She couldn't go to the hospital, so the doctor came over there and stayed with her three days. She went cutting the salmon berries in front of the shack where we was living. She say she never fell or anything—just that while she was doing that she felt something warm running down her legs, and she was bleeding. She never knew anything about how she got hurt. She almost died that time. This was after my second daughter, Beatrice. They had to leave a nurse with her. After three days she began to get well, but she wasn't allowed by the doctor to go and work at the cannery. The doctor say that she must have overworked—must have lifted up something. We were at Seymour Inlet when she had her last miscarriage. She didn't feel it the same as the first. She

just lay in bed for a while, and then she felt all right. I was
seining there for the cannery.

My brother and his second wife used to quarrel a lot. He
was married three times. This second wife was married to
him while I was a child. He just left her when he wanted to
have this third wife. He simply told her to get out of the
house—that he was going to get another wife. We were living here at Alert Bay, and I was living in the house I built
with my wife and children. While the second wife didn't
want to leave the house, my brother went to Fort Rupert
and got his third wife there. Before that, my brother arranged with the Indian agent at the time he built his house,
that he was building that house for my son Alfred. So when
my brother got married to his third wife he came over, knowing that the second wife don't want to leave his house, and
took out all the windows of that house and the front door
to Fort Rupert. His second wife didn't want to live in the
house without any windows and doors to it, and left it. When
she left, he came to Alert Bay with his third wife and bought
more windows and doors. The reason my brother wanted to
leave her was because she was sick all the time, and he was
liking this third wife a lot. She wasn't able to cook for all
the visitors that comes to the house from other tribes, for
it is always the rule of the chief to call visitors into the house
to feed them.

The third wife was a strong woman and could do all the
work that a chief's wife should do in housekeeping and cooking. But the people thought that she was not fit for a chief's
wife; she was low-down—not in the same position as my
brother. I was one of them that didn't like her. I always used
to go in and make trouble between them. I would tell her
anything that I think would hurt her. I would tell her she
is not a chief's daughter and is not fit to be the wife of my
brother, that she was the child of a man from Honolulu or
some place, and he was dark brown—almost black. And
that he is not a chief, and only her mother was the part of
her that was Indian, and that her father weren't married

according to the Indian custom or by the white man's way
either.[2] She used to cry when I speak rough words to her,
and my brother used to come to me and say, "Why did you
say such a thing to my wife?" I told him straight that I
didn't like her, because she wasn't fit to be his wife. I told
him that I have heard people making fun of him having
this wife. "I am ashamed of it," I says. He says, "She is
strong and cooks for the visitors, and the main thing that
she is able to bear us children." He was right in that. He got
two children out of her. After she had the first child, a girl,
I never used to go and scold her. After that she had a baby
boy.

WILLY HARRIS was our cousin—Lagius' father's brother's
grandchild. He was the first chief of the Nimkis tribe. As
Willy was too young to be a chief when his grandfather,
Tlakodlas, died, Lagius was the head chief. Willy was Lagius' nephew and would have become head chief when Lagius died. There was a time all the people went to Fort Rupert to attend to the potlatches there, and during that time
Willy came into my brother's house. I was married and had
six children then and he was about twelve years younger
than me. He tells Lagius and my brother he wants to get
married with a Kingcome Inlet woman whom he went around
with while they were in Fort Rupert. Lagius told him to go
to Fred Dixon to help him out with some blankets to use for
marriage. He was a relation to Willy.

Willy went out that evening to talk to Fred. What they
say I couldn't tell, but we all thought that Dixon didn't
want to help him. We knew he didn't like this Kingcome
woman for she was not in the same position as Willy Harris.
Besides that, she was going around with many other boys.
Lagius knew that Fred Dixon would not agree to Willy
marrying this woman, and that is why he sent Willy to go
and ask him to help. Lagius didn't want him to marry this

[2] Charley probably enjoyed this. His brother had kept him from marrying
a girl below him in rank. Now the tables are turned, and Charley feels justi-
fied in making his brother squirm.

woman either, but he didn't like to hurt his feelings. Willy came back and told Lagius and my brother that Fred Dixon didn't want to help and said, "I'm going away and leave you people, and I'll never come back to see you again." We all thought he wanted to go to River's Inlet where his mother was from. We all went to bed that night.

I and my brother got up the next morning, and my brother lit the fire. While I was splitting wood outside, a man named Monday Crow from Knight's Inlet came along, and he was not out of sight ten minutes when he came back saying that he saw a man hanging on a tree about fifty yards away from the trail. When he saw this man hanging on the tree, he got scared and ran back to tell us. I and him ran to where this tree was, and at once I recognized it was Willy Harris. He ran back and went into my brother's house and told my brother that Willy Harris is dead, hanging up on a tree with a rope around his neck. Everybody in the house begin to yell out and cry. I ran back, to where the tree is, with my brother. I held the body while my brother cuts the rope with his knife. When we got the body down to the ground, I turn and sees a lot of people there standing by, and they are all crying. Some were yelling, and all the village came running toward the place.

I told my brother that there should be a canoe sent to Alert Bay to notify the police about the suicide. The Indian agent came back with the police and the people that told him the news. The police try to find out right away why he did it, and nobody seems to know the cause. Some says that they heard him fighting and quarreling in the woman's house that night, and some says they think he was knocked off while he was fighting and was only taken to the place where he was hanging up, for we all saw his blankets stretched out close to the tree and the four corners of the blanket was twisted where it seemed like someone had been holding them. Everybody liked Willy Harris. He always spoke good to everybody and never quarreled with anybody. The policeman turned to me and my brother and says, "Who took the body down?" We told him how we did it. He says, "If I didn't know you and your brother, I would have arrested you, because you should have left him hanging there until the police come." I told him we didn't know this was against the law, and we were so shocked to see our cousin hanging there that we couldn't stand it. The Indian agent spoke and says he doesn't blame us for doing that.

All the people appointed Joe Harris, a cousin of Willy's, to take one of his positions in the first clan of the Nimkis, and Lagius appointed Fred Dixon to take Willy Harris' other position. They both gave a potlatch of one thousand dollars in cash to all the people who were at Fort Rupert. Both of them put my son in position where he takes their places when they die. Joe Harris took Willy Harris' copper. The next year Joe Harris sold the copper to Charley Hunt, and Charley Hunt paid ten thousand blankets for it. Joe Harris called all the people together and gave a potlatch, and he showed all the dances that Tlakodlas used at his potlatches. My son, Alfred, was the one that was dancing.

Some time after Willy Harris died, I was called to go and see Billy Sunday from the Kwekwesotenox tribe which are living at Village Island. Billy was sitting outside the village. He had his clothing all bleeding. I went to him and asked him what the blood was on his clothes for. At first he says, "I don't know," and laughed. I looked at his clothes, and they were soaking with blood. I ask him again, "What is this blood?" He says, "I shot myself." I says, "Why?" "Oh, I tried to kill myself, but I didn't kill myself." I says, "Where did you shoot yourself?" And he says, "Right here in the stomach." I says, "Aren't you feeling weak?" He says, "No." So I and Spruce Martin told him to get into the house where he was staying, and we ask him where he did the shooting. He says, "At the cannery wharfs." "What did you do with your gun?" He says, "I guess it is there yet." So we went to the wharf, and we found a rifle tied on a post, lying on top of a box. He had a string on the trigger, and we think he pulled the trigger with a string. I went and stood on the end of the barrel to see how far up on my belly it comes and it was just above my buttonhole. We went back and asked him to take off his pants so we can see the wound. We couldn't find any hole in front, for it was closed. We told him to roll over, and he got mad at us and says, "Leave me alone." He got up and just rolled over and got weak. Then we saw a big opening on the right side of the back bone, and this is where all the blood comes from.

I went to the police to tell him of what happened. He came over and examined the wound. Then we showed him where the gun is. He got the watchman at the cannery to see how the gun is tied. The watchman, Spruce Martin, and myself was summoned not to go anywhere. He went to the hospital and got the stretcher and took Billy Sunday to the hospital. About an hour after that he died. The doctor say his stomach was just full of blood and that it was too late for him to do anything. While we was asking Billy questions in the house why he did it, he only say he was tired of his life because he wasn't right, and doesn't know what he is doing sometimes. But he wasn't doing any harm to anybody, so the police say it was suicide. He was about my age. He wasn't married at the time. His wife left him after they lived together for two years, and he didn't have any children. Those are the only two suicides I ever saw. I've heard about others, but I don't know the stories. None of them I ever heard about was women. Mostly they were men Indians from River Inlet.

THERE was a man called Young Paul from Fort Rupert. He was a good deal older than me. The first thing we know, he was going around at night to some of the houses at Alert Bay and tried to open the windows in back of the houses. The people got suspicious and begins to talk about what he is do-ing—if he wants to steal, or whether he wants to get things for witchcraft. He was known as a witchcrafter, and there-fore the people were scared of him. The Indian agent was told about it, and he got a doctor to examine him. The doc-tor says that he is sometimes out of his mind, and the Indian agent tried to find out if he was doing anything serious. He find he never try to hurt anybody that he knows. So he left him alone for some months, when he started to do these things again. He made a lot of noise in the back of the houses, and kept some of the people awake. He takes a bar of iron and tries to open the back doors of the houses, so the policeman take him down to the asylum at New Westminster. He was there about four years when I went over to Vancouver to see him. I was allowed to have a talk with him. He was tickled to death when he saw me and begin to ask me questions about how the people at Fort Rupert are, and he says, "Why am I here imprisoned in this house?" I told him, "I don't know." I ask him if he knows about the people in the same house, and he says: "They is all bad people—all thieves. They steal each other's tobacco and begin to fight over it. One man tried to throw his shoes at a man I was fighting with and hit me instead, and broke two of my teeth." He seemed all right at the time I was there. I went to the man that looked after them and ask him how Paul was. He says: "Paul is a good man. He is the best of our patients, and nothing seems to be wrong with him. Only once in a while when these other patients are fighting he gets mad." I ask him why he is not sent back to Fort Rupert. "Why," he says, "nobody comes to get him." He says that his nearest relatives should come and get him and sign the papers—that he will be responsible to look after him. I says, "If any of his relations come and ask him, would he be able to take him home?" He says, "Sure, if he brings a note from the Indian agent showing he is some relative." I came home and told the people, and nobody seems to care to go and get him out. He was there until he died.[3]

At the same time, about fifteen years ago, I saw a woman who was sent down there. Her name is Jenny. While she was here, she used to act as if she doesn't know what she is doing. Her daughter used to say she would get out all her clothes, pile them up, and then put them in a basket and say she was going away, mentioning different places where she wanted to go. When she was alone in her bedroom, she take her blankets and cut it up in small pieces and put it back in

[3] Charley has done all that his culture demands. It is up to Young Paul's kin group to help him out. If they do not, it is none of Charley's business.

the bed. When her daughter come and tell her to go to bed
at night, they say she didn't want to sleep at all, and they
had to put her to bed. When they lift the blanket up, it was
in small pieces, and when they went to change her clothes,
they find her clean clothes cut to pieces. And she used to get
mad with them for touching her clothes. They say that when
she came downstairs in the kitchen, she break up the dishes
and then fit them together again. She had two brothers,
Harry and Dick, and her husband was crippled long before.
She was about my age. She was taken down to the asylum,
and at the time I went to see Young Paul, I went to see her,
too. She asked me about her daughter and grandchildren. I
told her they were all well. She says, "Why don't they come
and see me some time?" She speaks then as if she knows
where she was. Then she says, "You know it's very cruel of
them not to come and see me." I ask her if she gets tired of
staying there. She say she is not tired of it, because she is
looking after the houses of her grandfather. I now see she
thought she was in Village Island. She says, "I suppose I
have to stay here until my grandfather comes back." The
lady that looked after her seems to understand what we are
saying when we talk our language and was smiling all the
time. During the talk Jenny knocked me on the lap and say,
"Wasn't you awful in going after girls," and laugh and
laugh. Then she looks at me serious and says, "When I
wanted to marry you, why didn't you?" She looked awful
fierce then and I looked at the lady and motioned that I better go. She was holding my arms and wasn't she strong!
"You're going to marry me yet," she says, and I says, "Sure,
sure." The lady says, "Come along now; we'll go." She
cursed Harry while I was there. She wanted him to come
there so she could kill him. Harry was younger than she and
had a different father.

WHILE I was working for the Brunswick Cannery, before
Mr. and Mrs. Lagius died, I built a house here in Alert Bay.
The lumber was given to me by the B. C. Packers, because I
was working for them. I built a small house, 24 by 24, with

six rooms in it—three upstairs and three down. My wife and
I and my children lived there. When Mrs. Lagius died, Lagius came to my house and lived with us until he got married
again, and then he went back to his house and lived there
with his wife. When his second wife died, he came back and
lived with us until he died, not quite a year after Willy Harris committed suicide. When he died, my wife gave the potlatch for him, and she put our son Alfred into his place. She
invited all the different tribes in the Kwakiutl agency except
the Cape Mudge, Campbell River. They all came to the funeral. In the potlatch she gave out the blankets. That was because she herself held a position, and because Lagius didn't
have a son. She was young when she was put in that position, and it was not given to a nephew in case she should have
a brother later on. Then he would take the position instead
of her, but only when she dies, and that depends upon what
Lagius says.

When my wife called all the people to come to the funeral
of Lagius, it was told the people that her son had taken Lagius' position, and that he has the right to everything that
Lagius owns. When she had her first monthly, Lagius gave a
potlatch, and he says: "My daughter is grown up now, and
at that position where she is, I'll let that go to her now, and
she will receive the gift and use it herself. She is away from
me now and is a different person, and I'm not going to look
after her." This is what we call "to put a person away where
you don't have anything to say about what they do with
what they get in potlatches." From then on Lagius only received from the end of the clan. Before he had received first
in his daughter's position, and at the end as an old man. Lagius got this position from his father. If Lagius hadn't given
a potlatch when his daughter has her monthly, this wouldn't
have been settled. At his potlatch everybody that hears what
he says is the witness, and they all know it is she that takes
that position.

WHEN Alfred was sixteen, we wanted him to get married.
We went and asked Ewakalas, the chief of the Mamalele-

qalas, my brother and I, and spoke to him about my son getting married to his daughter. Her name is Lucy. When that was all arranged, we went to a potlatch at Turner Island, and there we got them to get married. We called the chiefs of the Nimkis, Tlowitsis, Tenaktak, Matilspe, Tsawatenox, Kwekwesotenox, Gwawa-enox, Hakwamis, Nakwaktox, and Lalisikwala—one chief from each tribe—to go and talk to Ewakalas about my son wanting to get married with his daughter. All these chiefs spoke at the potlatch in Turner Island. Before they went out from the house where we were staying, we put blankets onto the shoulders of these men; that was the belts for them to wear for their work in going to speak to this chief. When they have all spoken, the chief's answer was that he couldn't turn around and walk away from all these chiefs and say no, "I tell you now that while all you chiefs has come to me and spoken, you go back the way you came to who sent you and tell him that I have agreed." Then he also gave them blankets to put on their knees when they go back. When they all got up, each one of them was singing, and some of them was singing their great-grandfather's songs as they came out of the house. Some of them was speaking loud, to tell all the people that they have received a good answer from the chief, and that the chief has agreed to the marriage of his daughter. So they came into the house where we were and told the Kwakiutl people what the chief's answer was—that he has agreed. And that he tells us to go ahead any time that we want to, to get married to his daughter, and all the people that were in the house was feeling good and happy and talking. After that we gave them around a dollar apiece, all the people that were in the house, and we told them that we are going to hire all the different tribes to come to the marriage of Alfred to the daughter of the chief. They went home to where they were staying. Early the next morning, young men of the Kwakiutl went out in a canoe, and they came this side of Turner Island, and, before everybody got up, we heard a noise, singing as loud as they can—war songs. All the people got up wondering where this canoe came from. When they heard it was one of the Kweka

war songs, they found out that they came from me and my
brother, and that it was about the marriage. One man stood
up in the canoe when they got to the front of the village, saying, "We have come to hire you, Mamaleleqala; we have come
to hire you, Nimkis; we have come to hire you Tlowitsis,"
and so on through all the tribes. "You will come and help me
to get my wife." And then they came out of the canoe.

We called them into the house where we were staying and
give them something to eat, and paid them a dollar apiece
for their work, for that is part of the marriage ceremony.
Now we call two men to go and call all the people to come and
gather outside of the house where we were staying. The
speaker stood up and says that we are going to try to get
Owadi's son married to the daughter of a Mamaleleqala
chief. "Now we will try to get ready, so that we won't be upset in our canoes that we will use. We must all be ready not
to fail to get our wife." Then all the people says, "We will
try and get ready, since you have hired us to help in your
marriage." One of each tribe was sent to go and tell the
Mamaleleqala chief that we are coming now, and these were
also paid. When they get there, they tell the chief that we
are coming along now to get married with his daughter. The
chief's answer was, "I've already agreed, and my answer to
you today is to come along, for I am ready." He also gave
these men some blankets. They came back singing a war song
to where we were all assembled, and told us that the chief
says that he is ready and to come right along now. So we
gave out money to all the people that were there—everyone
—to put on for a belt around their blankets. They all
started—the chiefs of different tribes using their crests, that
is, holding their poles in their hands, and saying they represent their crests, although they have no carving on them.
Only the Mamaleleqalas didn't come with us because they
were on the other side and called by their chief to be with
them.

Our speaker asked Lagius and the chiefs of the other
Nimkis clans to stand up. Lagius spoke and told the Mamaleleqalas that they have come in their own canoe, which was

used by their great-grandfathers at the beginning of the world, when he used to go around to all the different tribes to marry chiefs' daughters. "And we are now using it. We are going to ask you to come toward us and listen to what we have to say." When he got through, the Tlowitsis chiefs were asked to stand up, and the head chief spoke in the same manner, and so on for the different tribes. None of the Fort Ruperts didn't speak this time.

When all the tribes, except the Fort Ruperts, got through speaking, a thing was put up that was made like a mountain where the ancestor of the Mamaleleqala chief was living. They say that sometimes the road going up to his house was flat, and then, when an enemy come to him, the road would slip back and be straight up and down, so the enemies couldn't get to where he was. This thing they had was an imitation to it—all made out of boards, about ten to fifteen feet high. Lucy, the chief's daughter, was sitting on top of this mountain with a mask of one of the wild women of the woods on her face, wearing a button blanket, and a man standing by her side is looking after the rope that pulls the board to make it steep. The speaker of the Mamaleleqala chiefs says to all the people that I hired, calling them by their tribal names: "Now you have come to get married with the chief's daughter, a descendant of the man who lived on that island," pointing to the other side of Turner Island, "and we have put it up in this village the same as that mountain. Now take care, all you tribes, because you are going to try to get up to this chief's daughter. If you don't get up to where she is sitting, you will not get her to be your wife, but if you do succeed, you will get her for your wife."

Odzistalis, the Tlowitsis chief, stood up and says to the people: "We have all heard what is said to us, and I also say that we will take care. Can we not get up to where the chief's daughter is? There are so many of us this particular time; there has not been as many as this before now. Besides that, Kwakiutls, take care and be strong for your chief, and you, Kweka, be strong and be brave for your chief who is going to be married. And you, Nimkis, be strong. I, for our part, the Tlowitsis people, is going to do the hardest thing for our chief that is going to get married. You, Tenaktak, have been hired, and you will all try all you can to get up to where the chief's daughter is, and you, Matilspe, will be the same," and so on to the other tribes. They started. Everybody beat the drums. All the Tsawatenox speech chiefs speak, saying, "We are big people, and we can't fail to get up there." We all thought that the boards would stay the way they were, but when he ran up to the first platform, he just stood and stared, because the board was pulled back by the man on top until it stood just straight up and down. He came down, and the Mamaleleqala chief gave him five pairs of blankets. All the different tribes had a young man that tried, and they couldn't make it.

After that a Nimkis young man got up and took off his shirt and tied up his belt tight and say that he is going, and the Nimkis chiefs say that they have a good young man that can almost fly like a bird. So he went while they beat the drums, and when he run up he never stop on the platform. He had been watching the others and just jump way up high to the top before the man could pull the board down. And there he stood by the chief's daughter. Then all the people on our side says, "Wee-ee-ee-ee, a-a-a-i-i-i." Then the Mamaleleqalas says: "Now you have done it. There was nobody before that could get up the road to that mountain. Now you have got her. Your wife will come down now. You have her. And you may also have this mountain that her ancestor was living on." This young man that went up there, received twenty-five pairs of blankets for getting up.

Then the Fort Ruperts, the chiefs, stood up and counted the money until they counted out $1,500, and there was eight hundred blankets piled up on the side of the mountain. Then the chief's daughter came down, and the Mamaleleqala chief said, "Now come and get your wife and lead her to your house, and also take these eight hundred blankets along with her as her mat." Then all the Fort Ruperts were called to sing their thanking song which says, "The chiefs will come on all sides of me to give food and blankets." There was two dishes, and before we went home the father of our wife says, "You take these home with you to use as a dish." This means that he is going to get some olachen grease to give to Alfred. And he says: "I am going to take my grandfather's name to give you. Your name will be Maxwa." When my son gives a potlatch with these eight hundred blankets, his name is to be called Maxwa. His name Melide that he had in the third position of our clan is put away not to be given to his son, but he stays in the third position with his new name.

Alfred took his wife into the house where we were staying, and that night they slept together. When we came away from Turner Island, we came to Alert Bay, and Alfred brought his wife and stayed in our house. When we got to Alert Bay, Jane, my eldest daughter, had her first monthly, and Alfred gave a potlatch for her. I had $250 and gave it to Alfred, and he gave it to his father-in-law secretly, and his father-in-law added another $250 to it and gave it to Alfred, and he gave the potlatch in honor of my daughter Jane.

Before the payment to him, Alfred died. After that my brother died. Alfred had a baby daughter from his wife, and that baby died soon after my brother. We didn't want to speak of the marriage, because they, the three of my family, died. When I was going to speak about it, Alfred's father-in-law died, too. Alfred's wife was the eldest of his children. His other children are grown up now, and I could go and ask them for the payment, but since the law has been enforced I couldn't do it. They keep on saying that the law might be amended, and we, on both sides, are waiting for that—so they can make the payments.

When Alfred died, his wife went back to her parents at Village Island. Some years after that, Odzistalis' son, a Tlowitsis, came to me and my wife and asked our permission to let him marry Alfred's wife. We says, "What have we to do with it, now that Alfred is dead?" He says he only thinks we might not let her get married soon after our son is dead. I told him not to think of that; we don't want her back from getting married, if she wants to get married. So she married him. This man died, too, and now she is married to Stanley Hunt. She comes and sees us. We are good friends, and she still looks upon me as her father.

When Alfred was married, his father-in-law gave him dishes and blankets and other things. Two of the dishes were the kind used in grease feasts. They represent that his father-in-law is going to buy a copper for Alfred to sell and give a grease feast. In this case my son died, and his wife's father died also, so the grease feast didn't come through, but all the money that I gave his wife's father is not paid yet on account of the Indian Act. Although the father of his wife is dead, his son would have finished the promise, but they couldn't do anything on account of the law. If we do, the Indian agent will go after us, and he has threatened those boys if they pay me they will be arrested.

WHEN Alfred died, all the Nimkis people went to the front of my house, and a man called Johnny Drabble stood up and says that they are very sorry for the death of Alfred and that they will show how sorry they are by his coffin and his tombstone and all the stuff that he is going to wear. He put a mat down in front of my house and put $15 on it. Then he told all the Nimkis people to put in what they think they could. Some of them put in the same, some put in $10, and it all came to $650. When that was finished, they went to Mr. Cook to order the coffin, for which they paid $175. They also ordered the monument, which didn't come for months, for they have to get this stone from the States. They bought all the clothing and blankets, and there was about $40 left. Then they got two twenty-dollar gold pieces, and they went into the house and put one gold piece in his right hand and one in his left, tying them on. They also bought two watches —one for each side of his vest—and a chain.

The morning when he died we sent a gas-boat to go around and tell the other tribes to come to the funeral. They came the same day and stayed here over night.

The next day the coffin came. Everybody came to meet the

boat, and they took the coffin in front of my house. The young men went in, opened the front window, took him out through the window, and put him in the coffin. Then they took him to the church and buried him. That evening they all went into a community house and sang lamenting songs that they used to sing for their chiefs in the olden days. After they get through singing, each man from each tribe spoke, making comforting speeches. A mask was brought in like at my brother's funeral, and it was the same mask—the Thunderbird. After this I gave them money, and his sisters took his positions at the potlatch which I gave that night. I gave $500 in that potlatch.

I gave them the positions that belonged to Alfred. My brother hadn't given the potlatch yet that put Alfred in his position with the name Owadi.

My brother died a year after this, broken-hearted. He loved Alfred just like his own son, although he had a son of his own, but Alfred was the eldest of the boys that we had. His son was only about four years old when my brother died. Before he was born, my brother put Alfred in the way to be his heir at his potlatch. This boy died about two years after my brother.

When each tribe was coming to Alfred's funeral in their gas-boats—three or four gas-boats coming tied together—the people were singing their songs. Each tribe sings four songs. The Nimkis and the Fort Ruperts were on the outside of the village singing their songs at the same time, while all the women in the houses were crying. The Mamaleleqalas came in first, singing as they came, and then the other tribes followed, all singing in the same way. The Tsawatenox came in last and also sang four songs. We sang four songs every time a tribe came in—one song from the Kwakiutl, two songs from the Kweka and one from the Nimkis. When they came they went into the houses to have something to eat, and the funeral took place after that.

We will take the Tlowitsis speech which was given by Od-zistalis that night:

You Mamaleleqala tribe has finished giving your speeches, which was all true, regarding how Alfred stood amongst us all. The Nimkis people has also spoken of their own chief, and I feel that they have felt very sad about their chief. Now we Tlowitsis people will try and give a speech. I feel for myself that I could not do this, for we are so sad. We feel badly because he was the one that was going to take our chief Tlatlilitla's position; he was going to be our chief. You Kwakiutl people, you see how we all feel and you know that you are not the only people that have lost your chief. He would have been your good chief, and a good chief of the Nimkis, and also our good chief. We all felt very badly about him, for we all wished that he had lived to old age. I for my part will try and comfort you and show you that we are not born into this world to live for a long time; we are all born to die. He is not the only chief that has died. Alfred has a child of his own, and Alfred has four sisters that are living yet. When they get married, we wish they will have boys to take our chief's place. You will have nothing to regret about. You have given potlatches, and have shown him to all the tribes, and have put him in his position. Lagius has put him in his position, and Mrs. Lagius has also put him in her position, and all of us would have done the same if he had lived longer. We would all have looked upon him as the biggest chief amongst us all. So I ask you all to try and.not feel so bad, although we will never forget him for all his goodness and kindness to everyone. He didn't look upon others to be lower than him. He went to old people and to young, and talked with them in the way that a good chief does. I don't think that we will ever have a chief like he was.

Then he sits down.

CHAPTER X

LATER YEARS

I WAS about fifty at the time my older brother died. He was about eighty when he died. He wasn't sick; he went to bed and never got up again. Then all the other tribes remembered what he said in his potlatch, that I am the one to take his place. I sent three gas-boats to all the different tribes to come over to Alert Bay and help us to bury him, for he was too heavy to be buried by the Fort Ruperts and the Nimkis. They all came and buried him. I gave a potlatch, and everybody received their gifts. At that potlatch I became the head chief of the Kwekas. I was called after his name, Owadi, and all the things he had is to be mine—the robe he uses in his potlatch, the talking stick he holds in his hand while giving a speech, and the whale headdress. All these I used in my potlatch after the funeral.

From then on I have been giving potlatches. I have put my grandsons in their places ready when I die. My eldest grandson I put in my place as head chief, and the others in my other positions. I have told all the people about it, so that there will be no argument about it after I die. That's the way the Indians do before they die. Each of them has his own paraphernalia to use, so that they won't try to take away each other's. They have their own names. If I had any coppers, I would give them each one. Coppers have different prices, and I would give the eldest one the biggest copper. They would sell them when I die, to give a potlatch with them. My brother used to have eleven positions, and in each potlatch he used to get eleven gifts. I used to have three, and in any potlatch I used to get three gifts. These places which my brother had I could have had when he died. I passed them around to my children. That is always done whenever anybody dies. It is given first to the son, then the grandson, and then the nephew, and the oldest of each comes first.

When I gave the potlatch after he died, I gave his positions to my children, but mine I kept for a while. Before they are old enough to take care of their blankets, I take them myself. When they are old enough to look after themselves, I give another potlatch and call it that one's potlatch, and I tell the people that he is going to take and keep the things for himself.

When my brother died, I sent three gas-boats to call the people together, telling them that the chief is dead, and that we Fort Ruperts and Nimkis are not able to bury him by ourselves. A big chief is too heavy for two tribes to lift the coffin, and it needs all the other tribes that knew him to be a great chief to come together to bury him. They all came the same day, and I called them into a community house in the evening. I gave them something to eat. Then all the chiefs from the various tribes takes turns giving a speech about what my brother has been doing in his lifetime—how good a chief he has been and how often he has given a potlatch. They say that all the people will miss him for the goodness to all the people that he did, and that he has been watching the beach in front of the village for visitors from other tribes to call them into his house and feed them and look after them as long as they are in his house.

The speeches start from the Mamaleleqala's chief. Then the Nimkis chief speaks, then the Tlowitsis chief, then the Tenaktak chief, then the Matilspe chief, then the Tsawatenox chief, then the Kwekwesotenox chief, then the Gwawaenox chief, then the Hakwamis chief, then the Nakwaktox chief, then the Tlatlisikala chief, and finally the Koskimo chief. After they finished, the three Fort Rupert chiefs stood up. One chief of each of the three tribes besides the Kwekas told them that we are downhearted for there will be no other chief that will do the same as he has done for all the various tribes, and also for his own tribe. "We will miss him," they say, "and we will always miss him who has been so good to us all, even to the little children. He has never spoken bad against anybody. He has always tried to lift other people's names—not trying to push them down but always doing his best to help them in every way. As you have heard him in his last potlatch giving his name and positions to his brother, now we will call him our chief's name, Owadi, and he will look after the other places to give around to his grandchildren, and he will be the Kwekas' head chief until he gives it to his oldest grandson, which will be told to everyone. Tomorrow we will go and bury our chief. We will put up his potlatch post in the graveyard to show everybody that he gave the biggest potlatch that has ever been known."

The next day we buried him. He was brought into the church first. The church was full of people inside and out. We had some men from the different tribes that knows the names and places of their own people to go and write out how much each person will get. After the funeral, they all come to the community house and begin to sing what we sing when a chief is dead. After that, in order, they sing their own potlatch song. After they finish, the Fort Ruperts sang four songs, and after that we sang my brother's potlatch song. Then money was given out to all the people. We paid the men that dig the grave, those that carry the coffin, those that put up the pole, and all the owners of the gas-boats that brought the people. After that, while I was giving away the money, each of the chiefs of the different tribes gets up and calls out my new name, and then they went out and went home.

The Indian says that the soul stays with the body while he is alive, and when a person dies his soul becomes a ghost. The ghost lives until he dies, and then goes to another world or returns to his relatives and comes to be born again. If he don't return to his relatives, he goes to another world. We call this the second death. They say this second death is long after the first and is when he has rotted and decayed. I've heard them say that there is a special part right in the head, where the soul, or that which makes you alive, is. When they took the heads of enemies, they used to take the skin off and dry it and keep it. These dried hair and skin they used to put on the blankets of the Hamatsas in the olden days. A warrior used to hold these skins in part of his ceremony. If they have no skins, they have hemlock twigs tied in a circle. He holds these to represent the heads of those whom he killed. If he killed two, he will have two. If he killed ten, he will have ten. It is only to show people how brave he was.

Now about my brother and how he died. He went to bed, and in the morning I went to call him to come and have breakfast with me in my house, as we were going to Village Island to see my son's daughter. My son had died maybe a month before this and we was going to give some potlatches. We was going to get my son's daughter to come and take his place. My brother wanted to have this all proved, because he could feel his heart breaking on account of my son's death. I went in and asked him to come to breakfast. He never answered me. I took his shoulder and shook him. I begin to feel he was stiff already. Some people was walking outside, and when I told his wife they heard her cry. They came in to see what was the matter, and they went out and told everybody in Alert Bay. They all came and stood outside my house. It was snowing at the time. I called them into my house, and some into my brother's house, and I told them to send the gas-boats to get all the tribes to come.

Some of the young men of Alert Bay fixed his body. They washed him, and put his suit of clothes on him, and wrapped him in four new Hudson Bay blankets. Then they took him outside through a window. They didn't want to take him out the door. They say that if he is taken through the door, all the family will soon go after him. He is put in the coffin outside, and was brought to the little house in back of the church. Then people came to see him—just relatives to look at him—the women crying and singing lamenting songs. They cried real loud, mentioning the dead name and how great a chief he was and how they would miss him. If we had had time, it would have been four days after, but this particular time the people had to go home, so we did it right after the funeral. After all the other tribes sung a lamenting song, the Fort Ruperts sing their song.

Then the chief of the Fort Ruperts told the people that they are going to call this chief that has died to come and see them. They say they will call him by all his crests, because we don't know which crest he has returned to. They says, if he does come, be stronghearted when you see him, so that you don't cry, because it is a very sad thing to see which crest he has returned to. One of them spoke in a loud voice, saying, "Chief! Come back and look at all these people that look upon you as their chief." This he says four times. The fourth time, we hear a whistle in the woods coming from the right side of the community house. The chiefs go out and come in again, and tell the people they have seen which way the chief has gone and say they are going to bring him in.

They come back surrounding a mask which a man has on his head covering his face. He comes to the door, where all can see the mask. The people open a path so that everybody can see him, and they see it is the Thunderbird man. He keeps on dancing around the front end of the house inside. Finally the Thunderbird opens his beak in four places, and it becomes like a sun mask, which is another of my brother's crests. All the points are sticking out in four places, showing inside it a man's face—a wooden face all ornamented with abalone shells. The parts close in again, and he dances to the back end of the house. The chiefs follow it with eagle-down feathers in their hand and keep blowing them toward the mask as it moves. When it gets to the back end of the house, it opens up again and lets the people see the face. From there he comes around to the other side of the house to go out.

While he is in the house, the Fort Ruperts sing a ceremonial song that belongs to the Thunderbird, and when the mask is going out of the door, all the Fort Ruperts make a yelling noise—"Wa-a-a-a-a-a-a-a-a!"—four times. Then it disappears. During the time it was inside, nobody makes any noise around the house. You couldn't hear anything except the Fort Ruperts singing. They keep quiet, knowing that the chief has returned to the Thunderbird and will never return again. Our chiefs watch and tell the people that they have seen which way he is going, and now we all know to which crest he has gone to. The Thunderbird has come to fetch him back to his own, what he was before he became a man. The Thunderbird is our crest on our mother's side. Our mother belonged to the Nimkis, and the Thunderbird was her crest.

About two weeks later, somebody died—I don't remember who it was—and we all went to the dead man's house. All his relations were there, and the Fort Rupert chiefs made speeches, and I made the second speech. I almost cried that time. I feel like choking. I think of my brother who used to make the speech. Although I heard him do it over and over again, and I knew how to put the speeches together, it was very hard at the beginning to make a speech amongst all the different tribes who were listening. From that time, I always make a speech in different ceremonies, for I have been taught how to put the speeches together in different ways, and taught how every man stands in his position. It was hard the first time, but now I have written down in my head what to say, and it seems to come easier every time.

I felt very bad when my brother died. I was left all alone. I and my wife just stayed in the house. People would come in to comfort me, telling me to just look around to the other people, and there was none of them that didn't have the same trouble as I had. I guess we stayed in the house like that more than a week. In the olden days, when I was young, I remember that when anyone dies, the relatives stays in the house for four days after the funeral. The fourth day is the time that the people gathers together to go into the dead man's house to comfort the son or relatives of the dead. After all the people finish comforting, the son begins to talk and tells the other chief he is going to have a dance to wipe away his tears. When he gives a potlatch, that means he has forgotten the dead and will go around with the other people. In those days, when a chief dies, nobody will make any noise or have any potlatch or feast until the fourth day after the funeral, and this man will be the first one to give a potlatch. They were very careful not to hurt the feelings of the dead's relatives in the old days. Now they don't seem to care; they play about and even make noise in front of the dead person's house. It was different when I was young.

The time I have a potlatch when my brother died, I was arrested for it about three months after. I went to the jail outside Vancouver for paying the people for helping at the funeral of my brother. I was sentenced for three months, but after I had been there for six weeks Dr. Newcombe came to see me and got me a parole from the Governor of Victoria, and they let me out.

When Jane was sixteen, two years after she had her monthly, she married Arthur Shaughnessy from Kingcome. This was after the law was enforced, so they didn't go through all the ceremony that they did for Alfred. Jane and Arthur went to the church and got married there. The money, which was $1,000, that Arthur gave me was given privately, and only the chiefs of the Tsawatenox was present. This was done in my house here at Alert Bay. Arthur's father was chief of one of the clans there. After they got married and come out of the church, they came to the day school and had a wedding feast there. All the people went in and feasted. After that they begin to dance in the white man's way and played games. When we got through there, I stood up and said that on Saturday everyone would go to the show free, that I will pay whatever it cost. That was the first time Dr. Mandy showed the moving pictures here. Mr. Corker, the minister, got up and says: "We thank our friend, Charley, for inviting us to the show. I will show my magic lantern pictures on Friday, and I am going to start at eight o'clock p.m. sharp." Everybody laughed because he was talking our language, and we don't use the word "sharp" like that.

After this feast, we came to the store, and I bought fifty boxes of apples, ten boxes of oranges, five pails of candy and cakes, and soft drinks, chewing gum—everything. All those things cost me $300. All the things they had at their wedding feast cost me $250, and to have all the people go to the show cost me $94. All the old people didn't go to the show, so

I got Arthur and Jane to go around to them and give them fifty cents each which was how much it cost to go to the show. Altogether it cost me for the show $140.

The name that was given to Arthur came from Jane's mother's side—Lagius, the name of my wife's father. One position from the Nimkis eagles went with this name. So Arthur has this position now, and is called Lagius.

Four years ago, old Whanuk, Peter Knox, and others from Fort Rupert had a meeting in my house, and I told them that I was going to pay Arthur. I mention the name of my copper which a man from Kingcome Inlet took from me and promised to pay for whenever I wanted him to pay. The name of the copper means "raven." Another one, called "too big a whale," was in the hands of a Gwawa-enox man. I told them that I am going to sell these—one for money and the other for articles. When I told them, they want to call the chief of the Tsawatenox. So Arthur went himself to call them. When they came in, old Whanuk got up, holding another copper, and says to them: "Thank you for coming in, for this is a great thing that we are going to talk about, which has not been happening these days, now that the law has been enforced. Owadi wants to pay Arthur for what he has paid him at the marriage of his daughter. This copper called 'too big a whale' you will sell, and get articles from the Gwawa-enox chief for this copper." And he called one of the chiefs to come and take it. When they have taken it, he picked up another copper and says: "This is the 'raven' which Tlatli-litla took from Owadi. Now you will sell this one for blankets to give a potlatch with." Then he picked up a box covered with a blanket, and he called his son, Ed Whanuk, who is a Hamatsa, to come there and carry this box, which is going to be given to Arthur Shaughnessy. He got up and held this box while Whanuk called one of the Tsawatenox to come and fetch it. They called one of their Hamatsas to come and take the box. Old Whanuk says that what is in that box is a winter ceremonial, and also potlatch names during the summer, which we will tell you when you have sold this copper. Old Whanuk says that these two chiefs were all ready to pay Owadi for the coppers, but instead Owadi is just giving them to Arthur Shaughnessy to sell.

About a year after that, Arthur went to Kingcome Inlet and asked those men who had the coppers and were going to buy them to buy them right now, and so they bought them from him. You see, I actually gave the coppers to Arthur, for I didn't want anybody to know that I was paying him. He sold the "raven" copper for thirty-three thousand blankets and the other copper for all kinds of articles which came to the amount of twenty-five thousand blankets, and he gave that to all the Kingcome people. Before he did that, he made me to write down what dances and masks and names were given to him in the box. So I did, and he used all those in his potlatch. There was no position went with it, but at his potlatch he mentioned the position that my wife gave him at his marriage and the name Lagius. He gave the name Lagius to his son, Alfred, and now Alfred has that name and that position. It has come back to the same family again, for Alfred is my grandson.

Arthur got $29,000 from those coppers in return for the $1,000 he paid me, but I didn't pay that much for those coppers. Lagius and I paid two thousand five hundred blankets for the "raven" copper, and the other copper was amongst the payment for the copper that my brother sold—three thousand blankets, which altogether amounted to $2,750. Both the chiefs that bought my coppers paid much more for them because they had broken those coppers for other chiefs. By paying more for them, they beat the other chiefs.

Besides this that I paid to Arthur, nearly every year I had to pay him something to give a feast. During that time, together with my wife, I have given him more than that $1,000 he gave me—just for feasts. Once or twice he gave me money secretly, and I added to it and gave it back to him. At the time Alfred was born and begin to crawl about, I gave his father money as a bandage to his wounds. Even if Arthur was not here in Alert Bay, if anything happened to Jane's children, she gathers up her clothing and says that Arthur is going to give a potlatch for his son's wounds.

Jane and Arthur had three children. The first is Alfred, then there was a baby born that died directly. Then came Rita and then another one that died when it was a baby. Jane died before I paid Arthur back. She had a sore throat and could hardly talk, and she died of that. I got out $300 and went around to the houses and gave out the money. That is, I sent three men to go around and give some to everybody who is here at Alert Bay. If the Indian Act hadn't been enforced, I would have called all the people here for a potlatch, and we would have gone through all the ceremonies. As it was, she was buried in the white man's way. When we went home that night, all the chiefs of the people that was here gathered themselves together and went into my house privately and comforted me and my wife. Then we announced we were going to put eagle down on their heads, which means we are going to give the money around. On the fourth day after her death, the three men went around and give out the money—the same amount to everybody. Alfred is the only boy that grew up to get married, but all four of my daughters got married.

Beatrice was my next oldest daughter. She married Jimmy Wadhams from the Tlowitsis. He came here with his near relatives to give me the money. All the Tlowitsis came to Alert Bay, but only the relatives came to my house. They gave me $450 to marry my daughter and $100 to Big Sam, who is one of my wife's relatives. When Jimmy Wadhams want that to be paid back, I and those three will work together and pay him. The next day they went to the church and got married. Jimmy is waiting for the time when the Indian Act is amended—for the Indian agents are promising all the time that it will be amended—so the potlatch and payment can be done in the right way. Beatrice had five children—all boys, all living. Three of them are in school. One is living with the father's mother and the other is gone to the Preventorium since last October. Beatrice died two years ago —of t.b. She got cold sitting up on the deck of a gas-boat coming to Alert Bay in rough weather. She was all wet when she got to Alert Bay, and she got cold and was coughing for

a long time, and it turned out to be t.b. She was a healthy,
stout girl before she took cold. I gave a potlatch at her first
monthly, too. This was done privately—not publicly like
Jane's. My wife gave the potlatch for my third daughter,
Agnes, when she first got the monthly. That was done privately, too. When Violet got her monthly, her mother also
gave one for her that was done privately. That was done by
sending people out to go around with money. One is carrying the money, and one is carrying a book where the names
are written and how much is coming to them, and the one who
is carrying the book tells the other how much is to be given.

Agnes was married in church—not in the Indian way. She
married Herbert Cook, a Nimkis. He is fishing now, and I
am living with him. She has six children living. She had one
more, but one of them died. Herbert Cook didn't pay me
anything; it was all done in the white man's way.

WHEN I was getting Indian fishermen and women to work
in the Brunswick Cannery, I used to get a bonus for doing
that, as well as my wages for looking after the men and
women. I used to get very tired when the cannery was working from morning until eleven o'clock at night. The China-
man boss told me to come and drink with him, that it would
help me from getting so tired. I had never drunk before, as
Mr. Hall had told me it would hurt my health. When I drank
some and found out I was feeling good, I wanted more. After
the fishing season I used to go right down to Vancouver and
bring back two dozen bottles, and when that's nearly all
gone, drinking with my friends, I go back to Vancouver and
get some more. When I was working for the cannery, I could
travel on the C.P.R. boats free, for they know me to be the
boss of the Indians. I was spending a lot of money on whisky,
and was beginning to be a heavy drinker.

When the Apostolic Faith Mission came to Alert Bay,
Brother Howard used to get me to go around from house to
house and interpret. When he preaches, I used to hear him
say that when a person is converted he quits all this drinking
and smoking. I wanted to quit them both. He used to pray to

God to help me quit, and I tells him it is very hard for me to quit them. I tried for a long time. I quitted smoking, but drinking I couldn't stop.

Just before my wife died, she called me to her bedside and said: "You know you have been a heavy drinker and spend most of your money for liquor. Now I'm going to leave you with the children. Promise me you will quit drinking, because you'll be the only one will look after our children. While I was alive, I looked after them while you was drinking, but there will be no one after I am gone to look after the children that you can trust." While she was talking to me, I felt a sharp thing just hurt my heart, and I saw what kind of a life I'd lived, and I was just staring at her without a word. Then she says, "Will you please promise me that you'll quit before I go?" I say, "Yes, I'll promise to do my best to quit my drinking."

When she died, I was invited to Vancouver by the head man of the Apostolic Faith Mission. He asked me about my wife, and I told him about the pain she had. He asks me what was the last words she said, and I says that she asked me to quit drinking. I told him that I promised her to do my best, but that it is very hard on me because I've been a very heavy drinker. He says: "There is nothing God couldn't do. Just trust on him and ask him to help you. Let us kneel down and pray." So we kneeled down, and he prayed. That night at eight o'clock we went to the A.F.M. house, and all the people there begin to sing. Brother Hall, the head of that Mission, told all the people we are going to pray especially for this brother of ours, Charley Nowell, that God will help him to stop drinking. They all kneeled down. Some was laughing, some was crying, and some was hollering, and pretty soon some just lay on the floor and rolled over and over. That's why they called them the Holy Rollers sometimes. It was funny. After that, I never thought of taking a drink. When someone asks me to take one, I just say, "No, thank you." I only says this three times, and then they don't ask me to have any more. Since that time I've been sober. Of course I have a drink now and then, but I don't drink hard liquor much any more.

When I was about sixty, my wife died of heart failure. It was a very solemn time when she died. She had a copper that was worth quite a lot of money. When she paid for the copper, it cost her twenty-four thousand blankets—some of it in canoes and other things. Her father loaned out the blankets, and she collected those debts and paid for the copper, buying it from a man named James Silas, a Nimkis. When she died, she said, "If that Kingcome man who has the copper don't pay for it right away, so my children can give a potlatch for my funeral, just say that you are going to put that copper on my grave as a monument." When all the people went to bury her, her uncle, her father's brother, says that his brother never finished giving a potlatch with that copper, that now his niece is another one that hasn't finished giving away the value of that copper, and that now that she has gone we will just put the copper on the grave and call it her monument. That was pretty hard on the man that got the copper now, because everybody is making fun of him. Now the copper is a monument, he is the one that is the coffin. It means that the man that has it now is supposed to be a monument because he didn't pay for the copper right away. He has been trying to get it straight, and he wants to pay for it, but we don't see how it could be done. It is too late now. They say that it has only been twice that a copper has been done in this way. If anybody said that in the old days, they would pay for the copper right away. If he gives the copper back now, we would just break the copper in pieces and give it back to him. She did it that way, because she tried to make him pay for it while she was still living, and he wouldn't. He promised to pay, and every time he says, "Next year I will." He isn't happy now and isn't even looked at by any of his own people. He wants to make it right, but he can't because she is dead and can't change her mind.[1]

---

[1] Again a man who fails to follow the rules is punished. He has waited too long; the person he owes is dead. If she had not asked him to pay, it would not have mattered, but, as it is, there is nothing he can do to regain the trust and good will of his fellows.

When my wife died, her daughter, who was her oldest child at the time, called all the tribes to come and bury her. The same tribes came as for my brother, except that the northern tribes didn't come, because they only wanted the near ones. After the funeral, they came to the community house and gave the speeches. She had the whale man, showing that she was going back to the whale crest. She was like a man, because she was the only child of that chief.[2] If she hadn't been a man, they would have come anyhow if she had been a chief's daughter and somebody had called the tribes.

On the fourth day after my wife's death, they all came and comforted my oldest daughter. They came to me at any time and comforted me and her uncle. In the olden days I would have stayed away from other people—even my own family—and at the fourth day they would come and bathe me, and would have hemlock branches rounded up as a ring and get me to go through it four times. They say it's bad for the husband to eat with the relations of the dead until all this is done. Then I would keep on bathing for four more days, then four more, then four more, and when I get through doing these things, I leave my clothing and hat in the woods. Somebody wraps these clothes around a stump about the height of a man, and puts a hat on it, and then I would come out and live amongst my family. I used to see the old people do this, and we used to be afraid to go near their clothing on the stump. But I didn't do these things; I only kept kind of quiet.

At change of life, which is what the white doctors call it, some of our Indian women have headaches, and sometimes they have their monthly for a week or more. My wife used to have her monthly for over a week, and went to see the doctor, and the doctor says she is almost over having her monthly. About two years before she died, she stopped having her monthly. She must have been about fifty-four. I was married to her about forty years, and she was about fourteen when I got married to her.

2 Charley's wife had an elder brother and two younger sisters, but she was the only one living when Lagius died in 1915.

Four or five years after she died I married again. I got
married because my people wanted me to have someone stay
with me to look after the house. She had married three times
before and was a Nimkis. She just died about five months
ago. She had a cancer on the womb. There wasn't any rules
about how quick you could get married after your wife died.
Some would marry quick, and some wouldn't.

It took me five years to make me think I might get along
with another woman. I didn't think so then, only my relatives persuaded me to. I was right. I didn't get along with
my last wife very good. She was quick-tempered and jealous
of other women. When I talked to another woman, she think
I was running after her, and she would bawl me out every
day. My first wife never did; we lived together really happy.
Although she knows I go around with other girls when I was
a young man, she never said anything about it. People would
go to her and tell her I am with another woman, and she
would say, "He is only young yet, and he will get over it."
All the young people tried hard to get her mad, but they
couldn't. It was pretty hard to make her get mad. They all
called her a fool, because she didn't want to bawl me out.
Even her own relatives would go to her and ask her to leave
me, and her answer always was, "He will soon get over it."
And she was right, too. I always did. This last wife was different. She bawled me out every time I come home. She says
that when I go to eat with my friends, I am going with a
girl. When I married my second wife, I didn't go through
any ceremony; we just went to the church. Only my people
went privately to the house to get us married. I didn't get
any crests or names, as I might have in the old days if she
was a chief's daughter and if she hadn't been married before.

When a man dies, the wife just comes home to her family.
This is changed by the white laws, and it is a great disgrace
to the Indians. Everything should go to the relations of the
man and not to his wife. If I have a son-in-law and he dies, it
is my duty to give some money or some blankets to the relatives of my daughter's husband. When I do that, it means
that my daughter is coming back to me. She leaves her hus-

band's home and everything her husband has. The children
stay there to get their father's position and name. She will
bring home a little baby if she has one, but it still has a place
on the father's side, and when he is old enough to look after
himself he goes back to his father's people.

My daughters' grandfather, Lagius, was chief here in
Alert Bay, and some of their children will have to be Nimkis
to take Lagius' place, because he had no sons and only one
daughter. She got his place, so now her daughters are looking after his place until her grandsons are old enough to
take his place. My wife became chief of the Nimkis because
Lagius didn't have any sons. Her mother was chief of the
Kwakiutl, and she had her mother's place, too. When our
oldest boy, Alfred, was living, he took all her positions. This
boy had all these places, and he was going to have mine.
After he died, his sisters took his places, and now they have
their sons and these boys will take all the places as well as
the ones I give them. The only case when a girl is in a position is when she doesn't have any brothers. Lagius' father
had first a girl, and then the second child was a boy. His
daughter had a name given to her, but not his position. The
way it is now, when so many people has no children, the
women, if they are any relation to a chief, would give a potlatch and take one of his places. In the old days it would
only be the men that would get these positions.

I know that I dream, but I don't remember what it is that
I dream. Sometimes I remember a little of it when I wakes
up, but I soon forget what it is. There is one dream that I
had that I remember, and that was after my first wife died. I
dreamed that she came toward me when I was sitting at the
table in my daughter's house. She came with a stick, and she
was mad with me, saying that I was fooling around with
girls. She tried to hit me with that stick, and I held up my
arm and try to get hold of the stick, and it hit me on the little finger. This was the time when I couldn't sleep good, and
my finger was paining me with the fish poison. I guess the
reason I dreamed about it was because my little finger was
awful sore that night. I think the reason I don't remember

my dreams is I sleep so sound, and when I wake up in the morning I could never go to sleep again. I had to get up and light the fire.

My youngest, Violet, married a Kitemat named Arthur Grant four years ago. They also married in the white man's way. They was married by the Anglican preacher and also a Methodist preacher, because Arthur is a Methodist and Violet is Anglican. She has three children; she would have got four, only the last one was miscarried. She had one child every year. She nearly dies when she has her babies.

Last October I came back to Alert Bay because we had a little trouble with a woman who came to our house drunk in Fort Rupert. She came looking for my second wife and wanted to beat her up, saying that my second wife said something against her. She got mad when I told her not to go into the bedroom, because my wife wasn't strong and wasn't feeling well. She was trying hard to get inside the bedroom, saying that she wanted to kill that woman, and I took hold of her arms and told her she better go home. I put her out of the house, and she came around to the front where the windows were and begin smashing them with her hands. There was no sleeves to her dress, and when she knocks through the windows her arms was bleeding. I never opened the door for her, but just tell her to go home and come back when she is sober. I told her she wouldn't be doing this if she wasn't drunk.

Next morning she and Frank Walker came to Alert Bay and reported that I was licking her, that I threw her through the window, and showed all the cuts on her arm. So the policeman went to Fort Rupert, and when he examined all the house and the windows, he saw that all the glass from the windows is all inside the house. He says, "That shows that you didn't throw her out, but anyway you better come to Alert Bay and get all this settled." So me and my second wife came to Alert Bay, and we was tried in court. The policeman got up himself and tells about examining the house and the windows, and I won the case.

When we went home to my daughter's house, the policeman came in again and says: "There is another trouble. You have to be back at the courthouse again at seven this evening." She made up another thing. She told somebody outside of the courthouse that she is not going to rest until I am sent down to jail, that she is going to find something that will sentence me. My granddaughter Rita told in court that she was already drunk when she came in. Her witness that she promised to pay, when they were asked by the judge whether I was drunk, every one of them says I was just eating my supper. I also got a witness that she told she is not going to rest until she has me locked up, and I called her to come and tell the court what she said. That won the case for me.

This woman went back and told the policeman that if they are not going to arrest me, at least I should pay for the wounds that she has on her arms. The policeman told her: "We have enough of your lies, so leave us alone. Charley has a chance to turn around and sue you for busting the windows and all the damages you have done. Charley has the right to get after you for saying that you want to kill his wife, so leave us alone." From that time she wouldn't look at me. I keep on smiling at her, and trying to talk to her, and going to see them. When we got back to Fort Rupert, my wife says: "I don't want to stay here, for she might come in while you are away. So let us go to Alert Bay." So we came, and from that time all my people at Fort Rupert is talking bad against her and feels sore that I am here instead of at Fort Rupert. They went after Frank Walker, who brought her, and told him to go away from Fort Rupert, because he is no good to anybody. The only thing he is good for is to make trouble, and they call him a troublemaker. The woman is one of his relatives, and when he comes to Alert Bay everyone calls him a stool pigeon.

This was the time I was met at the boat, hearing that my daughter Violet was sick and wanted to see me before she died. I got right back on the boat that was docking there, and I went up north to Bella Bella. When I got there, I was met by the chiefs who came and shook hands with me. One of

them called me into his house to have breakfast with him.
Before I went to his house, I went to see my daughter in the
hospital. She was very bad—she was pale. Before I could
see her, Dr. Darby says he will go in and see her first. I stayed
outside of the room where she was, and I heard Dr. Darby
say: "Violet, I have good news for you. Your father is here.
Shall I call him to come and see you?" I could hardly hear
her when she says, "Yes, please." I went in and went right
up to her and took hold of her hand and kissed her and told
her that I didn't think I would see her this way. "I thought
you was awful sick. You aren't as sick as I thought. You are
going to pull through with this," I says. She says, "Yes,
when you are here, I will feel better."

I stayed at Bella Bella three weeks, until she was ready to
go home to Kitemat. Dr. Darby says she is through the
worst part and she is going to live. This was the time she
had her miscarriage. She got there just in time; another day
or two and the poison would have been all over her and she
would have died.

While I was there at the hospital a man came and told me
that all the chiefs are in the house of the man that invited
me. So I went with him. As soon as I got in, food was served
around. We had boiled dried salmon with grease, and didn't
I enjoy that! It was so nice that I had a lot of it. And potatoes. After that we had some seaweed boiled—those Indians don't eat much of white man's food. After that herring
eggs. I felt myself full and hardly ate any of that, but the
rest of the men just keep on eating. After we finished that,
they brought in hemlock bark with wild rice mixed with it. I
asked the other one what are they trying to do—fill me so
full I'll bust? Then came a meat stew; the others had three
dishes each, and I couldn't finish one. After that they had
tea, cake, and the like of that. I says to myself, "This will be
the last." They all drank two cups each. I had to sit up
straight because I was full right up to my neck. When we
got through with that, the man alongside of me says to me:
"Do you know what the other chiefs does? They get up one
by one and go to the toilet, so if you want to get up you just

go. That is the way of our people." I says: "No, I don't want
to do that. We don't do that at a feast. It is a disgrace to
our people if we do that." When we get through with our tea
there was about seven girls called to come in. Each of them
had a bucket, and they beat some soap berries in it. That
was the last that we were to eat. When we got to the house
where I was going to stay, I told the man I was never going
to any of their feasts again. He and his wife just laughed.

The next day there was a feast for the whole tribe of the
Bella Bellas. They say a young man got married to a Bella
Coola girl, and they went over to see the girl's parents at
Bella Coola, and they came back with two cows that was
killed for them and fifty sacks of potatoes and fifty boxes of
apples and ten boxes of oranges and four hundred loaves of
bread that was given to him by his father-in-law to bring
back to his people. He is the one that called the whole tribe
to his feast in their hall.

I was at the hospital with my daughter when two men
came and told me they wanted me at the feast. I got up right
away and went with them. When we got to the door, one of
the two men sang out to the people: "The chief is now here.
Where will he sit?" A man called Moses Knight, that was
telling the people their seats, took out a chair and says,
"Here." When I got inside the door I saw a whole lot of
people there. They all turned around to watch me. Oh, I got
ashamed! I heard my ears whistling, and I could hardly see
where I was walking. Moses Knight was beckoning to me to
come and put me beside the head chief of that tribe, Moody.
I sat down and looked around and saw that the long table
had all the chiefs that was with me the previous day. At another table was what they called the second chiefs, and at a
third table was the third chiefs. The rest was all what they
call commoners. They give us a stew of the beef that they
brought, and we all ate it. Some of them asked for some
more, but I says that's enough; I thought it was going to be
like the day before, but that was all we ate.

Then a man stood up on the platform and says, "We will
start with the apples." They walked around and gave the

head chief three boxes of apples, Owadi three boxes, and three boxes for everybody at the first table. They gave two boxes each to the number two table, and one box to the number three table, and all the other people only two apples each. That is the first time I've seen a feast like that. Then the oranges were given out in the same way. At the head table two of us got a box between us. The rest of the people on the sides of the house didn't get any. Then at the first table we all got five loaves of bread each, and the rest got one. I kept on saying to Chief Moody: "Is that your ways? Don't they have to get the same as you get?" "No!" he says, "they are nothing." I says, "Why do they come into the feast if they are treated like that?" He says: "They don't care. They know they are commoners. They come here just to eat, that is all." Then the hind legs of the two cows was cut into pieces and given to the chiefs, and none was given to the commoners. I was wondering what I was going to do with all these things. When we got through, a man called out to the commoners to come and take these chiefs' apple boxes and things to their homes. So they all came and picked up our stuff and took it to the places where we stayed. When we got home, I simply told the wife of the man where I was staying to take them, I didn't want to keep them.

Sometime after that I took a walk. I saw a man that I fished with at Good Hope Cannery at River's Inlet. I says to him, "Hello, Alec." He looked at me and says, "Hello, Charley." I went up to him, and he looked around and seemed to be scared of something. I says to him: "I haven't seen you for a long time. Where have you been fishing?" He told me he has been fishing for Namu Cannery. I ask him how his wife was and he says, "All right." I says, "Is she home?" He says, "Yes." I says, "I'll go in and shake hands with her." I went in; the woman look at me, and I says, "Hello, Mrs. Alec." She says, "Hello, Charley," and just went on with her washing and never stopped to talk. She never even told me to sit on a chair. I had to go and take a chair myself and sit down. She didn't seem polite to me, and her husband walked away from the house and went somewhere. Finally a man came and says: "Charley, Chief Moody wants you right away. Come right after me."

I went with him, and he took me into Charley Moody's house. There were all these chiefs—the number ones—in the house. They all had their heads down, and none of them look up except Charley Moody. They told me to go and sit alongside of his father, old Moody. I sat down and looked around. None of them put their heads up, and I begin wondering and think they must have some trouble. For a long time they never says a word—just have their hands covering their eyes. Charley Moody says to his father: "Old man, what are you waiting for? Start and speak to him." So the old man sits up, and he never looked at me, although I was alongside of him. He sighed big, making a long breath, and then he says: "Charley, you make a very big mistake. Did you know that house where you went into, or do you not know?" I says, "What?" He says, "That you went into." "You mean Alec's house?" I says. He says, "Yes. You know Alec?" I says, "Yes, what about him?" "He is a real commoner," he says, "and you shouldn't go there. None of these chiefs ever goes into that house, and you shouldn't go into any of those houses that commoners lives in. I am going to tell you of one of our chiefs who went in that family's house in the olden days. He got stuck to a woman there, and he married that woman. When he went out hunting with his wife, they never returned, because one of our grandfathers went after them and killed them both. They were ashamed of this chief being married to a *xamala*[3] woman, and I'm scared lest they do the same to you if you go into one of these houses." Then Charley Moody says: "Is that all you have to say, old man? We don't think that what Charley did is good. We will get Hamtsit's wife to fill a bathtub and scrub him down tonight, so that the smell of the *xamala* won't stay on him." All the chiefs begin to laugh, and he turn around to me and say: "Charley, don't mind too much what the old man says. He is only jealous because you went in there. That is his sweetheart. All those women are his sweethearts because he doesn't

3 Xamala probably means "slave."

have to pay them anything. Tomorrow you and me will go
and look at that woman. She will have a black eye. The old
man will go and lick her."

After that all the chiefs were called by another chief. I am
always the last to be called because I am always in the hospital. When I went in there, they begin to get ready the food
we are going to eat. There was a big man sitting by the door
—coming on to old age. The one that calls us says to him,
"You better go and take a walk until these chiefs finish eating." I wondered why they sent him out instead of asking
him to come closer to the table and eat, and I asked a man
beside me why is that man sent out. They said that all the
chiefs wouldn't eat if he stayed in here. I says, "Why? Has
he got smallpox or what?" He says, "No, he is a *xamala*, and
he is not allowed to stay here while we eat." I says, "This is
crazy; we don't do that." He laughed and turned around to
the other and says: "You know what Owadi says? He was
thinking he had smallpox." They laugh and begin to tell
stories of the old people and how they used to look upon the
commoners.

IF a woman dies in childbirth, some of their relatives takes
the baby and raises it herself. If the father wants the baby
back, he puts the baby in his position, but the child still looks
upon its foster parents as its own. In marriage both of them
decide who the boy or girl will marry. For instance, my
granddaughter Jane was only about three years old when
her mother died, and I and my wife looked after this girl. I
have been her guardian ever since, and her father still has
the right to say what he thinks about her being married to
somebody, although he had nothing to do with that girl
while we was looking after her. Her brother was old enough
to stay with his father. He is three years older than Rita.
His father didn't marry again. He doesn't want to get married, in case his new wife hates the children.

Sometimes it happens that the new wife has trouble with
her husband's children, but some women are good and look
on the husband's children as their own. My new wife didn't

agree with my children. Although my children tried their best to be good to her, somehow they made her don't like them. She says that I love my children better than I love her, and that is her excuse of not wanting them near. I would rather talk to my children than talk to her, and when I am talking to them and she talk to me, I don't hear her and that makes her mad.

WHILE I and my second wife was roasting clams, we heard a dog yelling just behind where we was roasting. My granddaughter Rita was with us. I saw a dog standing with a cougar. I had a long wooden tongs in my hands that I fixed the fire with, and when I saw the dog and the cougar fighting I ran up to where they were. They rolled down from behind a rock. When I got to the rock, I jumped up on top of it and saw that the cougar had his mouth right on the dog's jaw, and the dog was yelling for pain. I just lift up the wooden tongs and smote the cougar right on the head. The cougar let go of the dog and got up and looked at me fierce. The dog got up and bit him right on the throat, and I hollered out to Mrs. Cadwallader, but she was in a family way and she didn't walk fast. While I was standing there watching the dog and the cougar fighting, my granddaughter Rita came running toward me with a little rifle No. 410, and gave me the cartridge. It was a shell with small shots in it. It wouldn't do any harm to the cougar, but it would tickle him. Finally, one of Mrs. Cadwallader's niece came up and gave a rifle to Rita and she shot the cougar three times before she killed him.

A YEAR ago I used to faint—whether at work or whether I am just walking along. I just dropped, and, the funny part of it, when I come to my conscious, I never feel anything what was the trouble with me. It is always when it is nearly high tide. The old people says that I was witchcrafted, and the thing is on a place at nearly high tide. Some of the people at Fort Rupert was trying to find it, but never did. Since I came up from there to Alert Bay I only had that twice, but

when I was at Fort Rupert I had that every day twice, and
sometimes during the night. I didn't think I was witchcrafted,
so I came to the doctor, and he says there is something wrong
with my heart. He gave me little pills to take and tell me not
to worry about anything, and to have a good rest, and to lay
down after meals for half an hour, and not to go uphill, and,
if I do, to go up slowly. I've got all right now. I feel now
that there is no witchcrafting against me. I think if you believe what they say when they tell you you are witchcrafted,
that makes you worse. When I was told that by several old
people, I begin to watch myself when it is nearly high tide. I
couldn't think of anybody who would do it, so it was hard
for me to believe I was being witchcrafted, and yet it seem
to be right when I would faint when high tide was nearly up.
I think if you believe you are being witchcrafted, you can
make yourself pretty sick worrying about it and getting
scared.

ABOUT three years ago I had a sliver from a rotten board in
my other hand, and I tried to get it out with a needle. While
I was trying to get it off, a boat came from Hardy Bay with
a lot of bluebacks, and they hollered out to me to go and get
some of the salmon. I went out and got some. I packed them
out on my fingers, and slime got into the wound, and I was
having the pain for a week before I came to Alert Bay. There
was no gas-boats there; they was all out fishing. The first
gas-boat that came to Fort Rupert brought me to the hospital here, and my whole hand was all swollen up. The doctor just cut it open. He saw it was all bad, so he cut way
down—three long cuts—and lift the skin and scrape the flesh
out from between the bone. I was watching him all the time.
He wanted to give me chloroform, but I says no. He put
something in to freeze it, and it still hurt a lot, but I wouldn't
grunt. After he finishes he says: "Why didn't you squeal? I
know it hurted you." I says, "That is my way." Every time
I go there, he looks at me funny and says, "You're a funny
man," because I wouldn't let him put me to sleep. I lie down

when he does it, and it don't make me feel faint or dizzy or anything. When I got the poison, everybody got scared that I would die of it.

I watched the doctor when he cut my finger off, too. I was tying a knot on a twine and it slipped. My hand went out and knocked against the lid of a tobacco tin and made a cut in my little finger of my right hand. In about two weeks this seem to heal up, and then I went out halibut fishing. I got some rock cod for my bait and put that on my hook and tried to get halibut, but a dogfish took my bait away. Every time I put my line down a dogfish take my bait, and so I come home. That night I couldn't sleep for the pain in my hand, and the next day I go to the doctor. He tell me to stay in the hospital, and begin to put my hand in hot water. When I was there about three weeks, it all got swollen up. One morning they told me to go to the operating room, and they cut my finger off. The slime of the bait got into the wound when it got wet all day, and it opened.

THE Indian women don't like to go to the hospital. They say they get worse there. Old Billy McDuff was in the hospital, and a woman that was carrying was brought in and had her birth there. When Billy heard there was a birth, and we told him who it was, he says: "Why is she allowed to come in the hospital and have a birth? That will make us get worse." I was in there with my finger at the time and tells him white people don't believe that. He says: "It is true though. It will make us get worse again." That very night he was very sick again and couldn't go to sleep. He had hurt himself while he was working, and fell on his balls and nearly busted them. One was as big as my hand. He ask me how I felt in the morning. He said, "Didn't you feel your hand got worse?" I says, "No." He says, "I did—all on account of that woman." When the nurse came to dress him, to put hot cloths on him, they say his ball was busted on one side, and want to get the doctor to come and look at it. He turns to me and says, "Look here now, that shows it is true." I says

to him, "That's too bad." They say that birth blood is the
worst. It is the smell of it that is the worst part. It may get
into your wound and make it worse.

BEFORE I stop, I want to tell you about how the ancestor of
my first wife got his crest. This is a true story of what happened in the past.

Yakotlalaseme, the ancestor of the Giksum, the second clan
of the Kwakiutls—which means, "where you believe you are
going to get the blankets from that were used in the early days"
—went out hunting, not with gun but with spear and harpoon.
He went northward on Vancouver Island, and then he went
past Shoshade Bay to a nice beach and camped there. Early
the next morning, before daylight, he heard a sound on front
of him in the water that made a terrible noise. He knew, when
he heard it, that it was a hok-hok—a bird kind of like a crane.
He looked toward the water to where the noise was and saw
it was a thick fog. When he saw a shadow like through the fog,
he covered his face again with his Indian blanket made out of
cedar bark. Then he heard another noise which sounded like
an eagle. Every time he take his blanket off his head, the noise
seems to stop. Then he knew he shouldn't look at it, and then
he covered his head up again. The hok-hok still make the noise,
and the eagle, and there was a grizzly bear noise added to them.
Then he took his blanket and bit a hole through it, where he
could put his eye to look through the blanket. Every time the
shadow became higher, the fog lifted higher. Soon he could see
the thing plainly. Then a whale came up on the bottom, and it
was a pole with a hok-hok on top and beneath an eagle and
beneath that a grizzly bear. When the whale was up, a wolf
came up under—a sea wolf. Last of all was a sea monster,
which was a large bullhead. The bullhead was a house under the
pole. The mouth of the bullhead was so wide that it reached
from one side of the house to the other. Then he saw people
and fishes going inside as the bullhead's mouth opened, and
then the mouth goes down again. Then he spoke while his head
was still covered. He saw a man outside the house, and spoke

A Hok-Hok Crest

to all those that went inside the house. He says to this man in a loud voice: "I have been watching you since the top of this totem pole appeared, until now, and I have seen what you have done. Do not move, for I will go inside the house to see what I can get out of the house." The man outside the house says: "Come, my friend, for you have done well when you did not disturb all these things that you saw while they were coming up. You will be welcomed by the rich chief that owns the house."

So he got into his canoe, and he watched the mouth as it opened and closed. He was near to the mouth, and the water was running into the mouth of the house very strong. As he was near the mouth of the house, he was backing his paddle not to get too close; as soon as he saw the mouth opening, he paddled as hard as he can to get in before the mouth closes again. When he got inside the house, his canoe landed on a dry place, and he stopped there still sitting on his canoe. Then the chief, "Rich Man," spoke to one of his servants that hears everything, even your thoughts, and the servant came up to him and stood beside him. "Rich Man" says, "What does our friend want in coming into my house?" Yakotlalaseme thought he would like to have the house and pole and what is in the house. The little man that was beside him spoke before Yakotlalaseme spoke saying, "Our friend wants to own your house and the pole and what is in the house." The "Rich Man" replies: "He shall have the house and the totem pole and this little box that contains riches. All that there is in this box, although he takes them out of it, the box will be always full. If he wants blankets, he will put it inside this box, and there will always be more and more. Now you will stay here four days until I show you all the dances of my people, and you will get whichever dances you like to have."

So he stayed there four days. He got hungry, and the "Rich Man" says, "Our friend better come to sit down by the fire, and we will give him something to eat." So he got out of his canoe, but his steerman had stayed on shore and never knew what had become of him. When he saw that Yakotlalaseme was nowhere, he walked back to Shoshade Bay. After Yakotlalaseme sat down, ready to have his meal, "Rich Man" said to his servant, "Take down what is in that bag hanging there." So his servant took it down and poured it into a dish. The dish was a seal, and it moved itself. Yakotlalaseme looked in the dish and saw it was dried frogs, and he thought to himself, "I have never eaten frogs in my life." This little man that always stood by him says to the chief, "He thinks he has never eaten these things before in his life, and he doesn't want to eat them." "Rich Man" says to this little man, "What does he want to eat?" He saw a lot of seals crawling along the floor, and he thought to himself, "Seal is what I would like to eat." The little man say to the chief, "He say he would like to eat one of your dogs." So "Rich Man" told some of the servants to club the seal's head. They burnt the fur off the seal, opened it, washed it out, and then built up a fire and put stones into the fire until it was red hot. Then they put kelp on top of it, and put the whole seal on top of stones, and covered it with kelp. When it was cooked it was put in a dish, and this dish was a sea otter. Every time "Rich Man" gave him something to eat, it was a different kind of a dish—a porpoise, sea otter, beaver, and other things. And every time he finished eating, "Rich Man" says, "You will keep that dish; it will be yours." That was why the Giksum clan had the most dishes.

At the fourth night, all the fishes came together and made a dance of their own dances. He liked the Rock-Cod dance, and he also liked the dance of the Blackfish, and some of the dances they showed him he didn't like. Every time he thinks that he like one dance, the little man beside him says, "He like that," and every time he think that he don't like that dance, the little man beside him says, "He don't like that one." Last of all, there came a dancer with four ghosts or skulls on the head and four skulls on the neck ring, and on her blanket there was the skeleton of a man. When the dancer gets to the rear end of the house, the people that went around covering the dancer opened up, and then the hok-hok on top of the pole begin to say, "Hau-hau-hau-hui-hui." He says to himself, "I like that." The little man told the chief, "Our friend likes that, and he wants to own it." The chief says, "He shall have it." Then he saw in the rear end of the house a harpoon; the ends of the harpoon keep shooting out, for it was a magic harpoon. He says to himself, "I would like to own that harpoon." The little man told the chief his thoughts, and the chief says: "He shall have it. But do not throw it when you want to kill anything, or else it will only turn to stone, but simply aim it without throwing it and whatever you aim it at will be dead."

So all these things that he liked was put in a box. It was a small box, and they took the totem pole down and folded it up and put it in the box. And all these things that he liked was folded and put in the box excepting the house. The chief says that as soon as he gets home to take out this totem pole and just put it out on the ground, not too close to his house, and, when this is set up, it will all come to life again and make all the noises. He must put it up the same time—early in the morning before daylight—and after it is put up the house will be there.

He was taken home to Fort Rupert by a blackfish. When he got there, he saw that his father's house was falling to pieces; his father had built a little shack to live in, for he thought that Yakotlalaseme was dead. He put up the pole, and it made all that was in the totem pole; the hok-hok, the eagle, the whale, the grizzly bear, the wolf, and the sea monster was making a terrible noise so that it waked all his tribe. When he had called all his tribe to come to the house, there was one man standing in front of the house telling the people when to get in, for if they are too slow in getting in, they will be chewed up by this bullhead.

He found out that he had been gone four years instead of four days. He made a winter ceremonial and showed everything that he saw as it was done by "Rich Man," after that the ghost dance. That is why the Giksum owns all these—the totems, the house, the dances, and the dishes. The people didn't know what to think how he get all these things, for when he put one in the box in the night it get full. The box was small when it was given to him, and when he put it inside the house it became a large box. Anything that he put inside this box, this box would be full of it in the next day. So he gave a potlatch all the time, and he was the biggest chief that ever lived.

That painting of Alfred now is the hok-hok on the top of that totem pole. My wife is a descendant of this man through her mother, for her mother was a Giksum, and her mother's father was a Giksum. Her mother's mother was a Tlowitsis. The old man called Wakias of that clan told my wife and me about this when I got married to her. And he told my wife to remember it all. At nights he used to tell that over and over again, so we would have it straight. That is the way the old people used to do in the nighttime when there is nothing else going on, so the stories won't be forgotten.

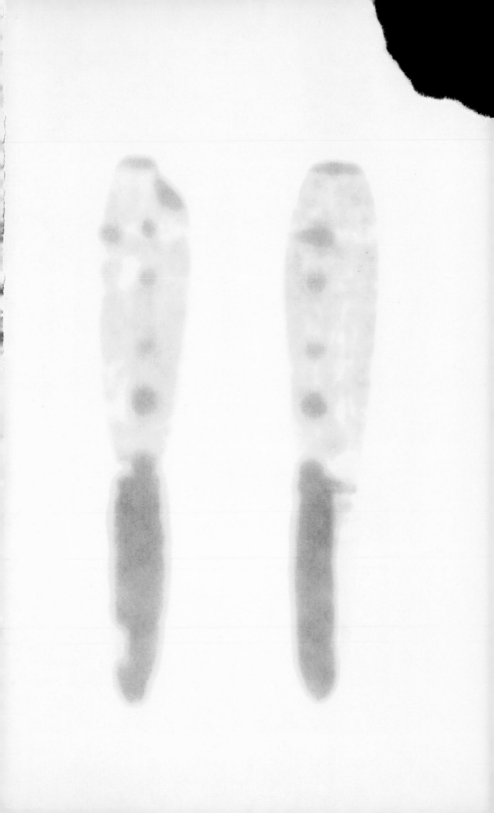